Isle of Skye
Inverness
Aviemore
SCOTLAND
Isle of Colonsay
St Andrews
Glasgow
Edinburgh
Limavady
NORTHERN
IRELAND
Belfast
Newcastle
Castlebar
Ambleside
Connemara
Kingscourt
ISLE OF MAN
Galway
Blackpool
Leeds
Kinnitty
Liverpool
Manchester
DUBLIN
Durrow
Nant Gwynant
Nottingham
IRELAND
Killarney
Birmingham
Rosslare
WALES
ENGLAND
St Davids
Cambridge
Brecon
Cardiff
Oxford
Bristol
Bath
Evershot
Amberley
Newquay
Brighton

CHANNEL ISLANDS
Guernsey
Jersey

Bury College
Woodbury LRC

BEST HOTELS

GREAT BRITAIN & IRELAND

INCLUDING THE CHANNEL ISLANDS AND ISLE OF MAN

HotelClub.com

APA PUBLICATIONS

L

Part of the Langenscheidt Publishing Group

Editorial

Project Editor
Ed Peters
Art Director
Harry Llufrio

Distribution

UK & Ireland
GeoCenter International Ltd
Meridian House, Churchill Way West,
Basingstoke, Hampshire RG21 6YR
Fax: (44) 1256 817988

United States
Langenscheidt Publishers, Inc.
36–36 33rd Street, 4th Floor
Long Island City, NY 11106
Fax: (1) 718 784-0640

Australia
Universal Publishers
1 Waterloo Road
Macquarie Park, NSW 2113
Fax: (61) 2 9888 9074

New Zealand
Hema Maps New Zealand Ltd (HNZ)
Unit D, 24 Ra ORA Drive
East Tamaki, Auckland
Fax: (64) 9 273 6479

Worldwide
Apa Publications GmbH & Co.
Verlag KG (Singapore branch)
38 Joo Koon Road, Singapore 628990
Tel: (65) 6865-1600. Fax: (65) 6861-6438

Printing

Insight Print Services (Pte) Ltd
38 Joo Koon Road, Singapore 628990
Tel: (65) 6865-1600. Fax: (65) 6861-6438

©2008 Apa Publications GmbH & Co.
Verlag KG (Singapore branch)
All Rights Reserved
First Edition 2008

CONTACTING THE EDITORS
We would appreciate it if readers
would alert us to errors or outdated information by writing to:
David.Wareing@HotelClub.com

www.insightguides.com
www.HotelClub.com

ABOUT THIS BOOK

This inaugural edition of *Great Britain & Ireland's Best Hotels* follows hard on the heels of similar and very successful guides to Asia and Oceania. Like its predecessors, it showcases hotels large and small, venerable and brand new, pricey and less so, but all terrific favourites of the travelling public.

The poll to seek out this guide's content - posted by HotelClub.com in early 2007 - provoked a huge response from all around the world. It seemed that Uncle Tom Cobley and all had myriad opinions on what constituted a really great hotel, be it in England, Scotland, Wales, Ireland or on one of the offshore islands.

While there are legion officially sanctioned star rating systems and awards schemes, the 300 hotels here have the ultimate stamp of authority - from genuine travellers. And you can't ask for a better recommendation. As in previous guides, the public choice has been

leavened with a select handful of Editors' Picks.

One of the great pleasures of overseeing such a democratically compiled hotel guide is that the outcome can often be something of a surprise. That hotels in London would garner a lot of votes was only to be expected; but Ireland's spectacular performance raised several editorial eyebrows. And while the appearance of stalwarts such as Chewton Glen and Le Manoir au Quat' Saisons was more or less a foregone conclusion, it was heartening to find lesser known establishments cropping up in the winners' circle, not sheltering beneath a chain's umbrella or part of some international marketing initiative, but simply dispensing hospitality with their own brand of gusto.

Great Britain & Ireland's Best Hotels is laid out to make it easy to choose where you should stay. Sorted alphabetically by country, destination and name, each hotel is summed up with a snappy pen portrait, supported by photos, a list of facilities and star ratings. More details are available at HotelClub.com, where you can also make reservations. As an added inducement, the guide also contains a discount card, unless somebody with uncontrollable wanderlust has got to it before you.

This series of Best Hotel guides was originally conjured up by **Jon Stonham**, who has long since left the cut and thrust of corporate life to sail around the world aboard his yacht with not one but *three* gorgeous females (wife and two daughters).

David Wareing and **Katharina Woergetter** of HotelClub headed up this project, with a fair amount of help from the company's London office in the perfectly formed shape of **Igor Jovicic,** who was ably assisted by the indefatigable **Kassandra Poulos**.

Gingerbreadman.net - principally **Harry Llufrio** and his wife, **Mina Chang Yim Ting** - handled design and layout while Insight's production team, **Derrick Lim** and **Angela Wong**, provided essential back-up.

Vivian Wong Ho Yee pulled numerous organisational rabbits from a variety of hats, and **Mariam Moore** - i-dotter/t-crosser extraordinaire - proofread the copy filed by the team of writers who had the wearisome task of checking out the countries' finest hostelries.

This was headed by veteran journalist **Bill Cranfield** who brought his vast experience of hotel living gained during a peripatetic reporting existence to bear on a host of witty and informative reviews.

Geoff Hill, author of the classic motorbike travelogue *The Road to Gobblers Knob*, weighed in with Northern Ireland, and **Yvette Dolan, Lynda Cookson, Karen Creed** and **Anthony Healy** looked after things south of the border.

In England, **Nigel Tisdall, Andrew Copestake, Teresa Machan,** and **Charlotte Swift** (whose bylines will be familiar to readers of *Marie Claire, Gay Times, The Daily Telegraph* and *Conde Nast Traveller*, respectively but not exclusively)

surfed the best of The Smoke. **Rebecca Gooch** fossicked about the West Country, **Carol Wright** (former chairman of the British Guild of Travel Writers) delved into Oxford, and **Dominic McGuinness** sorted out Manchester.

Scotland was embraced by **Greg Gordon, Amber Wilkinson, Mike Russell, Fiona MacLeod** and **Andrew Spooner,** while Welsh hotels were inspected by both **Ian Everett** (who celebrated finishing his task by decamping to Chicago to get married) and **Roger Thomas**.

Tom Birley, who turned down a promising career in the police force for more cerebral occupation, looked over the Channel Islands, together with long-time resident **Carl Walker**.

Other sterling contributors included **Tamara Peters, Kathryn Peat, Lydia Wilson, Paul Tarrant** and **Jane Brace**.

A huge thanks to one and all, and especially to those public bodies who helped with images, and the hotels for opening their doors to the inspecting team.

Ed Peters
Editor At Large
Edward.Peters@HotelClub.com

Picture credits
Front cover: *The Heritage Golf & Spa Resort.*
Back cover: *Dromoland Castle Hotel &
Country Estate, The Ritz London.* Page 2:
Image Source Black. Page 4: *Purestock.*
Page 5: *Jeremy Woodhouse.* Page 7: *Andrew
Ward/Life File.* Page 8: *Channel Islands
Tourism Board.* Page 14: *Allan Baxter (top),
Andrew Holt (bottom).* Page 15: *Allan Baxter
(top), Digital Vision (bottom)* Page 16: *David
Toase (top), Digital Vision (bottom).*
Page 132: *Dennis Flaherty (top), David Toase
(bottom).* Page 133: *Peter Adams (top),
Stockbyte (bottom).* Page 134: *Stockbyte
(top), Stockbyte (bottom).* Page 227:
Medioimages/Photodisc. Page 228: *Andrew
Holt.* Page 229: *Alan Becker.* Page 241:
*Wilfried Krecichwost (top left), Peter Adams
(top right).* Page 242: *Stockbyte (top),
ABEL (bottom).* Page 243: *ABEL (top),
Renaud Visage (bottom).* Page 284: *Peter
Adams (top), David Toase (bottom).*
Page 285: *Peter Adams (top), David Toase
(bottom).* Page 286: *David Toase (top,
middle and bottom)*

CONTENTS

About the ratings

In keeping with previous editions of
the HotelClub.com Best Hotels &
Resorts guidebooks, guests with
first-hand knowledge and
experience have selected the
properties listed. This guide pays
tribute to the most popular hotels
and resorts in the region as voted
by the most significant panel of all -
our consumers.

In 2007, HotelClub.com - in
conjunction with Sunday Times
Travel, Insight Guides, Waterstones,
German Wings, eBookers,
Vinopolis, Gay Times, Diva, Irish
Abroad and Carbookers - polled
users and consumers on their
favourite hotels throughout Great
Britain and Ireland.

More than 22,000 nominations
were received, citing over 6,500
hotels and guesthouses across
England, Ireland, Scotland, Wales
and the offshore islands. Each
nominated property was rated
across ten key criteria using a scale
of one to ten (ten being the best).

The overall rating was then
calculated from these scores using
a HotelClub.com formula.

Our team of reviewers and
independent writers then assessed
the ratings and the number of
votes to come up with a final list of
300 hotels across Great Britain
and Ireland.

All hotel finalists had to receive
a base number of votes as well as
an exceptional overall rating to
qualify. Our panel of travel experts
further added another 20 hotels as
Editors' Picks to broaden the
scope of the guide. In light of the
growing popularity of niche hotels
in Great Britain and Ireland, we
have highlighted these in this
year's Editors' Picks - many of
which are smaller properties, or
are the quintessential country
house experience for which Great
Britain and Ireland are renowned.
All Editors' Picks are clearly
identified in the overall rating
section of the hotel review.

Please note that the star ratings published are those nominated by the properties themselves. Where a hotel has not provided a star rating, we have indicated "n/a" in the star rating section. A scale of one to five stars has been used.

Room rates are normally influenced by a variety of factors, including seasonality and demand, and hence can fluctuate dramatically over time.

To provide a meaningful indication on pricing, we have benchmarked the properties accordingly to a Price Guide, ranging from affordable (💰) to seriously luxurious (💰💰💰💰💰).

Every effort has been made to ensure that all the information provided is accurate. However, we do recognize that hotels in Great Britain and Ireland are ever changing. If you spot any quirks, outdated or inaccurate information, or simply if you feel strongly about a property that should be (or should not be) included, please do let us know.

David Wareing
Global Brand Manager
HotelClub.com
David.Wareing@HotelClub.com

Price guide

	GBP	EURO	USD
💰	< 50	< 73	< 100
💰💰	50-100	73-146	100-200
💰💰💰	100-150	146-219	200-300
💰💰💰💰	200-250	292-365	300-400
💰💰💰💰💰	> 250	> 365	> 400

Rates from: 💰💰💰💰💰
Star rating: ★★★★★
Overall rating: 👍👍👍👍

Ambience :	1-10	Cleanliness:	1-10
Value:	1-10	Facilities:	1-10
Staff:	1-10	Restaurants:	1-10
Location:	1-10	Families:	1-10

Facilities

- Baby Sitting
- Bar
- Business Centre
- Casino
- Disabled Facilities
- Garden
- Golf Course
- Gymnasium
- Kids Club
- In-room computer ports
- Nightclub
- Restaurant
- Room Service
- Satellite / Cable TV
- Spa
- Indoor Swimming Pool
- Outdoor Swimming Pool
- Tennis Court
- Tourism Information
- Parking
- Wireless Internet Connection

Channel Islands

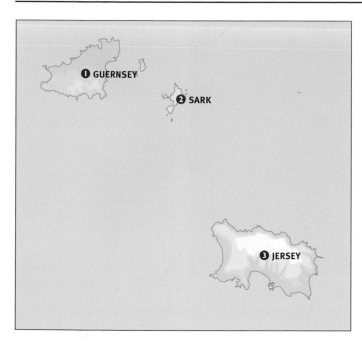

Distinguished by being closer to the French than the English coast, and the only British soil occupied by the Nazis in World War II, the Channel Islands are a pleasant bundle of contradictions.

Comprising Jersey, Guernsey, Alderney, Herm and Sark, and with a total population of around 160,000, the islands' relaxed attitude to taxation and related fiscal matters attracts a goodly amount of interested investors, while the gentle pace of life contributes to their reputation as a good family vacation spot.

The islands are part of the United Kingdom, but administered locally and mint their own currency and postage stamps. Each of the islands has a markedly different character. Jersey is the largest island, remarkable for its zoo which was founded by the naturalist and author Gerald Durrell, and with some excellent museums to boot. Guernsey is rather more laid-back, strikingly picturesque, and a point of pilgrimage for Victor Hugo fans. Hardly any development has taken place on

and nicknamed "donkeys", while Jerseyites are called "toads". Sark's inhabitants are dubbed "crows" and Alderney's "rabbits". The annual inter-island football match, the Muratti, is hotly contested, not least by the women's and junior teams.

While there may not be a huge range of choice of where to stay in the Channel Islands, the quality of accommodation is markedly high and is all the more enjoyable for the level of personal service.

Easily accessible by both sea and air from England and mainland Europe, the Channel Islands' chief attraction is being one step removed from the beaten track, with sandy beaches, an array of restaurants and sporting opportunities, pretty vistas and all the good things of life on offer without their being swamped by crowds.

Herm, which is run by a single family, while Alderney (reckoned by some to be the most British of the islands) sports its own railway as well as a number of lively pubs. Sark is sometimes cited as one of Europe's few remaining feudal communities, a status that's currently in the process of changing to a more representative democracy. In the meantime, its traffic-free, street lamp-less byways are a ready source of charm.

Wherever visitors pitch up in the Channel Islands, and whether they make the journey for reasons of business or leisure, they can be assured of a uniquely welcoming stay. A certain friendly rivalry exists between the islands: residents of Guernsey are supposedly stubborn,

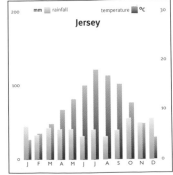

La Barbarie Hotel

Saints Bay, St Martin, Guernsey, GY4 6ES, Channel Islands

T: +44 1481 235 217 **F**: +44 1481 235 208

www.HotelClub.com

La Barbarie is tucked away deep in the quiet lanes of St Martin, one of the island's prettiest parishes; and although the hotel itself is not particularly elegant or imposing - and it certainly wouldn't lay any claim to be the grandest or

smartest on the island - it has an intensely friendly, welcoming feel about it. Managing director Andy Coleman has been running the place for years, and most of his key staff also have impressively long service records.

The en suite bedrooms are pleasantly furnished, well equipped and scrupulously clean, although again they're nothing spectacular in themselves. The jewel in La Barbarie's crown is really the restaurant, which produces outstandingly good food without affectation and with complete reliability. Rick Stein stayed there while making one of his television cookery programmes, and pronounced the lobster the best he had ever tasted - praise indeed from one of the country's most celebrated seafood chefs.

The dining room itself is so cosy and so cleverly lit that you would feel completely at peace finishing your meal there alone. The menus change daily according to what's in season and what's fresh; the wine list is decent and very fairly priced. All in all, it would be hard to find fault with it as a restaurant; as a hotel dining room it's quite simply an outstanding find.

Outside there are pleasant gardens, a pool, and a scattering of wooden tables and benches amongst the trees and flowering shrubs; ideal for an al fresco drink or two before dinner on a warm summer's evening.

Rates from: 🏨🏨🏨
Star rating: ★ ★ ★ ★ ★
Overall rating: 🪙🪙🪙

Ambience :	9.88	Cleanliness:	9.56
Value:	9.92	Facilities:	9.88
Staff:	10.0	Restaurants:	9.98
Location:	9.73	Families:	9.41

Longueville Manor

St Saviour, Jersey, JE2 7WF, Channel Islands
T: ++44 1534 725 501 **F:** +44 1534 731 613
www.HotelClub.com/hotels/Longueville_Manor_Hotel

If you're in search of elegance and luxury then the Longueville Manor is probably the first choice in Jersey.

Shielded away from the hustle and bustle of St Helier by its imposing granite wall, this deluxe property is especially distinguished by its restaurant, which certainly puts the epic in epicure.

A 14th century Norman manor house with just 30 rooms, Longueville offers the best there is, with everything from bathrobes, slippers and scented candles to fruit, fresh flowers and homemade shortbread.

For the business traveller, or indeed anyone with a mind to Google, there is free Wi-Fi broadband Internet throughout the hotel and its immaculately-kept grounds.

But if relaxing is the purpose of your stay, then try The Cottage Suite, a two-bedroomed Jersey farmhouse secluded in the grounds. Every luxury has been considered, and with a spacious lounge and dining area, you can entertain guests or put your feet up in absolute peace and tranquillity.

As previously implied, the restaurant offers fine dining at its best. Such is its reputation that even locals need to book well in advance to enjoy the treat of a meal at "The Manor". Its kitchens carry on the traditions of old, using original recipes enhanced and inspired by the fruit, vegetables and herbs grown in the walled garden and Victorian glasshouses.

The hotel's slogan is "consider us your home from home", something of a cliché but one must argue that if we all lived like this, we would never leave our homes.

Rates from: 🏠🏠🏠
Star rating: ★★★★
Overall rating: 🐻🐻🐻🐻 ½

Ambience :	9.64	Cleanliness:	9.82
Value:	8.91	Facilities:	8.06
Staff:	9.90	Restaurants:	10.0
Location:	7.82	Families:	9.67

Pomme d'Or Hotel

Liberation Square, St Helier, Jersey, JE1 3UF, Channel Islands
T: +44 1534 880 110 **F:** +44 1534 737 781
www.HotelClub.com/hotels/Pomme_dOr_Hotel_Jersey

Recently refurbished, the plush Pomme d'Or ("golden apple" for non-Francophones) is ideally located, whether you're in the island on business or pleasure.

The hotel overlooks historic Liberation Square, where thousands of islanders gathered to see the Union flag hoisted after five years of German occupation from 1940 to 1945.

Now, Pomme's upgraded frontage stands proudly at the gateway of the town centre. Literally metres from the front door is the main taxi rank, the newly-opened and state-of-the-art Liberation bus station and the tourist information office.

The preferred location for St Helier's popular business breakfasts, the hotel also sits within easy walking distance of its important "off-shore" finance centre. Unless you intend to explore the island at great length, a hire car will not be necessary here.

Inside you will find everything the modern traveller requires, including free Wi-Fi broadband Internet access in all public areas, conference and banqueting facilities and 143 spacious, air-conditioned, rooms.

Tucked into the street-side corner of the building is the Café Bar, which, once the sun begins to set over St Aubin's Bay, becomes one of the focal points for relaxed islanders to start their nights out. With a full-time cocktail shaker, and a selection of fine wines and Continental beers, the bar is a stylish way to begin an evening's entertainment.

And you needn't look any further for a place to eat as La Petite Pomme is one of Jersey's leading à la carte restaurants. It offers a mouth-watering selection of meals, inspired by the island's produce.

Rates from: 🍎🍎🍎
Star rating: ★ ★ ★ ★
Overall rating: 🐾🐾🐾🐾

Ambience :	9.00	Cleanliness :	9.17
Value:	8.75	Facilities:	8.33
Staff:	8.75	Restaurants:	9.27
Location:	9.58	Families:	7.67

Stocks Island Hotel

Smugglers Valley, above Pirate Bay, Isle of Sark, GY9 0SD, Channel Islands
T: +44 1481 832 001 **F:** +44 1481 832 130
www.HotelClub.com

Stocks Hotel is set at the bottom of a valley deep in Sark's heartland, in handsome stone buildings set around three sides of a lawn. To one side, and enclosed behind a high wooden fence, is an attractive pool complete with the requisite scattering of sun loungers, tables and chairs.

Inside the welcome from owner Paul Armorgie and his family is warm and genuine, and the establishment prides itself on a high proportion of repeat business. Paul presides over the hour of the cocktail in the comfortable bar, refilling glasses, taking orders for dinner, and expanding on the specialities of the day with considerable aplomb and great charm; and when the guests file through to the dining room they invariably discover that his enthusiasm is justified - the menu changes daily, and is always based on fresh produce, locally-reared lamb and beef, and freshly-caught seafood.

The décor is perhaps a little faded and a little dated here and there, but somehow that all contributes to the friendly feel of the place; the en suite rooms are all comfortable and prettily furnished, and a number have annexes equipped with bunk beds to cater for families.

Stocks doesn't rest on its laurels and let the charm of the island do all its PR. Former guests receive a personally signed Christmas card and next year's brochures as a matter of course; and all things considered it's no surprise that a large number of Paul Armorgie's guests take him up on the suggestion of a return visit.

Rates from: 🏨🏨🏨
Star rating: ★★★
Overall rating: **Editors' Pick**

Ambience :	n/a	Cleanliness:	n/a
Value:	n/a	Facilities:	n/a
Staff:	n/a	Restaurants:	n/a
Location:	n/a	Families:	n/a

England

One in four Londoners was born outside the capital. Manchester City and Chelsea football clubs are owned by Thai and Russian oligarchs. The chairman of the Peak District National Park comes from Zanzibar.

Stands the church clock at 14.50? And is there GM honey still for tea? Multi-culturalism might be a strong thread in England's zeitgeist, but even before the construction of the Tunnel the English Channel was no great barrier to foreign influence. Many major thoroughfares follow the course of roads laid out by the Romans two millennia back, the influence of the Vikings is still plain in the speech of parts of northern England, William of Normandy's Domesday Book might be regarded as an 11th-century precursor to Google, and while Queen Victoria (married to a German) saw the boundaries of her empire pushed to the four corners of the earth, the descendants of her former subjects (to say nothing of a swathe of Eastern Europeans) have flocked to Blighty in a neat reversal of colonisation. If, for example, babbling Bengalis hold sway over chirruping Cockneys in some parts of London, it is not so much a new trend but a more

visible (and audible) continuation of something that's been going on for centuries. Membership of the European Union dented the concept of Splendid Isolation somewhat, and while dictates from Brussels may cause some hiccups to traditional ways, pub barmaids

still pour pints (not litres) of beer even if greengrocers (a fast vanishing breed given the predominance of Tesco and other supermarket chains) sell spuds by the kilo.

The capital, the focus of the rather over-hyped Cool Britannia vogue, remains one of the wealthiest (and by the same token expensive) cities in Europe, while Heathrow is the busiest airport in the region. As a cultural centre, London brooks few rivals - whether you want to catch a concert by Arctic Monkeys, wander the many free museums, or take in the merry crew of buskers and mimes on the ultra fresh south bank of the Thames; however its prominence faces some challenges from secondary cities such as Birmingham and Leeds, which are reinventing themselves after spending much of the 70s and 80s in the economic doldrums. Smaller places, such as Brighton, provide

not simply a vivacious escape from The Smoke, but a glimpse of the new freewheeling breed of restaurants and shopping that has brought its influence to bear on England's leisure time. And the seaside resort's naturist beach, some 200 metres long and strewn with flesh-resistant pebbles, is a sure indication that the English penchant for eccentricity is alive and well.

For many visitors, England is represented not so much by its cities as its countryside. Despite being heavily populated (50 million and counting, or some 383 per square kilometre), and in some parts less picturesque than in John Constable's day, there are still vast expanses, criss-crossed with walking and biking trails and superbly mapped by the Ordnance Survey, where you can roam pretty much undisturbed. The Lake District, which so inspired the romantic poet William Wordsworth, contains some of the loveliest vistas in the country, which - strange to record - many visitors seem happy to absorb from the security of a car park.

England's hotels continue to run the full accommodation gamut, from country inns which have accelerated past mere bed and board to gastro pub status and beyond, to such well known metropolitan names as The Ritz and Claridge's. (Another grande dame, The Savoy, sadly does not appear here as it is being renovated by its new North American owners, and not due to reopen until 2009). In the

provinces, many rural estates now host golf courses and spas beside stately mansions, while tremendous plaudits are due to the current range of "style" properties, such as Malmaison and Hotel du Vin. Best of all, many would aver, are small, individually owned hotels like Estbek House

near Whitby, run with passion and a degree of hospitality that no corporate mission statement can ever hope to mimic.

No hotels in Torquay (home to the fictional, fantastic Basil Fawlty) appear in the following pages, but it's part of the *soi-disant* Cornish Riviera. This is a clever piece of

nomenclature, and the weather does its best to fall into line, however visitors used to balmier climes might do well to pack both umbrella and warm clothing, whatever the advertised season, and wherever they are headed in England. Talking about the weather is still a staple of native conversation, from Berwick-upon-Tweed to Land's End. And with good reason.

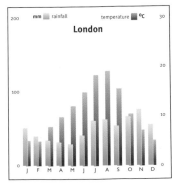

Amberley Castle

Amberley, Nr Arundel, Amberley, West Sussex, BN18 9LT, England
T: +44 1798 831 992   **F**: +44 1798 831 998
www.HotelClub.com

For anyone in search of a fairytale setting, Amberley Castle provides the classic answer. The stunning experience begins right from the moment of motoring up the gravel driveway beneath the oak portcullis which is lowered bang on the dot of midnight. In the lee of the South Downs, 900-year-old Amberley Castle ticks all the romantic boxes - the medieval stonework, the rose-covered arches, the statuesque curtain walls and the battlements.

Medieval kings and queens never had it as good as diners sampling breakfast by the window seat in the barrel-vaulted Queen's Room, though. Here, as well as in the larger Kings Room or the more intimate King Charles Room, menus are seasonal. Still, if this is not enough there is always the Mistletoe Lodge. A thatched roof treehouse and beneath the shady sycamore trees by the castle's entrance gate, the lodge encourages lingering after a meal with its comfy armchairs and window seat.

Owners Martin and Joy Cummings and their two Pyrenean Mountain dogs are a frequent sight around the immaculate grounds, and a stuffed toy version of those friendly canines lies atop the pillows in each of the 19 rooms. Other homey touches such as a Roberts radio, four-poster beds and fresh milk, as well as Jacuzzi bathrooms and spacious sitting rooms in the Bishopric suites, make staying in as tempting as exploring the rolling acres outside. All in all, few could dispute Amberley is a harmonious marriage of old world splendour and charm with new world practicality and comfort.

Rates from: 🏰 🏰 🏰 🏰
Star rating: ★ ★ ★ ★
Overall rating: 🏰 🏰 🏰 🏰

Ambience :	9.60	Cleanliness:	9.60
Value:	8.25	Facilities:	7.24
Staff:	9.60	Restaurants:	9.25
Location:	8.90	Families:	7.71

The Drunken Duck Inn and Restaurant

Barngates, Ambleside, Cumbria, LA22 0NG, England
T: +44 15394 36347 **F:** +44 15394 36781
www.HotelClub.com

If a certain gallant Commando officer and his not so blushing bride hadn't honeymooned here in 1944, this guide might have had a

different editor. But that's another story... The main point about the Duck - which is set on 24 hectares of private land - is that it epitomises

the hospitality revolution that has overtaken England in recent years. From a farmhouse that took in visitors, it meandered through the decades as a fairly ordinary chicken-in-a-basket pub, until it was taken over by the current owners in 1977, who've turned it into a boutique gastro inn.

The past 30 years have witnessed tremendous change, although the glorious surrounding countryside would be instantly recognisable to returning wartime honeymooners. The complement of 16 rooms - and it's a rare night when they are not all occupied - is split between the old inn and a new, more spacious extension to the rear. Antiques, prints, and tasteful upholstery make each of the rooms a mini haven that's full of character. The most popular, and

understandably so, is the Garden Room, whose French windows open onto a large private balcony overlooking the garden and tarn. An open-beamed ceiling, and floor-to-ceiling cantilevered windows looking up to the Langdales, adds to the sense of intimate rural luxury.

In the wildly inconceivable event of the Duck ever giving up its rooms, it could still prosper as an independent restaurant. Modern British cuisine flourishes in its low-ceilinged yet freshly modern interior, and most evenings there are few seats to spare as diners graze the likes of Cannon of Cumbrian lamb, roasted Scottish beef fillet, and Goosnargh duck breast. Failing to leave room for pudding is a definite sin helping of omission.

Of course, the heart of the Duck is its Bar. Many hotels nowadays make much of their policy of local sourcing: the bar here is made from Brathay Black slate quarried from a short way down Duck Hill. The atmosphere is compounded by wide oak flooring, old beams, an open fire, and swims to the heady atmosphere of the Duck's own brewery, Barngates, which now supplies many other inns around the north of England.

Tables outside provide one of England's best al fresco spots to drink and dine on a summer's evening.

Anglers should note that Duck Tarn, just behind the inn, is stocked with Brown and Rainbow trout, and there's no charge for fly-fishing guests in season.

Perhaps the Drunken Duck's greatest attraction is that it remains a "local". The crowd at the bar of an evening may well include as many Lakeland farmers as Londoners who've popped up for a couple of nights' break in what was an Area of Outstanding Natural Beauty long before any government agency so classified it.

Finally, anyone wondering about this inn's name will be intrigued to learn it dates from the day a long-ago owner returned to find her entire flock dead. It was only when she started to pluck them that she realised they were drunk, rather than deceased, a beer barrel in the cellar having seeped into the ducks' pond.

Rates from: 🪙🪙🪙
Star rating: ★ ★ ★ ★ ★
Overall rating: 🦆🦆🦆🦆

Ambience :	8.75	Cleanliness:	9.75
Value:	8.25	Facilities:	4.00
Staff:	8.50	Restaurants:	9.00
Location:	10.0	Families:	6.33

Ashdown Park Hotel & Country Club

Wych Cross, East Sussex, RH18 5JR, England
T: +44 1342 824 988 **F:** +44 1342 826 206
www.HotelClub.com/hotels/Ashdown_Park_Hotel_and_Country_Club

Seemingly this elegant country house was always destined to be a sanctuary - first to shell-shocked Great War soldiers; then to the Sisters of Notre Dame and now to modern-day guests in need of de-stressing.

Just 30 minutes' drive from Gatwick Airport but feeling isolated in its 75 Sussex Wealden hectares, it sits in the ancient royal hunting ground of Ashdown Forest, celebrated by AA Milne in his enduring tales of that honey-fixated bear.

Winnie the Pooh would be heartened to see that real honeycomb is served at breakfast in the Anderida Restaurant while one-time MP Thomas Thompson, who built the property back in 1867, would approve of the attentive army of black-suited, purple-waistcoated staff and the house rule banning denim in public rooms after 6pm.

With 106 rooms - many, like Monkey Puzzle, named after trees in the grounds, and some with four-poster beds and whirlpool baths -

there is a sense of peace and space, a lingering aroma of wood smoke mixed with the heady scent of endless vases of pink lilies, and an afternoon tea timelessness despite the steady tick of longcase clocks. And with a herd of wild deer in the grounds don't be surprised if you wake to see a stag strutting his stuff across the lawn.

You can lose yourself in woodland walks, head to the fitness centre or 18-hole golf course, discover the chapel or secret garden or play Pooh Sticks at the renowned nearby bridge. Completely restorative, even Pooh's heavy-hearted friend Eeyore couldn't be gloomy here.

Rates from: 💰💰💰
Star rating: ★★★★
Overall rating: 👐👐👐👐

Ambience :	9.50	Cleanliness:	9.38
Value:	7.57	Facilities:	9.08
Staff:	9.14	Restaurants:	9.64
Location:	8.57	Families:	8.40

The Victoria Hotel

Front Street, Bamburgh, Northumberland, NE69 7BP, England
T: +44 1668 214431 **F:** +44 1668 214404
www.HotelClub.com

If castles are your thing, this little corner of Northumbria is the place to find them, from the one on the historic, causeway-linked "holy" isle of Lindisfarne to the Duke of Northumberland's 700-year-old pile at Alnwick, location for atmospheric films from *Elizabeth* and *Becket* to *Harry Potter*. But Bamburgh Castle is reckoned to be one of the finest in England and it hovers over Bamburgh village like a medieval movie backdrop.

In the middle of said village, right on the green, is the Victoria Hotel, the perfect base for castle-hopping, island-exploring, wildlife-spotting or simply scuffing along the sands of one of Britain's most glorious beaches. Transport yourself back to a typical 19th-century holiday lifestyle: uncanopied four-poster beds, repro and genuine-antique furniture in all the rooms, log fires...

The private dining room off The Brasserie restaurant - which specialises in locally-grown produce - is named after the only man known to have amused the austere Queen Victoria, Gillie (John) Brown. And the bar boasts a superb selection of northern "real ales" - ask for a pint of the spectacular Black Sheep.

In true Victorian fashion, you are expected to make your own entertainment: a leisurely Afternoon Tea, for instance, with all the trimmings, or nodding off behind a newspaper in an armchair as ensnaring as the local sands, a quiet game of chess or draughts, or a pre-prandial snifter to the background strains of local anthem *Fog On The Tyne* (hopefully, the 1970s Lindisfarne original rather than footballer Paul Gasgoigne's forgettable revival).

Rates from: 🐻🐻
Star rating: ★★
Overall rating: **Editors' Pick**

Ambience :	n/a	Cleanliness:	n/a
Value:	n/a	Facilities:	n/a
Staff:	n/a	Restaurants:	n/a
Location:	n/a	Families:	n/a

Macdonald Bath Spa Hotel

Sydney Road, Bath, BA2 6JF, England
T: +44 1225 444 424 **F:** +44 1225 444 006
www.HotelClub.com/hotels/Bath_Spa_Hotel

Think Jane Austen, swish your crinolines for ten minutes and a rambling scenic stride from the sometimes car-snarled hub of Bath leads to this imposing 18th-century former nurses' home. Fronted by immaculate gardens and soothing fountains, it's a peaceful away-from-it-all green lung in a cream city; a sedate Georgian gem ideal for getaways and genteel, city-with-style resuscitation. With ornate plaster ceilings, flame fires, high windows and muted, soothing colours, it's five-star smart but not snooty. Around £10 million has just been spent on refurbs to the 129 variously sized bedrooms, along with luxy improvements such as the spa.

Continuing the *Aquae Sulis* tradition of feel-good, do-good water dermal appeal, it boasts sense-tingling aroma, salt infusion and ice rooms, a nifty indoor-outdoor swim-through pool kept to a flesh-cosseting 37 degrees, and a sun bathing terrace gagging for sun-kissed smoothy-sipping before one of the spa's signature treatment Algae Wraps. Every gram lost can then be restored at the colonnaded, airy Al Fresco restaurant with its Mediterranean menu, or the ballroom-sized Vellore dining room where the fare leans towards modern English and the ambience is more formal.

Although the general décor is traditional with an occasional modern twist, the mood is unstuffy, the staff user-friendly and creature comforts are as respected as the grand setting. Bedroom treats include a choose-your-tog duvet and pillow menu, and there is butler service in the 21 more contemporary Imperial Suites, across a courtyard from the main building. No surprise that this is the flagship of the Macdonald's chain.

Rates from: 🛏🛏🛏🛏
Star rating: ★★★★★
Overall rating: 👐👐👐👐

Ambience :	8.91	Cleanliness:	9.32
Value:	7.72	Facilities:	8.80
Staff:	9.00	Restaurants:	9.13
Location:	9.16	Families:	8.33

The Royal Crescent Hotel

16 Royal Crescent, Bath, BA1 2LS, England
T: +44 1225 823 333 **F:** +44 1225 447 427
www.HotelClub.com/hotels/The_Royal_Crescent_Hotel_Bath

Persuasion? There's little of that needed to tempt you here. Keira Knightley - who's been filmed outside so often she's almost qualified for a parking permit - couldn't drag you kicking and screaming from this relaxed but ravishing Regency gem, plopped grandly slap bang in the middle of one of the world's finest architectural crescents, which took eight years to build and has ever since been the smartest address in Jane Austen Central. Arriving at its chic-discreet front door, marked by subtle green tubs of manicured box, the urge is to exhale, step back in time and swoon like a period damsel/swain onto the sumptuous bedding in one of the 45 bedrooms.

But slump-not: the atmospheric lure of the candle-lit, churchesque spa pool is sensual enough to stir even "Damp Trews" Darcy from his stiff-lipped brooding....

Add to all this the ultra delicious dining in The Dower House, while The Library and The Pavilion Conservatory are ideal for more intimate gourmeting.

Rates from: 🐘🐘🐘🐘🐘
Star rating: ★ ★ ★ ★ ★
Overall rating: 🐾🐾🐾🐾 ½

Ambience :	9.62	Cleanliness:	9.58
Value:	8.38	Facilities:	8.62
Staff:	9.27	Restaurants:	9.46
Location:	9.65	Families:	7.60

Burgh Island Hotel

Burgh Island, Bigbury-on-Sea, South Devon, TQ7 4BG, England
T: +44 1548 810 514 **F:** +44 1548 810 243
www.HotelClub.com

Guests heading to this 1930s country house hotel can choose to walk across from the coast of Devon just 200 metres away or be picked up by the hotel's Sea Tractors at high tide.

This quiet hideaway, where dolphins frolic in the bay and rare birds breed, is also home to what's reckoned to be one of the country's sexiest hotel rooms - the Beach House. It is here that Wallis Simpson and Edward Windsor whiled away the time and Agatha Christie wrote two of her novels. Like the other 22 rooms, the Beach House is individually furnished with original pictures and a retro radio. It's simply perfect for 21st century flappers.

Centuries ago, Britons bartered tin and iron for wine, oil, spices and silk with Mediterranean traders on the beach that today fronts the art deco-style Burgh Island Hotel.

Rates from: 🐘🐘🐘🐘🐘
Star rating: n/a
Overall rating: 🐾🐾🐾🐾

Ambience :	9.57	Cleanliness:	9.00
Value:	7.57	Facilities:	6.40
Staff:	9.29	Restaurants:	9.21
Location:	9.71	Families:	8.40

City Inn Birmingham

1 Brunswick Square, Brindleyplace, Birmingham, B1 2HW, England
T: +44 121 643 1003 **F:** +44 121 643 1005
www.HotelClub.com/hotels/City_Inn_Birmingham

Brindleyplace is the epitome of bright new Birmingham - all pastel brick and tinted glass - and the stylish City Inn fits it like a USB plug-in. Almost next door to the huge Convention Centre, National Indoor Arena and Symphony Hall, it attracts a mix of business types and night-on-the-towners, as such proximity would suggest. The entertainment scene on Broad Street and the vibrant canalside nightlife are added attractions of the location.

Of the 238 minimalist rooms (showers only, but all contemporary such as free Wi-Fi Internet access, flat-screen TVs, stereo system and free DVD library), ask for one overlooking the canal (did you know that Birmingham has more of them than Venice?)

If you don't have time to try one of the trendy new restaurants in which the area abounds, the in-house City Café, with two terraces, makes a reliable alternative.

A couple of tips: if the hotel car park is full, you can obtain a reduced rate at the public one opposite as a guest of the City Inn.

And, for inspiration-seeking couples, the adult TV channel is FOC, to coin a phrase. Oh, and although the breakfast buffet closes early (9.30am) during the week given the nine-to-five needs of most guests, it stays open till a leisurely 11am on Sunday mornings.

The traditional city-centre shopping district and revamped Bull Ring are a mere ten-minute walk away and you're within easy reach of most other places of interest, such as the Art Gallery and the Botanical Gardens, the Jewellery Quarter and Chinatown.

Rates from: 🏠🏠🏠🏠
Star rating: n/a
Overall rating: 👍👍👍👍

Ambience :	8.88	Cleanliness:	9.13
Value:	8.50	Facilities:	8.21
Staff:	8.75	Restaurants:	8.64
Location:	9.25	Families:	8.00

Crowne Plaza Hotel Birmingham City Centre

Holiday Street, Birmingham, B11HH, England
T: +44 870 4009150 **F:** +44 121 643 9018
www.HotelClub.com/hotels/Crowne_Plaza_Hotel_Birmingham

As dependable a property as you would expect from the four-star brand of one of the world's largest hotel groups. Its 284 rooms (including an Executive Floor) are exceptionally large and amply furnished and come with CD/DVD player, satellite and cable TV, pay-per-view movies, sound system, free tea, coffee, bottled water, biscuits and morning newspaper, plus ice-making machines in the corridors.

Light meals are served in the club-style Terrace Bar, while the Conservatory Restaurant does breakfast, lunch and dinner, with plenty of healthy-eating options - and kids get to eat for free! The extensive buffet breakfast runs to steaks for those looking to stoke up for the day or repair the damage of the night before.

There is a health and fitness centre and Wi-Fi Internet access is available in the reception area and the bar.

But perhaps this place's biggest selling point is its location - just round the corner from New Street Station, a major rail hub, and slap bang in the middle of the trendy canalside bar-and-restaurant area known as The Mailbox. From one side, you have exhilarating city views, from the other, the Canal - and the International Convention Centre, National Indoor Arena and new shopping developments are but a short stroll away.

With Hong Kong billionaire Carson Yeung's recent interest in Premiership football club Birmingham City, you can expect an influx of visitors from Asia - who should feel very much at home here, as a high proportion of the staff are Chinese. Go Blues!

Rates from: 🪙🪙🪙🪙
Star rating: ★ ★ ★ ★
Overall rating: 👍👍👍👍

Ambience :	7.67	Cleanliness:	8.72
Value:	7.50	Facilities:	8.11
Staff:	7.63	Restaurants:	8.29
Location:	8.72	Families:	7.36

Hilton Birmingham Metropole

National Exhibition Centre, Birmingham, B40 1PP, England
T: +44 121 780 4242 **F:** +44 121 780 3923
www.HotelClub.com/hotels/Hilton_Metropole_Hotel_Birmingham

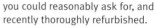

If you have a reason for visiting Birmingham's National Exhibition Centre - and plenty of people do, it hosts some 80 percent of the nation's exhibition business - then this is the place to stay since it is literally next door. A huge (794 rooms) hotel with all the facilities you could reasonably ask for, and recently thoroughly refurbished.

It is the only property on the NEC site to boast a swimming pool (indoor and heated, and a toddlers' pool to go with it, plus free aqua-aerobics lessons). It also offers the LivingWell Health Club, with fully equipped gym, Jacuzzi, sauna and massage. A business centre and 33 meeting rooms cater for the largely executive clientele.

As is usually the case with hotels that offer upgrades, stepping up to an Executive Room is well worth it, granting access to the Executive Lounge, with its free breakfast and cocktail-hour snacks.

Dining options range from an imaginative 24-hour room service menu (chicken balti or BLT baguette any time) through the long, always-open lobby Lounge Bar, where you can grab a club sandwich, to Millers Gastro Pub and a brace of restaurants, La Primavera and Boulevard .

Downsides are that Internet access has to be paid for and drinks are a tad pricey. Upside, proximity to the airport, to which there is a half-hourly shuttle-bus service. On the other hand, it's a hefty 30-minute taxi ride to the centre of town. If you're a music fan, watch out for the special offers to tie in with concerts at the NEC.

Rates from: 🛏🛏
Star rating: ★★★★
Overall rating: 🛏🛏🛏🛏

Ambience :	8.35	Cleanliness:	8.94
Value:	7.94	Facilities:	8.81
Staff:	8.65	Restaurants:	8.14
Location:	8.94	Families:	7.90

Hotel Du Vin

Church Street, Birmingham, B3 2NR, England
T: +44 121 200 0600 **F:** +44 121 236 0889
www.HotelClub.com/hotels/Hotel_Du_Vin

When the mattresses are hand-sprung and the bistro produce is hand-picked, you know you're off to a rattling good start. With 66 rooms dotted around a central courtyard, hard by the glittering revitalised Jewellery Centre, this branch of the deservedly successful Vin chain is symptomatic of the new hum in Brum. Chef Nick Turner helms the bistro's kitchen with more than a little éclat, while Ben Mulvaney, with the mouth-watering title of Head of Bars and Cigars, is thoroughly *au fait* with both cellar and humidor. Five spa treatment rooms, plus sauna (worth checking in here simply for the drench shower), steamroom and gym, spell just about every conceivable need being catered for under one roof. And what better use could there possibly be for a former Victorian Eye Hospital? Given the current state of the National Health Service, perhaps the public can look forward to more and similar Hots DV.

Rates from: ☾☾☾
Star rating: n/a
Overall rating: ♨♨♨♨

Ambience :	9.36	Cleanliness:	9.64
Value:	8.50	Facilities:	7.87
Staff:	8.93	Restaurants:	9.08
Location:	9.29	Families:	7.11

Hyatt Regency Birmingham

2 Bridge Street, Birmingham, B1 2JZ, England
T: +44 121 643 1234 **F:** +44 121 616 2323
www.HotelClub.com/hotels/Hyatt_Regency_Hotel_Birmingham

The world-wide Hyatt chain has a grand total of three outposts in Britain; besides having the most modern exterior, this - a city centre skyscraper - is the only one outside London. Regulars (both out-of-towners who make a habit of staying here and locals who like to pop in for a bite or a drink) speak respectfully of the swish environs of Bar Pravda and the culinary symphonies dished up in Aria. Potential guests given pause for thought by seven different sorts of room should note that major differentials include a) size and b) price. Quite the best on-property accessory is the 16-metre indoor heated pool, plus attendant sauna and steam room, which offer quite the best antidote to a long day's slog around Brum till well after dusk. The cold water plunge pool is all together a different proposition...

Rates from: ☾☾☾☾
Star rating: ★★★★
Overall rating: ♨♨♨♨

Ambience :	8.96	Cleanliness:	9.52
Value:	8.29	Facilities:	8.89
Staff:	8.64	Restaurants:	8.67
Location:	9.08	Families:	8.40

Malmaison

The Mailbox, 1 Wharfside Street, Birmingham, B17 9AN, England
T: +44 121 246 5000 **F:** +44 121 246 5002
www.HotelClub.com/hotels/Malmaison_Hotel_Birmingham

Is it the little touches or the really basic stuff that sorts the hotel sheep from the lambs? Birmingham's Malmaison manages to get both of them right - for example, speakers for your iPod in the rooms, and some of the comfiest beds this side of a Harrods showroom. No prizes for guessing that this, and other properties in the group, are among Britain's top hotel trendsetters.

Set above Harvey Nicks in the trendiest part of town, The Mailbox (named after the old PO sorting office, but now a hip haven of waterside bars, boutiques and bistros), the hotel is unremittingly funky, from its individually designed, different-sized rooms to its welcoming green apples, plus all mood lighting and mirrors.

Its Brasserie (which has some private dining rooms) prides itself on spotlighting home-grown produce such as smoked meats air-dried with Shropshire oak, hand-crafted cheese from England's oldest cheesemaker, and the country's finest organic fudge. Room-service breakfast is presented in a Muji-style box. The weekend crush at the Bar is testimony to the place's popularity with the locals, always a good sign.

There is a gym and a Petit Spa, with sauna and steam room and all sorts of exotic treatments. All in all, it's the perfect big-city getaway for a couple with romance in mind. Splash out on a suite with complimentary iced champers, chocolate-dipped strawberries, aromatic oils and candles, and a Malmaison mood-music CD. The legendary Josephine, who built Chateau de Malmaison for Napoleon Bonaparte, would certainly have approved.

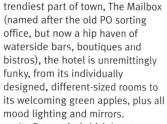

Rates from: 🏠🏠🏠🏠
Star rating: n/a
Overall rating: 👍👍👍👍

Ambience :	9.22	Cleanliness:	9.59
Value:	8.04	Facilities:	8.04
Staff:	8.56	Restaurants:	8.67
Location:	9.00	Families:	7.58

Radisson SAS Hotel Birmingham

12 Holloway Circus, Queensway, Birmingham, B1 1BT, England
T: +44 121 654 6000 **F:** +44 121 654 6001
www.HotelClub.com/hotels/Radisson_SAS_Birmingham

Newest kid on Birmingham's newest block - on Holloway Circus between the modish Mailbox and the bustling Bull Ring - is a 39-storey circular glass skyscraper that were it not for the proximity of the airport would have been Europe's tallest residential building. The first 18 floors house the 211-room Radisson SAS, a strong contender for Brum's best.

The Matteo Thun-designed rooms are labelled Chic, Fashion or Fresh; further up the scale there's both Business Class and Suites; and then there's the pop-star-sized 1820 Presidential Suite. All have flat screen TVs and free broadband access and are reached via curved corridors with atmospheric padded-silk walls and cleverly angled lighting.

The first-floor Filini Restaurant (and adjoining Bar), named after a matchstick-thin pasta, offers Sardinian specialities and boasts bay and olive trees to give a truly Mediterranean feel. Or there's the Lobby Bar, where the busy business person can order a "Grab & Run" breakfast!

Views from the 18th-floor gym would be spectacular if Birmingham had rather more vistas worth drooling over, and there are three treatment rooms under the somewhat puzzling name "Obsession" (unless that's what some folk's interest in their appearance is deemed to be).

Amidst all this modernity, in a nod to the industrial heritage of England's second city, the hotel's meeting rooms are named after all the things that made Birmingham a power in the land, not to say the world - Water (its canals), Light (after local lad James Watt), Mini (its cars), Steam (its engines), and Oxygen (its contribution to anaesthesia).

Rates from: 🪙🪙🪙
Star rating: ★★★★
Overall rating: 🐾🐾🐾🐾

Ambience :	9.00	Cleanliness:	9.57
Value:	8.07	Facilities:	9.07
Staff:	9.21	Restaurants:	9.25
Location:	8.71	Families:	8.50

The Norbreck Castle Hotel

Queen's Promenade, Blackpool, Lancashire, FY2 9AA, England
T: +44 845 838 1001 **F:** +44 845 838 0720
www.HotelClub.com/hotels/Norbreck_Castle_Hotel_Blackpool

Whether or not the Norbreck Castle is your kind of hotel rather depends on whether Blackpool is your kind of town. Do you think the faux turrets on what looks like part of a post-war housing estate resemble prison watchtowers or a Las Vegas-style themed hotel-casino? Tacky and downmarket, or whacky and working-class? Whatever your verdict, there's no getting away from the fact that it is great value for money.

With 480 rooms, meaning that at peak periods it could be catering for up to 1,500 guests, there is no getting away from a slightly holiday-camp atmosphere, nor would you expect cordon bleu cuisine.

But there is bags of choice - from the Castles and Boston restaurants to the Conservatory Bar and Copper Face Jack's pub. Blackpool holidays are family affairs and the kids are well provided for with nightly live entertainment and a 36-seat cinema, as well as free entrance to the Leisure Club, which boasts an 18-metre heated pool, splash pool, sauna, steamroom and Jacuzzi.

The place has just undergone a £10 million refurbishment and niggles about windows not opening or shutting properly should be a thing of the past (at least many of the rooms still have proper windows!). The biggest drawback is probably its out-of-town location on the North Shore, though there is a frequent tram service to the centre. The castle has Wi-Fi Internet access and is very wheelchair-friendly. As they say in this neck of the woods, you pays yer money...

Rates from: 🐨
Star rating: ★★★
Overall rating: 🐨🐨🐨🐨

Ambience :	7.27	Cleanliness:	7.40
Value:	7.60	Facilities:	8.29
Staff:	7.60	Restaurants:	7.73
Location:	7.53	Families:	8.07

Bournemouth Highcliff Marriott

St Michaels Road, West Cliff, Bournemouth, Dorset, BH2 5DU, England
T: +44 1202 557702 **F:** +44 1202 292734
www.HotelClub.com/hotels/Marriott_Highcliff_Hotel_Bournemouth

"Tony Blair slept here" may not have quite the same cachet as being told you're frequenting the same hotel as the Virgin Queen, but at least the former can be proven historically. How so? The Marriott stands adjacent to the Bournemouth International Centre, host of many a party conference. Pols love the place, so do your homework first if you wish to avoid spending the night next to the future Cabinet.

The chief asset of this stately, dolled-up Victorian gem of a hotel is really its location, perched atop the cliffs with gob-smacking sea vistas from many of its 160 recently-refurbished guest rooms. But here's a tip: for even greater peace and privacy, plump for a room in one of the original coastguards' cottages alongside the main building but with equally spectacular marine views (the coastguards have long gone). The hotel's public areas include a plush, sprawling reception area, speckled with antique clocks and mirrors, full of cosy nooks and crannies perfect for a bit of political intrigue. The charming Sea Breezes restaurant serves international cuisine with many a Dorset twist. You'll find lighter fare in the elegant Mountbatten Bar. Dorset cream teas taste even better on the terrace - except, perhaps, when you're being buffeted by a force nine sou'wester. After all that clotted cream, work off the calories in the hotel's generously equipped health and fitness suite. With Bournemouth's main shops and entertainment facilities just minutes away, and a quirky funicular to the beach opposite the hotel's main entrance, you'll recognise that few places in this town can rival the Marriott.

Rates from: 🛏🛏🛏🛏
Star rating: ★ ★ ★ ★
Overall rating: 🏵🏵🏵🏵 ½

Ambience :	9.06	Cleanliness:	9.47
Value:	8.41	Facilities:	9.20
Staff:	9.00	Restaurants:	9.25
Location:	9.53	Families:	8.70

De Vere Royal Bath Hotel

Bath Road, Bournemouth, Dorset, BH1 2EW, England
T: +44 1202 555555 **F:** +44 1202 292421
www.HotelClub.com/hotels/De_Vere_Royal_Bath_Hotel_Bournemouth

This low-rise, turreted, chateau-like edifice sprawls across a sizeable chunk of Bournemouth's East Cliff, in stark contrast to its brick-and-concrete neighbour, the Imax cinema/aircraft hangar which was voted the second ugliest building in Britain. A busy municipal car park - used (at cost) by Royal Bath guests when the hotel's own spaces are full - separates the contrasting pair.

The Royal Bath opened amid some fanfare in 1838 when Bournemouth was in its infancy, on the day 18-year-old Princess Victoria became Queen. It went on to entertain some of her most illustrious subjects - including prime ministers Benjamin Disraeli and William Gladstone. The majestic public rooms, with their monster chandeliers, lavish furnishings and forest of pillars exude Victorian elegance, and provide a sumptuous setting for breakfast and dinner. For a more intimate culinary experience, guests can dine in Oscar's restaurant, named after a certain Mr Wilde, another frequent visitor.

Many of the 135 well-equipped guest rooms boast gorgeous views across the bay to the Purbeck Hills and the Isle of Wight, though some can be a bit on the small side, while a few visitors have complained of creaky floorboards.

Meanwhile, those with creaky joints should head for a circular structure in the sub-tropically planted grounds where they'll find a well-equipped leisure club with a large indoor pool to complement the al fresco one. The hotel's central location - just a few minutes from the main beaches, 50 metres from the not-to-be-missed, lavishly over-the-top, recently-restored Russell Cotes Museum and Art Gallery, and a five-minute walk to Bournemouth's main shops - is another very good reason for staying here.

Rates from: 🛏🛏🛏🛏
Star rating: ★★★★
Overall rating: 🦢🦢🦢🦢

Ambience :	8.95	Cleanliness:	8.39
Value:	7.84	Facilities:	8.63
Staff:	8.95	Restaurants:	9.22
Location:	9.37	Families:	7.86

The De Vere Grand, Brighton

King's Road, Brighton, East Sussex, BN1 2FW, England
T: +44 1273 224 300 **F**: +44 1273 224 321
www.HotelClub.com/hotels/De_Vere_The_Grand_Hotel_Brighton

When Dr Richard Russell described bathing in seawater as beneficial to people's health in the 18th century, he started a trend that has yet to die out. So perhaps one could say he is indirectly responsible for the presence of the 200-room De Vere Grand with conference facilities for up to 5,000 located right on the seafront in this now thriving sea town.

Listed among the things to do in Brighton is getting stuck into afternoon tea at the Grand, in truly Victorian surroundings. For those with a healthier appetite, there is the modern European decorated King's restaurant. Specialties such as smoked haddock and salmon fishcakes and the crab terrine are sourced locally - in keeping with tradition that dates back to 1310 when the first fish market set up shop after Brighton was granted a charter. Ain't life Grand?

Rates from: 🛏🛏🛏
Star rating: ★★★★★
Overall rating: 🕊🕊🕊🕊

Ambience :	8.76	Cleanliness:	9.14
Value:	7.86	Facilities:	8.34
Staff:	8.77	Restaurants:	8.71
Location:	9.56	Families:	8.18

Hilton Brighton Metropole

King's Road, Brighton, East Sussex, BN1 2FU, England
T: +44 1273 775 432 **F**: +44 1273 207 764
www.HotelClub.com/hotels/Hilton_Metropole_Hotel_Brighton

Not for nothing is Brighton is synonymous with trendy getaway for Londoners, and the Hilton likes to let its guests get away from it all by offering them a light-filled interior with sea-viewing terraces, al fresco dining (Bar 106), and plenty of windows looking out toward the Continent.

For those wanting to be reminded that London is only a 50-minute train ride away, there is the Windsor restaurant with its ornate ceilings and European cuisine, and the Metropole Lounge Bar with its Victorian surroundings and even more tempting deep sofas.

Not groovy enough? Step into Lo Lounge and you could be in your favourite hip London bar. And for those here on business, let's not forget that with 28 meeting rooms and nine exhibition halls, this Hilton is host to Southern England's largest conference facilities. Who says you can't mix business with pleasure?

Rates from: 🛏🛏🛏
Star rating: ★★★★
Overall rating: 🕊🕊🕊🕊

Ambience :	8.58	Cleanliness:	8.92
Value:	8.24	Facilities:	8.52
Staff:	8.83	Restaurants:	8.79
Location:	9.24	Families:	8.70

The White House

6 Bedford Street, Brighton, East Sussex, BN2 1AN, England
T: +44 1273 62 62 66
www.HotelClub.com/hotels/White_House_Hotel_Brighton

To find the real heart of Brighton, forget The Lanes or the Royal Pavilion or the Pier - go to Kemp Town, about ten minutes' walk from the city centre in the direction of the Marina. This is the Brighton of Laurence Olivier and Max Miller and Graham Greene, of illicit weekends in sleazy B&Bs, of idiosyncratic pubs, gourmet restaurants and antique shops that exhort lengthy browsing.

The White House is a gem of a boutique hotel in the heart of this heart. A converted four-storey Regency dwelling, it has only ten bedrooms. All are equipped with TV, free Wi-Fi Internet access, hairdryers, facilities for making tea and coffee (fair trade, of course, as befits this liberal-thinking enclave), Gilchrist & Soames toiletries in the bathrooms, and - a much-appreciated touch, this - free chocolate bars.

As an upmarket B&B, only breakfast is served - but what a breakfast! Kippers and poached eggs, smoked salmon, a vegetarian Full Monty... served either in the dining room or al fresco in the small garden if it's a sunny morning. Proprietors Sean and Kathryn are the antithesis of the fierce types usually reputed to run such establishments and a great deal of the hotel's success is down to the personal touch of this friendly couple.

If you're looking for five-star luxury, this place is not for you. Rooms are on the Lilliputian side and the décor is minimalist bordering on sparse. But it is spotlessly clean, meticulously maintained and more like staying with exceptionally good friends than being in a hotel.

Rates from: 🏷🏷
Star rating: ★ ★ ★ ★
Overall rating: **Editors' Pick**

Ambience :	n/a	Cleanliness:	n/a
Value:	n/a	Facilities:	n/a
Staff:	n/a	Restaurants:	n/a
Location:	n/a	Families:	n/a

Bristol Royal Marriott Hotel

College Green, Bristol, BS1 5TA, England
T: +44 117 925 5100 **F:** +44 117 925 1515
www.HotelClub.com/hotels/Marriott_Royal_Hotel_Bristol

With a suitably regal statue of Queen Vic at the front, the majestic vibe of this city centre hotel is obvious even before you set a monogrammed slipper over its marbled threshold. With 242 recently re-souped-up bedrooms, it's a spacious multi-purpose treasure, in a traditional "tick-the-box" polished mahogany, gleaming brass, pillow menu, business and leisure kind of style. The Champagne Bar, with its plasma screen, red walls and black granite bar, has a mellow, moody feel, while the airy Romanesque interior atrium of the main Palm Court restaurant will have you half expecting Romeo and Juliet to pop out for a quick balcony snog while you savour a *bouchée*. But the jewel in this accommodation's crown is its fabulous location: smartly neighbouring the cathedral and a pleb' s-throw away from the historic waterfront, theatres and shops. Even the notoriously not-easily-amused Victoria would have to admit Herself pleased hereabouts.

Rates from: 🍸🍸🍸	
Star rating: ★★★★	
Overall rating: 👣👣👣 ½	
Ambience : 9.29	Cleanliness: 9.36
Value: 8.71	Facilities: 8.82
Staff: 8.86	Restaurants: 9.23
Location: 9.14	Families: 7.91

Hotel Du Vin & Bistro

The Sugar House, Narrow Lewins Mead, Bristol, BS1 2NU, England
T: +44 117 925 5577 **F:** +44 117 925 1199
www.HotelClub.com

suite. Dining, quaffing and inhaling are other specialities: the land-sea menu aims to offer a plate with everything hailing from within 50 kilometres, they sell at least one bottle of the £1,500 St Petrus a month, and the humidor contains tobacco-sausages that are similarly pricey and equally toothsome.

Sing along now - *sugar, sugar, dahdadadadada, ahh, honey, honey... you are my* - well no, not candy girl obviously, but bo-hotel nectar, creatively carved into a restored 18th-century sugar factory. Each of the 40 rooms is syrup to the senses, oozing pretty much designer everything: mega wooden beds, orgy-sized showers, even fresh milk for tea! Close to the old (and less second world war bombed/more picturesque) business hub of the city, this is a place for listening to live jazz in the wood-floored bar on Sundays, or sipping a Mojito in His'n'Ners baths in the split-level Veuve Cliquot

Rates from: 🍸🍸🍸	
Star rating: ★★★★	
Overall rating: 👣👣👣👣	
Ambience : 9.28	Cleanliness: 9.48
Value: 8.22	Facilities: 7.35
Staff: 8.96	Restaurants: 9.45
Location: 9.08	Families: 6.89

The Lygon Arms

Broadway, Worcestershire, WR12 7DU, England
T: +44 1386 852 255 **F:** +44 1386 858 611
www.HotelClub.com

and technology of today. Dining at the Great Hall - in a setting of oak panelling, a barrel-vaulted ceiling and 17th century Minstrel's Gallery - is reminiscent of the grand traditional three-hour meal served in great medieval castles. The extensive grounds and country club provide the icing on the cake.

One of the more remarkable facts about The Lygon Arms (500 plus years old, and an ultra traditional, classic Cotswolds village inn) is that it hosted both Oliver Cromwell and Charles I - arch adversaries at the time of the Civil War. Warm welcomes continue to

be a hallmark of the hotel; many of the 69 rooms and suites - split between the original building and the more recent Garden and Orchard wings - include four-poster beds, fireplaces and antique furniture. In sum, this is country house style but with all the comfort

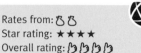

Rates from: 🐚 🐚
Star rating: ★ ★ ★ ★
Overall rating: 🐚 🐚 🐚 🐚

Ambience :	9.18	Cleanliness:	9.00
Value:	7.86	Facilities:	7.92
Staff:	8.95	Restaurants:	8.81
Location:	9.41	Families:	7.60

Hotel Felix

Huntingdon Road, Cambridge, CB3 0LX, England
T: +44 1223 277 977 **F:** +44 1223 277 973
www.HotelClub.com/hotels/Felix_Hotel_Cambridge

just the bitter chocolate cream), with an inventive menu (fish with lamb can work), a good wine list and great staff. Breakfast is similarly high-quality and imaginative - chef's granola, fruit compote, and waffles accompany the classics. On the outskirts of Cambridge, this is an oasis of indulgence.

Set a little out of town, the Hotel Felix breathes luxury in an attractively arty style: from the restaurant to the rooms, there is a wide range of contemporary painting, photography and sculpture throughout. All 52 rooms share a understated style which

comes with highest-quality materials such as Egyptian cotton sheets, goose-down duvets and raw-silk curtains. Despite all this opulence, the biggest selling point here is the food. The restaurant alone is worth the serious trek up the hill from Cambridge (in fact,

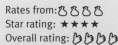

Rates from: 🐚 🐚 🐚 🐚
Star rating: ★ ★ ★ ★
Overall rating: 🐚 🐚 🐚 🐚

Ambience :	8.67	Cleanliness:	9.17
Value:	7.67	Facilities:	6.83
Staff:	8.67	Restaurants:	8.50
Location:	8.17	Families:	6.50

De Vere University Arms Hotel

Regent Street, Cambridge, CB2 1AD, England
T: +44 1223 273 000 **F:** +44 1223 273 037
www.HotelClub.com/hotels/De_Vere_University_Arms_Hotel_Cambridge

An ongoing refurbishment at The Cambridge University Arms is gradually turning this property into an environment that's far more chic than at present; two rooms which have already had the facelift are both stylish and luxurious in grey and white. But while this is just the latest development in the long life of this Victorian hotel, it is clear that much will stay the same - not least the wooden lift, one of the last of its kind. This has always been a hotel, and the staff are proud to assert that it is "a traditional hotel in the deluxe mode". Breakfast, served in the magnificent ballroom with huge windows overlooking parkland, certainly fits this upper-crust description; there is the English fry-up, and Scottish classics such as porridge, kippers, haddock, smoked salmon and scrambled eggs - all with locally sourced ingredients whenever possible. The separate restaurant for lunch and dinner is slightly less grandiose; and there are also many good restaurants in the area, so guests certainly have plenty of choice. The 120 bedrooms vary as to size but all have the same facilities (ensuite, Internet, all digital channels, movies, PlayStation, tea, coffee, chocolate, fruit and so on); surprisingly, there are no mini-bars at all, only room service, a nice touch for those who feel the personal element is lacking in some hotels nowadays. And the location is as good as it gets if you travel by train to Cambridge. Altogether this is a pleasant and charismatic hotel that is facing a very much more interesting future. Watch this space.

Rates from: 🏨🏨🏨🏨
Star rating: ★★★★
Overall rating: 🏨🏨🏨🏨

Ambience :	7.75	Cleanliness:	8.00
Value:	6.25	Facilities:	4.25
Staff:	7.75	Restaurants:	6.67
Location:	8.75	Families:	6.67

The Grove

Chandler's Cross, Hertfordshire, WD3 4TG, England
T: +44 1923 807 807 **F:** +44 1923 221 008
www.HotelClub.com

An oasis off the roaring cataract that is the M25, and a very accessible bolthole from The Smoke, The Grove lives up to its name in more ways than one.

Like many of England's grand retreats, this one started life at a time when its surrounds truly justified the term "country house". Subsequent development notwithstanding, its stately lines and 120 hectares of grounds insulate it perfectly from the outside world. A hotel since 1996,

The Grove's 227 rooms are broadly luxurious, with a very select bunch of Mansion suites boasting four-poster beds and open fire places.

Rural weekends of yore were traditionally centred around excellent meals interspersed with country pursuits, and The Grove follows this theme heartily. To deal with the former - an inspired wine cellar backs up three restaurants, each of which has its own bar: Colette's (fine dining), the rather more relaxed Stables, and all-

singing and dancing Glasshouse, an international theatre of cooking. And betwixt breakfast, lunch and dinner, entertainment runs from an 18-hole, par-72 championship golf course ("The greens... are perfect." T. Woods) to the very much less strenuous Sequoia spa.

Needless to say The Grove attracts conference types in droves, hosts a fair few weddings, and is adept at catering to the demands of youngsters not yet won over by the joys of fairway, full-body-scrubs or the finer subtleties of grain and grape. A snazzy art collection sets the seal on this remarkable capital escape, somewhere that's ultra smart and the antithesis of stuffy.

Rates from: 🐿🐿🐿🐿🐿
Star rating: ★★★★★
Overall rating: 🐿🐿🐿🐿

Ambience :	8.82	Cleanliness:	9.41
Value:	6.82	Facilities:	8.99
Staff:	8.41	Restaurants:	8.59
Location:	8.18	Families:	7.55

The Chester Grosvenor and Spa

Eastgate, Chester, CH1 1LT, England
T: +44 1244 324 024 **F:** +44 1244 313 246
www.HotelClub.com/hotels/Grosvenor_Pulford_Hotel_Chester

Opened 28 years into Queen Victoria's 64-year reign, this Grade II listed building, with its period black-and-white timbered façade, in the very centre of one of Britain's most historic cities, is what Britons of a certain generation were brought up to regard as the epitome of a grand hotel. But don't let the liveried porters, doormen and valets fool you - its 66 rooms and 14 suites all contain the latest in 21st-century mod cons, including air conditioning, plasma TVs, CD and DVD players and broadband Internet access.

You approach it via the pedestrianised old section of town (lots of covered walkways, so you can shop and sightsee in the rain without getting wet), and a gatekeeper will let your car through - then phone the hotel to tell them you're on the way. Just dump it at the imposing front door and it will be valet parked for free (they'll even have it washed for you).

An added attraction to the impeccable Victorian-style service at this "hoteliers' hotel" is a luxurious spa that offers a steam room, herbal sauna, ice fountain, foot bath, "themed" shower and salt grotto among many other delights. Highlights of the spacious guest-rooms are the Hollywood-type illuminated vanity mirrors and Molton Brown toiletries in the bathrooms, morning tea delivered in silver pots, and a door between bed and corridor to keep out extraneous noise.

The fine-dining Arkle restaurant (named, presumably, after the legendary racehorse) has held on to its Michelin star for nearly two decades now, while La Brasserie and The Library are more informal options.

Rates from: 💧💧💧💧💧
Star rating: ★★★★★
Overall rating: 🌀🌀🌀🌀 ½

Ambience :	9.19	Cleanliness:	9.38
Value:	8.15	Facilities:	8.88
Staff:	9.08	Restaurants:	9.38
Location:	9.54	Families:	8.50

Crabwall Manor Hotel & Spa

Parkgate Road, Mollington, Chester, CH1 6NE, England
T: +44 1244 851 666 **F:** +44 1244 881 000
www.HotelClub.com/hotels/Crabwall_Manor_Hotel_Chester

This imposing, redbrick, crenellated country-house hotel is a Grade II listed building that dates back to the mid-17th century, though there has been a manor house on the site since before the Normans began their civilising mission to England (William the Conqueror presented the estate to his nephew in 1077). Hence the medieval ambience that pervades the place, despite its having been largely rebuilt in the early 19th century.

With 48 rooms, including two with four-poster beds, it offers an out-of-town option for visitors to the old Roman city who, when sightseeing is done, can stroll its five hectares of private woods, looking out for foxes, hedgehogs, rabbits and squirrels. Shooting can be arranged (but not of the resident wildlife), though most guests prefer to do that with a camera, before lunch or dinner in the Conservatory Restaurant (great wine cellar).

Even more relaxing is a session in the spa (complete with Jacuzzi, sauna, steam room and solarium)

or a swim in the 18-metre indoor pool. For fitness enthusiasts, the gym is particularly well equipped, providing Pilates balls, ankle weights and skipping ropes in addition to all the usual paraphernalia. While she is having a facial, he can enjoy a quiet game of pre- or post-prandial snooker. And golf addicts will need no reminding that the property is just a short drive from some of Britain's best courses, including Formby, West Lancashire, the Royal Liverpool and Birkdale.

Altogether, then, a low-key, refreshingly old-fashioned alternative to today's more familiar bells-and-whistles accommodation experience.

Rates from: 🏰🏰🏰
Star rating: ★ ★ ★ ★
Overall rating: 🏰🏰🏰🏰

Ambience :	8.85	Cleanliness:	9.54
Value:	8.08	Facilities:	9.19
Staff:	9.33	Restaurants:	8.85
Location:	8.77	Families:	8.78

De Vere Carden Park

Carden Park, Nr Chester, Cheshire, CH3 9DQ, England
T: +44 1829 731 000 **F:** +44 1829 731 032
www.HotelClub.com/hotels/De_Vere_Carden_Park_Hotel_Chester

The Great Outdoors vs The Great Indoors debate continues to rage, and nowhere with such acuity as at Carden Park, a short way outside Chester. Count two 18-hole championship courses and a challenging nine-holer up against the hotel itself, which sports 196 rooms (31 specially adapted for families with two double beds). A spa, indoor pool and fitness centre vie with archery, mountain biking and tennis courts built among vineyards. On which subject, the wine lists at the Brasserie, and Redmond's restaurant, have been intelligently compiled, and more than complement the fine menus. Catering to golfers, executive gatherings and families - though not necessarily in that order, and certainly with no mutual exclusion - the Carden Park, originally a 17th century country estate, is a marvellous rural retreat, both within and without its walls.

Rates from: 🛏🛏🛏🛏🛏
Star rating: ★★★★
Overall rating: 📷📷📷📷 ½

Ambience :	8.92	Cleanliness:	9.63
Value:	8.92	Facilities:	9.11
Staff:	9.35	Restaurants:	9.17
Location:	8.54	Families:	8.67

Highbullen Hotel, Golf & Country Club

Chittlehamholt, Umberleigh, North Devon, EX37 9HD, England
T: +44 1769 540 561 **F:** +44 1769 540 492
www.HotelClub.com

The Highbullen has so many activities on offer it could be mistaken for a boot camp were it not so gentrified in that manner only the English do to perfection. Fly-fishing fans will appreciate the proximity of the trout filled rivers Mole and Taw (novices can take advantage of the hotel's tutors); there are four Wimbledon-class tennis courts for practising your backhand; an 18-hole golf-course; three swimming-pools; and an indoor Bowls Hall where you're welcome to kick off your shoes and play in your stockings. In fact it's exactly what you'd expect from a weekend in the English countryside - roaring log fires, soaring views across the wilds of Dartmoor, cosy rooms to cuddle up in, and a traditional dinner that will inevitably include classic cuts of beef or guinea fowl.

Rates from: 🛏🛏
Star rating: ★★★★
Overall rating: **Editors' Pick**

Ambience :	n/a	Cleanliness:	n/a
Value:	n/a	Facilities:	n/a
Staff:	n/a	Restaurants:	n/a
Location:	n/a	Families:	n/a

Coombe Abbey Hotel

Brinklow Road, Binley, Coventry, CV3 2AB, England
T: +44 2476 450 450 **F:** +44 2476 635 101
www.HotelClub.com/hotels/Coombe_Abbey_Hotel_Coventry

Playing up the historical angle for all its worth, this former Cistercian Abbey (dating from the 12th century) goes the whole hog with medieval banquets - candlelight, daggers, mead *et al* - haunted Halloween nights and events inspired by H Potter Esq. Sidestep this, and you're left with a staggeringly lovely building, surrounded by topiaried gardens and lush countryside, whose 83 guestrooms add an extra dose of vigour to the word sumptuous. These are capped by eight Grand Feature (something of an understatement) rooms with the Princess Elizabeth's "hidden" bathroom an added treat. Naturally, there's more than enough space at the hotel for conventioneers and meeters, as well as those inspired by the concept of team building, and as a backdrop for plighting your troth there can be few more imposing venues.

Rates from: 🛏🛏🛏🛏
Star rating: ★★★★
Overall rating: 🐾🐾🐾🐾

Ambience :	9.73	Cleanliness:	9.67
Value:	8.40	Facilities:	7.44
Staff:	9.13	Restaurants:	9.00
Location:	9.20	Families:	7.33

Crewe Hall

Weston Road, Crewe, Cheshire, CW1 6UZ, England
T: +44 1270 253 333 **F:** +44 1270 252 322
www.HotelClub.com/hotels/Crewe_Hall_Hotel

It's hard to feel sorry for the high-ranking German officers held prisoner here during the second world war, but there again perhaps they weren't in the best mood to appreciate their bucolic surrounds or indeed Crewe Hall's richly designed ceilings, exquisite marble fireplaces, ornate carved wood and stained glass features. Nowadays, there are 25 bedrooms in the main house, and 40 more in adjoining more contemporary wings, all thoroughly mod con and a tremendous place to put up for the night. Two restaurants, the fine diner Ranulph and a surprisingly modern brasserie, cater impressively to hunger pangs, and with a host of sporting activities at hand (not least a golf course) there should be no lengthy pondering on how to build up an appetite.

Of course, like all good Jacobean houses, this one has its own chapel.

Rates from: 🛏🛏🛏
Star rating: ★★★★
Overall rating: 🐾🐾🐾🐾

Ambience :	9.25	Cleanliness:	9.38
Value:	8.25	Facilities:	8.90
Staff:	9.00	Restaurants:	9.13
Location:	8.63	Families:	9.00

Lumley Castle Hotel

Chester-le-street, County Durham, DH3 4NX, England
T: +44 191 389 1111 **F:** +44 191 387 1437
www.HotelClub.com/hotels/Lumley_Castle_Hotel_Durham

"Touristy", yes, but then, the castle really is more than 600 years old, the scenery - glorious parkland overlooking the River Wear and Durham County Cricket Ground - really is lovely, so where's the harm in highlighting ye olde-worlde vibe with such theatrical touches as serving wenches in period costume and "Elizabethan" banquets.

The corridors are dark and narrow enough to convincingly conjure up the ghost of Lady Lily Lumley, murdered wife of soldier hero Sir Ralph, who just had time to get the battlements built before being executed by King Henry IV for treason - how's that for a theatrical touch?

Lumley Castle's 73 rooms, or "bedchambers" as they are predictably dubbed, have most of the facilities you would expect (and some you wouldn't - like entering the bathroom through the middle door of the wardrobe). The fare in the Black Knight restaurant is excellently prepared and presented. And the plush Library Bar, complete with roaring log fire and oil paintings on the walls, is perfect for pre-dinner drinks or afternoon tea.

There is a golf course next door and the grounds are eminently strollable, but there is nothing much else to do except wind down - after a day spent visiting the nearby cities of Durham, Newcastle or Sunderland, perhaps, or tramping the wild Northumberland coastline. All in all, an ideal base for exploring England's Northeast - if you don't mind the theatrical touches. Most people love them - this has been a very popular tourist hotel since it opened as such in 1984.

Rates from: 🏰🏰🏰🏰
Star rating: ★★★★
Overall rating: 🏰🏰🏰🏰

Ambience :	9.63	Cleanliness:	9.50
Value:	8.56	Facilities:	7.44
Staff:	9.44	Restaurants:	9.13
Location:	9.06	Families:	8.08

The Grand Hotel

King Edwards Parade, Eastbourne, East Sussex, BN21 4EQ, England
T: +44 1323 412 345 **F:** +44 1323 412 233
www.HotelClub.com/hotels/Grand_Hotel_Eastbourne

English afternoon tea has become a staple of five-star hotels the world over, but to sit in one of the cosy rooms leading off the long lobby of The Grand Hotel Eastbourne, probably in front of a roaring fire if it's a typical summer's day, and be presented - by a tail-coated waiter - with a tiered salver of cucumber sandwiches, strawberries and cream, cakes and a pot of Earl Grey is to appreciate the ritual in all its ethnic splendour.

This 152-room "wedding cake" building, known locally as The White Palace, dates from 1875 and counts Winston Churchill, Charlie Chaplin and Edward Elgar among its distinguished late patrons. Debussy wrote his symphony *La Mer* here, the BBC used to broadcast orchestral music from its Great Hall every Sunday night and it has been the setting for many a period film and TV series. But don't worry, the place is not set in dust-covered aspic: television sets are craftily hidden in antique-looking cabinets, and the *Upstairs, Downstairs* maids in their frilly pink outfits are au fait with anything

that a comtemporary guest might see fit to request.

Its award-winning Mirabelle and Garden restaurants, serving predominantly French haute cuisine, are among the best of their kind in the country. Facilities include indoor and outdoor pools, a health spa with sauna and steam room, a gym, massage and manicure parlours. The Grand is right on the seafront and ideally placed for visits to the South Downs and the magnificent 15th-

century moated castle of Herstmonceux, or just a bracing walk along what is still arguably one of Britain's finest piers.

Rates from: 🏰🏰🏰🏰
Star rating: ★★★★★
Overall rating: 👻👻👻👻

Ambience:	9.10	Cleanliness:	9.35
Value:	7.95	Facilities:	8.07
Staff:	8.90	Restaurants:	9.15
Location:	9.20	Families:	8.54

The Acorn Inn

28 Fore Street, Evershot, Dorchester, Dorset, DT2 0JW, England
T: +44 1935 83228 **F:** +44 1935 83707
www.HotelClub.com

rooftops, is simply called Evershot. Modems and colour televisions there are aplenty, but there are far more pressing diversions to hand.

The two bars chorus quintessential English rural pub - log fires, beams, oak panelling and flagstone floors - while the restaurant serves the very best of country cooking. The patio comes into its own on those long English summer evenings, while the skittle alley - a recreation that predates the inn even - doubles up as a function space. David and Bebe Parry, who run The Acorn, state that well-behaved dogs are very welcome. Suffice to say that the same applies to their owners.

Emma Woodhouse, wrote Jane Austen, was handsome, clever, and rich, with a comfortable home and happy disposition, and seemed to unite some of the best blessings of existence; and had lived nearly twenty-one years in the world with very little to distress or vex her.

On parallel lines, there's very little to distress or vex in the handsome village of Evershot, some 200 metres above sea level, where the comfortable and happily disposed stone-built Acorn Inn has

been welcoming visitors for something like 421 years. The period drama *Emma* was filmed here, and the producers would have needed to make very few changes to the scenery as the village backdrop is picture postcard perfect.

Continuing the literary theme, The Acorn's nine regular rooms take their names from Thomas Hardy's *Tess of the D'Urbervilles*, while the single suite, up in the loft with views over the tiled

Rates from: 🝊🝊🝊
Star rating: ★★★★
Overall rating: **Editors' Pick**

Ambience :	n/a	Cleanliness:	n/a
Value:	n/a	Facilities:	n/a
Staff:	n/a	Restaurants:	n/a
Location:	n/a	Families:	n/a

Babington House

Babington near Frome, Somerset BA11 3RW, England
T: +44 1373 812 266 **F:** +44 1373 813 866
www.HotelClub.com

As mellow as the Bath stone it was built from 300 years ago, Babington is the blueprint for the supremely modern country hotel, where boho chic meets self-indulgence. And ooh, what a marriage... They fall in love over a Russian Spring Punch in the laid-back bar, propose while feeding the ducks, wed in the candle-lit 18th century church in the grounds and produce lots of unstuffily stylish offspring called Chill, Hang-Loose and Pamper.

This early Georgian haven of welly-wearing hedonism, hidden unexpectedly in the heart of the Somerset countryside, is a place where you can forget restaurant hours and eat when you want; chew over the papers in one of the hanging chairs in the Playroom; take a tipple of choice into the private cinema and catch a pre-release movie; have muscles massaged in one of the cute Cowshed Spa wood cabins dotted by the lakeside; or glide like one of the visiting swans over the bath-temperature outdoor pool...

All of the 28 luxurious rooms have plenty of treats and gizmos, with beds the size of aircraft carriers, two-bod clawfoot baths and ahead-of-the-crowd uber-trendy décor. Room Six even sports an outdoor Jacuzzi on a massive terrace overlooking the lake and garden, while the five split-level family rooms in the stable block host their own balconies, and the three-bedroomed lodge cottage at the top of the drive has its own kitchen. It's rural, but rocking; a bit of funky amid the farmland, and being a private member's club has a welcoming buzzy amiability lacking in its more soulless copycats.

Rates from: ☙☙☙☙
Star rating: n/a
Overall rating: ♘♘♘♘

Ambience :	9.00	Cleanliness:	9.25
Value:	7.75	Facilities:	8.83
Staff:	8.25	Restaurants:	9.00
Location:	9.25	Families:	8.00

The Balmoral Hotel

16/18 Franklin Mount, Harrogate, HG1 5EJ, England
T: +44 1423 508 208 **F:** +44 1423 530 652
www.HotelClub.com/hotels/Balmoral_Hotel_Harrogate_The

Visitors to the sedate old Balmoral Hotel in Harrogate who haven't been there for a while will be as surprised at its new incarnation as a vicar finding his church full of tarts: the old Victorian terrace building - three houses knocked into one and turned into a hotel by its original owner, a chef to the Queen Mother who named it after Ma'am's Scottish retreat - has been given a stunning makeover by the people responsible for the trendy Room restaurant in Leeds and the Grille in Hoxton, London.

A bold mix of hi-tech (plasma TV screens with HDML, for checking out that conference presentation) and period opulence, the 23-room boutique property is now dripping with designer wallpaper, faux-antique furniture, dark wood and plush velvet, mango-yellow leather sofas and gilt-edged mirrors. Bathrooms have black-marble walls and slate floors.

The restaurant, as you might expect, has also hurtled into the 21st century, with the bistro-style Harrogate Grille offering everything from breakfast martinis through to classic rump-and-*frites* (and 20 different wines by the glass), with all-day snacks in between. Private dining is available and there is a Members' Bar.

Hotel guests also have complimentary use of the Academy Spa, five-minutes' drive away, where they can work out in the huge gym, swim in the four-lane pool or undergo various relaxing body and facial treatments. They can even play tennis there - and it has a creche, too.

Lots going on, then, from the leafy sanctuary of the ex-royal cook's old B&B. Would she have approved - or is she doing a spot of grave-turning?

Rates from: 🛏🛏🛏🛏
Star rating: ★★★
Overall rating: **Editors' Pick**

Ambience :	n/a	Cleanliness:	n/a
Value:	n/a	Facilities:	n/a
Staff:	n/a	Restaurants:	n/a
Location:	n/a	Families:	n/a

De Vere Slaley Hall

Slaley Hall, Slaley, Hexham, Nr Newcastle-upon-Tyne, NE47 oBX, England
T: +44 1434 673 350 **F:** ++44 1434 673 962
www.HotelClub.com

Just half an hour's drive from Newcastle city centre, this stately Edwardian country house - part of the De Vere portfolio of unusual properties - is just outside the market town of Hexham (great National Hunt racing there during the winter season).

Essentially a conference hotel, its 400 hectares of Northumberland forest and moorland offer a smorgasbord of outdoor activities to imbue delegates with that gung-ho corporate spirit - fishing, archery, clay-pigeon shooting, mountain biking, quad-biking, hot-air ballooning and paint-balling, plus of course the two championship golf courses. Its 139 air-conditioned rooms range from standard to suite, with varying levels of amenity, but all have bath/shower, tea/coffee machines, hairdryer and trouser press, plus Sky TV. Then there are the Lodges, which can sleep from four to eight. And some rooms have been specially equipped for the disabled. You can dine in the Restaurant, overlooking the golf courses, or in the Clubhouse Bar & Grill. And while the chaps are out testing themselves with rod, gun or golf club, the gals can preen in the Health & Beauty Spa, based around a 20-metre "tropical" pool and offering hydrotherapy, thalassotherapy and aromatherapy as well as plain old steam room and sauna, solarium and Jacuzzi. There is also a straight up-and-down gymnasium.

The idea is to provide enough for guests to do for them not to need to leave the premises, but if you're using this as a Northumbrian excursion base, you're in easy driving reach of Durham (Cathedral and Castle), Hadrian's Wall, Derwent Reservoir and, of course, the fleshpots of Newcastle.

Rates from: 🏰🏰🏰
Star rating: ★★★★
Overall rating: 🏨🏨🏨🏨

Ambience :	8.68	Cleanliness:	9.32
Value:	8.14	Facilities:	8.90
Staff:	8.68	Restaurants:	8.45
Location:	8.55	Families:	8.93

Four Seasons Hotel Hampshire

Dogmersfield Park, Chalky Lane, Dogmersfield, Hook, Hampshire, RG27 8TD, England
T: +44 1252 853 000 **F:** +44 1252 853 010
www.HotelClub.com

British doctors' and dentists' waiting rooms are often strewn with outdated copies of the magazine *Country Life*, a weekly glossy festooned with adverts for rich and rare properties that are the stuff of dreams for the average National Health patient.

However the Four Seasons - a Georgian manor house set in the rock 'n' rolling Hampshire countryside - is a chance to make those dreams come true, however briefly, and play 21st-century squire.

Melding the manor's perfectly designed proportions with the most modern of cons, the Four Seasons is the rural retreat par excellence. Its 133 guestrooms (which include 22 suites) look out over the central courtyard or the heritage-listed gardens; however there is a huge amount to admire within, not least the spectacular marble bathrooms.

In Seasons, the main restaurant, Dogmersfield Park is framed by French windows and the cuisine continues the theme with Gallic and European accents. The emphasis is on fresh and healthy dishes in Café Santé, adjoining the spa; this is housed in the former stable block, a repository of holistic pampering and an effective counter measure to the cream teas served in The Library.

The hotel's indoor-outdoor pool might be regarded as a spa treatment in itself, as the uncovered (yet heated) part contains a number of tingly water massage features. A brace of all-weather tennis courts offers alternative recreation, as do more countrified pursuits such as falconry and clay pigeon shooting.

As devotees of *Country Life* will aver, staying at the Four Seasons is akin to Alice stepping through a rural looking glass.

Rates from: 🛏🛏🛏🛏🛏
Star rating: ★★★★★
Overall rating: 👌

Ambience :	8.83	Cleanliness:	8.83
Value:	7.83	Facilities:	7.40
Staff:	8.33	Restaurants:	8.33
Location:	9.17	Families:	7.75

Hell Bay

Bryher, Isles of Scilly, Cornwall, TR23 0PR, England
T: +44 1720 422947 **F:** +44 1720 423004
www.HotelClub.com

There's no escaping the old adage that very many of the best hotels are family-run. There are few better examples of this than Hell Bay, on the miniscule island of Bryher, which is nurtured by the guiding hands of Robert and Lucien Dorrien-Smith.

It's not overstating the obvious to say that Hell Bay (the area was once notorious for ship wrecks) is not far short of heaven. Some 23 suites are dotted about the property, swathed in Lloyd Loom and Malabar fabrics as fresh as the sea breezes that waft in from the Atlantic.

Hell's kitchen, to coin a phrase, is overseen by chef Glenn Gatland, scooping up crab, lobster and farm-grown vegetables more or less from outside the back door and onto patrons' plates. Small wonder that guests staying on other islands frequently make a pilgrimage over here to dine.

While this is a marvellous place to kick back and relax (and who could resist despatching a post card or two from this address?) there's also a great deal in the way of recreation. White sandy beaches patrolled by puffins and seals are only a few minutes' walk away, and if the ocean looks a tad chilly, there's a heated outdoor swimming pool as well as sauna and Jacuzzi. The nine-hole, par three golf course presents a nice challenge, while boules provide a Continental alternative.

Depending on your approach, this is the last, or the first, hotel in England. Either way, you're assured of a deliciously warm welcome.

Rates from: 🛏🛏🛏
Star rating: ★★★
Overall rating: 👣👣👣👣👣

Ambience :	10.0	Cleanliness:	10.0
Value:	9.00	Facilities:	9.57
Staff:	9.00	Restaurants:	9.00
Location:	10.0	Families:	9.57

42 The Calls

Leeds, West Yorkshire, LS2 7EW, England
T: +44 113 244 0099 **F:** +44 113 234 4100
www.HotelClub.com

While at first blush the fact that such a redoubtable and very English hotel is owned by Sheikh Mohamed Bin Issa al Javer (who numbers the island nation of Bahrain among his other assets), it's fair to state that His Majesty may have more than a little in common with the league of merchant princes who raised Leeds to such prosperity in the 19th century.

Quite apart from its reputation as the Knightsbridge of the North, the city is now the country's biggest financial centre outside London, and where better for high ranking number crunchers to put up and browse and sluice than a converted grain mill?

Numerologists as well as bean counters will find much in the way of figures to entertain here. There are 41 rooms and suites (each individually and imaginatively decorated), bathroom shelf brackets are shaped as a large "4" and "2"; Brasserie Forty 4 fairly buzzes; and the Pool Court at 42 wears its Michelin star with more than a touch of deserved pride.

And while other hotels may have a routine Do Not Disturb sign, of course this establishment puts it rather differently: "Quiet Please, I'm Having 42 Winks".

Many of the accoutrements of the former mill have been retained, though there is not a trace of twee olde worlde. Indeed, the whole property (which assumed its current incarnation in 1991) neatly espouses 21st century Leeds, and is run with considerable élan by long-serving general manager Belinda Dawson. It's by the banks of the River Aire, and in staggering distance of the city's clubs, bars and pubs.

Rates from: 🐚🐚🐚
Star rating: n/a
Overall rating: 🐚🐚🐚🐚

Ambience :	9.25	Cleanliness:	9.31
Value:	8.00	Facilities:	6.45
Staff:	8.81	Restaurants:	8.60
Location:	9.50	Families:	6.88

De Vere Oulton Hall

Rothwell Lane, Oulton, Leeds, Yorkshire, LS26 8HN, England
T: +44 113 2821000 **F:** +44 113 2829084
www.HotelClub.com/hotels/De_Vere_Oulton_Hall_Hotel_Leeds

beautiful formal gardens or a gentle game of croquet - which today's guests can still enjoy.

There's nothing particularly "wuthering" about Oulton Hall (the word describes the sound made by a strong wind), but its fans claim that it reaches the heights of a great hotel experience. A Grade II listed, Italianate country mansion, the 152-room property has to be seen to be believed: from the imposing drive to the tiled entrance, from the Great Hall to the Grand Staircase, from the crystal chandeliers to the mahogany-pannelled walls, it is elegant living epitomised.

Its original owners, however, did not have the luxury of a heated indoor pool, spa with sauna and steam rooms as well as a beauty salon, gym and aerobics studio, and two golf courses (nine and 18 holes respectively) plus driving range in the grounds. They had to make do with strolling in the

And whether they would have eaten better than in the Bronte Restaurant (French and English cuisine - "elegant casual" dress code) or the more informal Blayds is debatable. Their bedrooms may have boasted a decanter of port (provided for suite occupants), though their bathrooms would undoubtedly have lacked a heated mirror (to prevent misting after a shower) and radio extension speakers.

The golf complex, incidentally, has just had £7.5 million pumped into it and is ranked one of the best in the north of England. It is a lure for corporate groups, who can also "bond" by means of archery and paint-balling. Then or now? Hard to say.

Rates from: 🛏🛏🛏🛏
Star rating: ★★★★★
Overall rating: 🐾🐾🐾🐾

Ambience :	9.25	Cleanliness :	9.25
Value:	8.46	Facilities:	9.00
Staff:	8.96	Restaurants:	9.21
Location:	8.50	Families:	7.27

ENGLAND'S BEST HOTELS

Hilton Leeds City Hotel

Neville Street, Leeds, LS1 4BX, England
T: +44 113 2442000 **F:** +44 113 2433577
www.HotelClub.com/hotels/Hilton_Leeds_City_Hotel

Yorkshire folk have a reputation for being dour and down-to-earth. They hate what they call "side", or showing off, and prefer value for money to luxury. This Hilton should suit them to a tee, then: it has everything the public has come to expect from the brand name - convenience, professional service from well-trained staff, comfortable rooms, excellent if unadventurous food, and rates that should certainly appeal to bargain-hunters.

The unostentatious glass and concrete building is ideally situated for train travellers, being right next door to the main station, though light sleepers are advised to ask for a room that doesn't adjoin it. And it's only a five-minute walk from the centre of town.

You can work out at the LivingWell Health Club, relax in the spa pool or sauna, and swim a few lengths of the heated pool before a sumptuous buffet breakfast (it sensibly opens at 7.30am). The City 3 Restaurant and Caffe Cino coffee-shop are informal eating venues (no "side" here) and the City 3 Bar does light lunches and some very tasty tapas in the evenings.

But it is the small efficiencies that most impress the practical citizens of Leeds: such as keycards that control the use of electricity, vibrating fire-alarm pillows, special provision for the disabled (including Braille lift buttons), an express check-out on demand (the bill is slipped under your door the night before you leave), and security cameras in all public areas. It's enough to make you wonder whether Conrad Hilton didn't come from solid Yorkshire stock.

Rates from: 🐾 🐾
Star rating: ★ ★ ★ ★
Overall rating: 🐾 🐾 🐾 🐾

Ambience :	8.33	Cleanliness:	9.38
Value:	8.33	Facilities:	8.47
Staff:	8.90	Restaurants:	8.90
Location:	8.57	Families:	8.76

Leeds Marriott Hotel

4 Trevelyan Square, Boar Lane, Leeds, LS1 6ET, England
T: +44 113 236 6366 **F:** +44 113 236 6367
www.HotelClub.com/hotels/Marriott_Hotel_Leeds

It may be on Boar Lane, but it's anything but boring. For a fine example of a chain hotel in the provinces, Marriott Leeds fits the bill more than adequately. The 244 rooms function highly efficiently, conference and meeting facilities follow the template to a T, and John I's, the main restaurant, is both welcoming and hearty. And within easy walking distance lie yet more eateries, closely allied to the Marriott, such as Georgetown, with a Malaysian theme and pan-Asian menu, a spicy Thai and the enigmatically named Est Est Est, which serves Italian. An indoor pool and fitness centre both lie within the confines of the hotel, however the Waterfall Spa - check massages, scrubs, pedicures and therapy baths - is only a short way off. All in all, a very satisfying stay.

Rates from: 💰💰💰
Star rating: ★ ★ ★ ★
Overall rating: 🏵🏵🏵🏵

Ambience :	8.77	Cleanliness:	9.45
Value:	8.64	Facilities:	8.35
Staff:	8.91	Restaurants:	8.68
Location:	9.41	Families:	8.00

Malmaison Leeds

1 Swinegate, Leeds, LS1 4AG, England
T: +44 113 398 1000 **F:** +44 113 398 1002
www.HotelClub.com

At times one almost wonders if there are enough old buildings left in Britain to be turned into Malmaisons. This one used to be a tram depot, and the 1999 conversion was undertaken with all the group's characteristic style and finesse. Egyptian cotton duvets invite rather more than a long lie in the 100 bedrooms, and there's power showers and lots of space in the monochrome bathrooms. The main suite, naturally called The Depot, is semi-circular with a terrific centrepiece window. For a gin and tonic, head to the bar that's part of the 90-seater Brasserie; for Gymtonic head to the bonsai fitness centre that's so named. Four meeting rooms are flooded with both natural daylight and Wireless connections. This, as they say in Yorkshire, is a rattling good hotel.

Rates from: 💰💰💰
Star rating: ★ ★ ★ ★
Overall rating: 🏵🏵🏵🏵

Ambience :	8.86	Cleanliness:	9.50
Value:	8.43	Facilities:	8.85
Staff:	9.07	Restaurants:	8.79
Location:	9.07	Families:	7.33

Park Plaza Leeds

City Square, Boar Lane, Leeds, LS1 5NS, England
T: +44 113 380 4000 **F:** +44 113 380 4100
www.HotelClub.com

This 186-room property is part of the huge US-owned Carlson group, which has everything from hotel chains to travel agencies to cruise ships to fast food restaurants in its multinational portfolio, yet it manages to exude the kind of stylish personality you'd expect to find in a place with a far more pro-active corporate pedigree. Ah well, perhaps that's the result of globalisation for you.

It has certainly livened up the Leeds accommodation scene, with its minimalist Post-Modern décor and its funky food. Chino Latino, as its name suggests, fuses the best of the Orient - Chinese, Japanese and Southeast Asian - with South American specialities: from sea bass in banana leaves to green-tea noodles with truffles, duck salad in hoi sin sauce to coconut cappuccino and ginger ice-cream, and sushi and sashimi galore (you are even

presented with a couple of very welcoming tidbits on arrival).

A small supplement to the reguair rate will get you free wine and mineral water, fresh fruit, a newspaper, bathrobe and slippers and a late check-out from an executive room, whose occupants are also entitled to free use of the nearby LA Fitness gym, which has a pool, sauna and sun beds (the hotel itself runs to a small work-out area). And four suites on the 20th floor offer panoramic city views.

Best of all, Park Plaza is right on City Square in the heart of the shopping and restaurant district, and opposite the railway station. These global monoliths may have a reputation for putting profit before "soul", but they sure as hell know what the public wants.

Rates from: 🏰🏰🏰🏰
Star rating: ★★★★
Overall rating: 🦋🦋🦋🦋

Ambience :	8.71	Cleanliness:	9.29
Value:	8.53	Facilities:	7.69
Staff:	8.31	Restaurants:	8.86
Location:	9.18	Families:	6.88

Quebecs

9 Quebec Street, Leeds, LS1 2HA, England
T: +44 113 244 8989 **F:** +44 113 244 9090
www.HotelClub.com/hotels/Quebecs_Hotel_Leeds

If a sense of place, character, beauty and history form any part of your expectations when choosing somewhere to stay, you cannot miss this Leeds city gem. Originally the site of the old Cloth Hall, it was rebuilt in 1891 as the premises of the Leeds and County Liberal Club. Now it is a 45-room boutique hotel. The name? After the address - in Quebec Street.

The redbrick Victorian façade has been preserved, as have various stunning features inside -

such as the magnificent oak staircase, the stained-glass windows and oak-panelled lounge (the Oak Room, which is as relaxing as its laid-back "honour" bar would lead one to hope).

Air-conditioned rooms are all different, but all warmly welcoming, with classic, unfussy furnishings and decisive décor. All have CD and DVD players, free movies, books, magazines - and apples. There is a spiral staircase in the middle of each of the two

mezzanine suites, leading to the sleeping quarters.

No restaurant, but with the city centre just minutes away, there are plenty nearby to pick from. And you do get 24-hour room service and a full buffet breakfast (with vegetarian options) in the delightful rooftop conservatory.

Quebecs is for romantics - and if it's an actual romance you're celebrating, the setting is perfect. They'll even strew rose petals on your bed if you ask them to, and all the suites are named after confectionery, with a big jar of sherbert fountains in the Sherbert Suite, and so on. Talk about sweets for my sweet...

Rates from: 💰💰💰💰💰
Star rating: ★ ★ ★ ★ ★
Overall rating: 🌀🌀🌀🌀

Ambience :	9.10	Cleanliness:	9.30
Value:	7.90	Facilities:	7.17
Staff:	8.50	Restaurants:	8.00
Location:	8.60	Families:	7.50

The Queens Hotel, Leeds

City Square, Leeds, LS1 1PJ, England
T: +44 113 2431323 **F:** +44 113 2425154
www.HotelClub.com/hotels/The_Queens_Hotel_Leeds

Time is not only a great healer, but a great revealer. When this hotel was built some seven decades ago, just before the outbreak of World War II, it took everyone's breath away - and became an instant city landmark.

But who then could foresee what its effect would be on jaded 21st-century tastes? The answer, thanks to a meticulous £10-million makeover that has seen every detail of its original art deco splendour lovingly recreated, is that the place is just as stunning as it must have been when it opened. Indeed, even if you were not staying here, it would be worth a visit just to wander around and gawp at the opulence and artistic audacity of a style that, far from looking dated, comes across today as fresher than ever.

Its central location, next to the railway station in the city centre, its size and its state-of-the-art meetings facilities make it a top conference venue, but it is equally favoured by business travellers and weekend getaway types. The 217 rooms are commodious and attractively furnished, with double-glazed windows to allay any noise from the rail terminus. There are on-demand movies and games consoles to while away those rare rainy Leeds days.

Buffet breakfast is served in the basement, while the Queens Bar & Grill is as imposing as it sounds. No gym or spa, but all guests have free access to nearby LA Fitness. A men-only barber-shop and beyond-the-call-of-duty concierge add to the pre-war grandeur of it all.

Rates from: 🪙🪙🪙🪙
Star rating: ★ ★ ★ ★
Overall rating: 🦢🦢🦢🦢

Ambience :	8.83	Cleanliness:	9.11
Value:	8.61	Facilities:	8.13
Staff:	8.94	Restaurants:	8.65
Location:	9.72	Families:	9.00

Britannia Adelphi Hotel

Ranelagh Place, Liverpool, L3 5UL, England
T: +44 151 7097 200 **F:** +44 151 707 9107
www.HotelClub.com/hotels/Britannia_Adelphi_Hotel_Liverpool

Any visitor to Liverpool - which recently celebrated its 800th birthday - will want to poke his or her nose into the Adelphi because of its historic role in the city, dating back to pre-Victorian days; since then it's played host to VIP passengers from the great cruise liners that docked here (but not from the *Titanic*, which sank the year the hotel re-opened, though there is a suite modelled on that tragic vessel's Smoking Room).

The huge, 402-room property has an iconic place in the hearts of Scousers (its address is Maggie May's Lime Street, a short walk from the station). And it was the setting for a national TV series. Partially refurbished, it retains the air of Edwardian grandeur that would probably have impressed the young Beatles when they splashed their first royalties here.

There are three restaurants - the fine-dining Cromptons, the popular Jenny's Carvery (a carnivore's delight) and The Overstuffed Pizzeria, a kids' favourite. Plus Jenny's Bar, which attracts a lot of locals, and Fridays Pub, with big screen for the footie. A residents' bar stays open late for nightcaps.

An ultra-modern leisure centre offers a heated marble pool, Jacuzzi and sauna, as well as a gym and Spindles Salon, for spa treatments, hair and beauty care. There are those who maintain that standards have slipped since the hotel's glory days, but others who would no more think of going to Liverpool and not staying at the Adelphi than they would give the Mersey a miss.

Rates from: 🐾🐾
Star rating: ★★★
Overall rating: 🐾🐾🐾🐾

Ambience :	8.35	Cleanliness:	7.85
Value:	7.35	Facilities:	8.25
Staff:	7.85	Restaurants:	8.44
Location:	9.45	Families:	8.21

Crowne Plaza Liverpool

St Nicholas Place, Pier Head, Liverpool, L3 1QW, England
T: +44 151 243 8000 **F:** +44 151 243 8111
www.HotelClub.com/hotels/Crowne_Plaza_Hotel_Liverpool_City_Centre

Steps away from the rather grisly, pretentious new-build Malmaison, the Crowne Plaza is light years away when it comes to being genuinely accommodating. A bright, airy lobby, and an immediately recognisable do-as-you-would-be-done-by hospitality, form the best of welcomes for both snappy exec and happy tripper.

Liverpool has been dubbed the European City of Culture for 2008, and - some ten years on from when it first opened its doors - the Plaza could not ask for a nattier location, hard by the Royal Liver Building in the heart of rejuvenated Princes Dock.

Inside the hotel, all is fresh and bright. The 159 rooms and suites are well fitted out, comfortable and sleeper-friendly; naturally those overlooking the River Mersey are at a premium. Of particular note, the brace of double beds in the family rooms are a smart choice for two plus 2.4s, not least for their trampolining capabilities.

The main dining venue is the Brasserie, with a menu that's straightforward but none the less toothsome, while guests can eat more informally in The Lounge, and knock back a pint or two at the bar if that's all the sustenance required.

Most mainstream hotels nowadays include a gym, routinely described as state-of-the-art, with attendant health facilities. The Plaza manages all this (the indoor 18-metre heated pool is a boon) but sensibly keeps it all running till 2am.

As an endnote, the sea of red and white when Liverpool FC's playing at home of a Saturday makes this hotel but one place removed from the Spion Kop.

Rates from: 🛏 🛏 🛏
Star rating: ★ ★ ★ ★
Overall rating: 🐾 🐾 🐾 🐾

Ambience :	9.00	Cleanliness:	9.79
Value:	7.71	Facilities:	8.96
Staff:	8.62	Restaurants:	8.77
Location:	9.07	Families:	8.88

Liverpool Marriott Hotel City Centre

1 Queen Square, Liverpool, L1 1RH, England
T: +44 151 476 8000 **F:** +44 151 474 5000
www.HotelClub.com/hotels/Marriott_City_Hotel_Liverpool

Smoking has shifted from debonair habit to demonisation in the past few years, and like hotels all over the country, the Marriott is fag-free; with the notable exception of 21 of its 146 bedrooms, which are exclusively reserved for those for whom quitting is at the top of their list of New Year's Resolutions for 2009. Other aspects of this remarkable property which are well worth puffing include its main restaurant, Olivier's, which does a nice line in vegetarian dishes, and the VivaCity Café, which adopts a slightly more casual approach to dining. Seven dedicated rooms serve those needing to meet to discuss business or similar, and there's a pool, sauna and gym to wind down in afterwards. And as it's just across from Lime Street Station, the Marriott could hardly be more central.

Rates from: 🐚 🐚 🐚
Star rating: ★★★★
Overall rating: 🐻 🐻 🐻 🐻

Ambience :	8.77	Cleanliness:	9.45
Value:	8.73	Facilities:	9.03
Staff:	8.91	Restaurants:	8.82
Location:	9.32	Families:	8.62

Radisson SAS Hotel Liverpool

107 Old Hall Street, Liverpool, L3 9BD, England
T: +44 151 966 1500 **F:** +44 151 966 1501
www.HotelClub.com/hotels/Radisson_Hotel_Liverpool

There's nothing like a really stunning atrium to announce a hotel's general brio, and the Liverpool Radisson's is a case in point. Zoom from here up to the 194 rooms and suites, rainbowed with colour that's both practical and fun, capped by The River Suite which lays claim to being the largest in the city. You'll find similar hues at Filini's (Sardinian flavours and Mediterranean classics) which kicks off each new day with a dazzling super-size buffet breakfast - pitch up early for tables overlooking the River Mersey. And guests head by the score, rather than two by two, to The Ark, which dangles everything from spin bikes to hot stone massages to a 12-metre pool. Well adapted to both executives and those on The Beatles trail, this hotel is an utterly fabulous four-star.

Rates from: 🐚 🐚 🐚
Star rating: ★★★★
Overall rating: 🐻 🐻 🐻 🐻 ½

Ambience :	9.15	Cleanliness:	9.55
Value:	8.65	Facilities:	9.28
Staff:	9.20	Restaurants:	8.94
Location:	8.80	Families:	7.89

Andaz

40 Liverpool Street, London, EC2M 7QN, England
T: +44 207 961 1234 **F:** +44 207 961 1235
www.HotelClub.com/hotels/Great_Eastern_Hotel_London

Officially opened in 1884 as The Great Eastern and retaining many original features, a recent makeover to this already ebullient hotel in the crutch of Liverpool Street reflects the nature of East London and those who inhabit its surrounds. Strolling into the Andaz, one does not think of entering a hotel of five-star status so much as a Guggenheim exhibition in a semi-casual environment - artwork abounds and the music soothes. There's no official reception desk *per se*, and the staff welcome you as an old friend.

This is the way they want it. You're finally home.

No airs and graces, no conventional checking in. A unique and original approach that whets the appetite for a little indulgence without the stiff back and starch shirt; casual luxury.

A personal escort to one's room is the norm, at which point pride will become apparent - reason being that none of the hotel's striking yet simple 267 rooms is the same; however each has an eco-friendly loo which uses 80% less water than a conventional model, giving one the sensation of being airborne with every vacuum flush. A practical novelty. Sleek furnishings and a bed you will be reluctant to leave feature predominantly.

Clean, comfortable and spacious (especially in central London), the typical amenities are readily available and if not they can be requested. Upon exploring the hotel, five restaurants, four bars and 14 event spaces (including a former Masonic Temple) await discovery, each unique and lively and fundamental to the nature of this "uber cool" dwelling.

Rates from: 🏨🏨🏨🏨🏨
Star rating: ★ ★ ★ ★ ★
Overall rating: 🦋🦋🦋🦋

Ambience :	9.16	Cleanliness:	9.16
Value:	7.68	Facilities:	8.23
Staff:	9.11	Restaurants:	8.81
Location:	8.84	Families:	7.82

Ascott Mayfair, London

49 Hill Street, Mayfair, London W1J 5NB, England
T: +44 20 7499 6868 **F:** +44 20 7499 0705
www.HotelClub.com/hotels/Ascott_Mayfair_Hotel_London_The

As Dorothy memorably decreed at the end of *The Wizard of Oz*, there's no place like home and she's probably right. However perfect a hotel might be, with the slickest service, the best Michelin-starred cooking and interior designed bedrooms, nothing beats being in the comfort of your own home. But when travel's on the agenda what can you do? Serviced apartments could well be the best answer and in many cases are found in locations that most people could only dream of having a property. Sharing a postcode with some of the wealthiest people in the capital, in the heart of exclusive Mayfair, The Ascott is just such a place. The 1920s art deco building has 56 apartments ranging from studios (complete with fold away beds) to a 100-square-metre three-bedroom suite that will sleep up to eight. Executive apartments come with sofa-beds making them a great choice for families and each is equipped with the entire inventory you might need to make it feel like home. Living rooms are spacious and furnished with dining tables, full-size desks as well as DVD and CD machines. Kitchens have all the tools you need to whip up a feast (or to serve takeaways) while washer/dryers ensure you'll not be lumbered with extortionate laundry charges on check-out. If you want a change of scene without leaving the building, head to the ground-floor lounge for breakfast and evening drinks or, in the summer, make the most of the serene private terrace. It's really all rather homely.

Rates from: 🏵🏵🏵🏵
Star rating: ★★★★★
Overall rating: 🦋🦋🦋🦋

Ambience :	9.14	Cleanliness:	9.21
Value:	7.71	Facilities:	7.94
Staff:	8.79	Restaurants:	8.85
Location:	9.36	Families:	7.78

Bonnington Hotel

92 Southampton Row, London, WC1B 4BH, England
T: +44 20 7242 2828 **F:** +44 20 7831 9170
www.HotelClub.com/hotels/Bonnington_Hotel_London

If you're the sort of guest who judges a book by its cover (not inappropriate in this part of town), and likewise, a hotel by its main watering hole, head straight for the Bonnington's Malt Bar. The range of whiskies would gladden any drinker's heart (or throat) and -

especially when there's some live sporting action on the quartet of plasma screens - it's a highly convivial spot to pause and take stock. The same could be said for the entire property, from its bedrooms (recently given a very plush upgrade) to the crisp

Waterfalls restaurant (with resident harpist and pianist) to the select fitness centre. The hotel is also a regular venue for Masonic dinners, and other gatherings of a similar nature. Almost a century on from its opening by Lord Strathcona, the Bonnington's blooming in Bloomsbury.

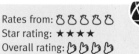

Rates from: 💰💰💰💰💰
Star rating: ★★★★
Overall rating: 🐾🐾🐾🐾

Ambience :	8.00	Cleanliness:	8.67
Value:	7.82	Facilities:	7.17
Staff:	7.25	Restaurants:	8.06
Location:	8.83	Families:	6.86

Brown's Hotel

Albemarle Street, London, W1S 4BP, England
T: +44 20 7493 6020 **F:** +44 20 7493 9381
www.HotelClub.com

The capital's fashionable districts come and go but Mayfair remains a constant, as does the success of the 170-year old Brown's Hotel. Don't be fooled by its age; a £24 million renovation has kept things comfortable, while making this London institution effortlessly contemporary. Behind the elegant

18th-century façade you'll find rooms with iPod docking stations, flat-screen digital TVs and interactive video on demand from a vast library of films. A nod to the hotel's more genteel roots is accented by the use of antique accessories and photos of established celebrities who have

stayed here. Perhaps they too sipped a cuppa in the English Tea Room where traditional scones with clotted cream are served. The Terence Donovan-decorated Donovan Bar is more boisterous, but whichever you choose you can work it all off in the state-of-the-art cardiovascular gym.

Rates from: 💰💰💰💰💰
Star rating: ★★★★★
Overall rating: 🐾🐾🐾🐾

Ambience :	9.43	Cleanliness:	9.43
Value:	8.07	Facilities:	8.35
Staff:	9.08	Restaurants:	9.00
Location:	9.86	Families:	9.17

The Cavendish London

81 Jermyn Street, St James, London, SW1Y 6JF, England
T: +44 20 7930 2111 F: +44 20 7839 2125
www.HotelClub.com/hotels/Cavendish_StJames_Hotel

your à la carte breakfast kippers. But what most surprises at the Cavendish are the stunning vistas of London's iconic landmarks. St Paul's, Sir Norman's Gherkin, Canary Wharf, the London Eye, Centrepoint, Big Ben, the Houses of Parliament and even Battersea Power Station are all swept into the Cav's well-endowed viewfinder.

Current owners Thistle reduced the room count when they purchased the hotel - even standards have a desk with high-speed Internet access. Suites enjoy a wall-to-wall sweep of iconic London sights. The chic bathrooms, with their stand-alone washbasins, heated chrome towel rails and Gilchrist & Soames toiletries deserve a special mention. Unusually for London, there are many plasma TVs (though not all rooms have them yet) while nice biccies, herbal teas, a kettle and token bottles of water are not to be sniffed at in a city where very little comes for free.

Back in Edwardian days The Cavendish was run by Rosa Lewis, the so-called Duchess of Duke St, and the Regency dandy Beau Brummell, whose statue marks the entrance to the nearby Piccadilly Arcade, would surely nod his approval at the latter-day Cavendish.

That it's a popular choice among Scandinavians says a lot about this contemporary bolthole located at the heart of salubrious Piccadilly. A short stroll from Green Park, and tucked into the prestigious gentlemen's tailors' enclave that is Jermyn Street, the Cavendish is

anything but stuffy. In fact, its informal boutique personality and intimate lobby and public areas belie a large room count: 230 - all with magnificent views, uncluttered, contemporary and you can peer into Fortnum & Mason's hallowed tearoom while devouring

Rates from: 💰💰💰
Star rating: ★★★★
Overall rating: 🏨🏨🏨🏨

Ambience :	8.93	Cleanliness:	9.08
Value:	8.57	Facilities:	8.36
Staff:	9.14	Restaurants:	8.55
Location:	9.64	Families:	8.00

City Inn Westminster London

30 John Islip Street, London, SW1P 4DD, England
T: +44 20 7630 1000 **F:** +44 20 7233 7575
www.HotelClub.com/hotels/City_Inn_Westminster

The name may sound bland; the hotel - next to the Thames and the Tate Britain - is anything but. For a start, the entire property moves to the invigorating rhythms of the contemporary artworks displayed as part of a rolling exhibition. And, continuing the theme and just in case you get the idea that this is somewhere solely on the hunt for the corporate quid, they even host art classes for children.

There's more in the way of zest to be found elsewhere in the hotel. The City Café is the obvious source, augmented by al fresco dining in summer, and with a neat pre-or post-theatre supper menu.

And the Millbank Lounge was aptly summed up by one visitor's comment: "classy cocktails and mellow moods for the young Machiavellian set - you're assured of a good seat".

And so to the main event, that is, the 460 guestrooms, which include 16 suites. The hallmarks are freshness and modernity, and while the windows are of the floor-to-ceiling variety, they also open. Flat-screen screen satellite TV is a given, ditto CD and DVD player. Shave in the power shower's mist-free mirrors, dabble with the free Broadband, or pop the laptop inside the safe (it's quite big enough) and hit the

fitness suite. This is a hotel that's designed with the 21st-century guest in mind.

Finally, anyone with some sort of event in mind should check out the Sky Lounge, with private bar and mezzanine dining area, and whose name needs little elucidation.

Rates from: 🐍🐍🐍🐍
Star rating: ★ ★ ★ ★
Overall rating: 👋👋👋👋

Ambience :	8.63	Cleanliness:	9.38
Value:	8.31	Facilities:	8.21
Staff:	8.97	Restaurants:	8.41
Location:	8.78	Families:	7.92

Claridge's

Claridge's, Brook Street, Mayfair, London W1K 4HR, England
T: +44 20 7629 8860 **F:** +44 20 7499 2210
www.HotelClub.com/hotels/Claridges_Hotel_London

London remains a city of characterful neighbourhoods, and - as the veteran Monopoly board attests - Mayfair is its most prestigious. A traditional playground for dandies and toffs, its strollable mix of handsome avenues, quaint shopping arcades and leafy squares is in resurgent mood thanks to a wave of openings that has included a swanky new food hall at Fortnum & Mason, the revival of Scott's seafood restaurant in Mount Street, and the arrival of fashion stores such as Luella and Marc Jacobs.

In the midst of this glamorous swirl stands Claridge's, a ruddy-faced, seven-storey hotel that was built in 1898 by CW Stephens, who later designed Harrods. With a long tradition of welcoming the daring and the distinguished into the glittering heart of London, its pedigree is unassailable. This is where flappers danced and Winston Churchill plotted, where the late Queen Elizabeth, the Queen Mother loved to dine and supermodels like Kate Moss now trip along corridors built wide enough for two ladies in crinolines to walk side by side. On one celebrated occasion there were so many royals in residence that when a diplomat rang up and urgently asked for the King, the receptionist calmy replied "Certainly sir, but which one?"

In the late 1920s Claridge's received an art deco makeover that would today be deemed cutting edge. Its mirrored halls and graceful bedrooms still gleam with flourishes from that period: a naked female statue holds up a moon-like lamp, a chunky clock stoically ticks on, your bathroom taps could double as propellers. With the recent appointment of a new General Manager, Philippe Leboeuf, the commitment to impeccable design has continued with the opening of eleven suites with absorbingly detailed interiors by Viscount Linley, the renowned furniture maker and nephew of the Queen. Here the customary plush furnishings are still present, but now matched with a custom-made TV cabinet decorated with intricate marquetry, or chairs upholstered in a contemporary toile de Jouy printed with police cars.

For anyone with the good fortune to stay in one of Claridge's 203 bedrooms, the hotel is simply the most elegant and well-appointed address from which to launch yourself onto town. Nothing here is fake. There is no corporate

gloss sent from above. That sun-ray chandelier above you really has been there since 1929. The lilies exploding in The Foyer (a dining room and not a foyer) are as

cheerful as the waiter who delivers your superlative luncheon of Claridge's traditional game pie served with greengage chutney.

Gordon Ramsay, Britain's

rumbustious three-Michelin star chef, has had an eponymous, apricot-toned restaurant here since 2001 - and it is booked solid. Claridge's Bar, with its silver-leaf ceiling and foxy red leather banquettes, is a permanent fash-pack favourite. The lesser-known Fumoir is ideal for a wicked cocktail with your *amour*. Let's put this another way: at Claridge's everyone has so much fun they get through 36,000 bottles of Champagne every year. Next time you're bowling through Mayfair, it would be rude not to join them.

Rates from: 🏨🏨🏨🏨🏨
Star rating: ★★★★★
Overall rating: 🐾🐾🐾🐾 ½

Ambience :	9.65	Cleanliness:	9.67
Value:	7.76	Facilities:	8.76
Staff:	9.36	Restaurants:	9.63
Location:	9.53	Families:	8.53

The Connaught

Carlos Place, Mayfair, London W1K 2AL, England
T: +44 207499 7070 **F:** +44 207495 3262
www.HotelClub.com/hotels/Connaught_Hotel_London

Fans of the Connaught may have felt bereft when it shut its doors in March 2007 for a nine-month, multi-million pound restoration, but they should take comfort in the fact that this 1897 landmark is not about to forget its traditional appeal. Antique fittings have been carefully removed to get their own spit-and-polish before being returned *in situ*, while the redoubtable staff were merely temporarily relocated to one of the Marylebone Hotel Group's sister hotels to keep their skills well-oiled before their return home. For home is what interior designer Guy Oliver and architect Michael Blair are aiming to keep with their 21st-century interpretation of Edwardian aristocracy. They have added lots of glass - especially to a terrace extension to the Red Room bar - but kept the iconic colonnades, sweeping staircase and stone griffin sculptures; they have also rewired, replumbed and redecorated each guest room (which should obliterate any complaints about creaky pipes or dog-eared wallpaper), but will keep the doormen in top hats and chamber maids who know every guest by name. In short they have done everything they can to avoid scaring off old school regulars (which, in the past, included Grace Kelly and Cary Grant) while trying to attract the newly curious. This new breed of gentlefolk may opt for the spanking new 33-room extension, which, though far from trying to ape postmodernist irony, will include such modern design features as a "green" roof complete with succulents to absorb rainwater and release oxygen back into the environment.

Rates from: ☕☕☕☕☕
Star rating: ★★★★★
Overall rating: 🦢🦢🦢🦢

Ambience :	8.75	Cleanliness:	9.56
Value:	8.25	Facilities:	7.33
Staff:	9.00	Restaurants:	9.07
Location:	9.00	Families:	6.88

Copthorne Tara Hotel London Kensington

Scarsdale Place, Kensington, London, UK W8 5SR, England
T: +44 20 7937 7211 **F**: +44 20 7937 7100
www.HotelClub.com/hotels/Copthorne_Tara_Hotel_London

Kensington High, dominated by art deco buildings, is one of west London's most iconic shopping streets. Though old favourites such as Biba, the store that epitomised London 60s street style, and the alternative fashions of Kensington Market are long since gone, equally popular hangouts still magnetise the crowds. America's Whole Foods Market opened the UK's first organic superstore here, while both sides of the street heave with well-known brands (including the Mecca that is Top Shop) and more specialised boutiques. Just around the corner is Kensington Palace, while well within bag-carrying distance - and away from any traffic rumble - is the perfectly positioned Tara Copthorne. As a member of Millennium hotels the 833-roomed property bears all the facilities that might be expected - flight crews from Singapore Airlines and JAL wouldn't choose to spend layovers here if it didn't. Standard rooms are generously sized and equipped with broadband, roomy en suites and, cleverly, they've dropped the stocked mini-bar (available anyway from room service 24/7) in favour of an empty fridge - handy for all those Whole Foods purchases. If you can delve into the coffers a little deeper it's worth spending the extra to upgrade to a Club room up on the top two floors. Broadband and an ample breakfast will then be complimentary, so will access to the small but handy fitness room and evening alcoholic drinks in the private Club lounge. The views over London in both directions are enough to make you stay in your room all day.

Rates from: 🏠🏠🏠🏠
Star rating: ★ ★ ★ ★
Overall rating: 🐻🐻🐻🐻

Ambience :	7.85	Cleanliness:	8.65
Value:	8.05	Facilities:	7.64
Staff:	7.90	Restaurants:	8.22
Location:	8.74	Families:	7.88

Covent Garden Hotel

10 Monmouth Street, London, WC2H 9HB, England
T: +44 20 7806 1000 **F:** +44 20 7806 1100
www.HotelClub.com/hotels/Citadines_Holborn_Covent_Garden_London_1

From the moment you walk into Tim and Kit Kemp's Covent Garden Hotel you know you're in safe hands. Not that this is an insalubrious part of town; you're just a hop to that notable restaurant The Ivy, a skip to the Donmar Warehouse (and dozens of other West End theatres) and a scant few metres to the designer fashion boutique The Loft, where discount price tags can soon add up. Back at the hotel things are as traditional as a country inn, with all the cosy comfort that implies. On pea soup fog nights you can snuggle up in front of a log-burning fire in both the Tiffany Library and the Drawing Room, pour yourself a warming toddy from the honour bar or nestle beneath sumptuous Frette bed linen in one of the 53 guest bedrooms. Among the hotel's particular boasts are London's largest four-poster bed and a two-floor Loft that can convert into a grand two-bedroom, three-bathroom suite. But its real appeal is not in those Guinness Book of Record-breaking statistics, and if, unlike its sister Soho Hotel it has failed to grab too many lifestyle magazine headlines, that's because what it does exceptionally well is unostentatious pleasure. It's as polite as an English country gent, without any jarring eccentricities.

Even the state-of-the-art, surround-sound private cinema (for all its THX technology) is underplayed with cool, cream leather seats by Poltrona Frau, and if you can't be bothered to wander out on Saturday night the Film Club comes complete with dinner at the hotel restaurant Brasserie Max.

Rates from: 🛏🛏🛏🛏
Star rating: ★★★★★
Overall rating: 🛡🛡🛡🛡

Ambience :	9.21	Cleanliness:	9.86
Value:	8.36	Facilities:	8.41
Staff:	9.21	Restaurants:	8.83
Location:	9.71	Families:	8.13

Crowne Plaza London St James

Buckingham Gate, London, SW1E 6AF, England
T: +44 20 7834 6655 **F:** +44 20 7630 7587
www.HotelClub.com/hotels/Crowne_Plaza_Hotel_St_James

Pause for a second, and ignore the Crowne Plaza's 342 elegant rooms, its spa and bistro - respectively branded Fifty One and 51 - the impressive stack of conference and private dining rooms, the business centre that's open 24 hours a day, and the regularly uproarious, 48-metre Zander bar, reportedly the longest in Europe. Instead, take time to admire the central courtyard and fountain, which really underlines this Westminster hotel's claim to be metropolitan haven. This is the heart of the property, and something to be thoroughly appreciated, particularly when they're serving floral afternoon teas. Of course the hotel's other offerings - especially The Quillon, sister restaurant to the celebrated Bombay Brasserie - measure up to what is generally a very high standard. Note that many London hotels charge for newspapers nowadays - they're free here. This is a very worthy property, as its staff will proudly tell you unprompted.

Rates from: 🛏🛏🛏🛏🛏
Star rating: ★ ★ ★ ★
Overall rating: 👣 👣 👣 👣

Ambience :	9.07	Cleanliness:	9.50
Value:	8.71	Facilities:	8.37
Staff:	9.36	Restaurants:	8.85
Location:	9.36	Families:	8.38

The Cumberland Hotel

Great Cumberland Place, London, W1H 7DL, England
T: +44 870 333 9280 **F:** +44 870 333 9281
www.HotelClub.com

This one's a show-stopper, and guests would be forgiven for thinking they'd walked into an extension of the Tate Modern. Packed with sculptures, art works and installations, it's inspiring and enthralling in equal measure. The interior design team was given free reign in the suites and apartments, which are gloriously invigorating, packed with the latest hi-tech thrills, while remaining supremely comfortable. Gary Rhodes' signature restaurant leads the dining pack, while both Carbon and Espresso bars are equally lively.

Kua Bar is more chill, and the five open kitchens of The Market start the day with a breakfast sizzle. Some 26 conference and meeting rooms (zoned Aqua, Blue, Green and Ocean) provide a dazzling but thoroughly workable space. London would benefit from a few more hotels with the Cumberland's sense of exhilaration.

Rates from: 🛏🛏🛏🛏🛏
Star rating: ★ ★ ★ ★
Overall rating: 👣 👣 👣 👣

Ambience :	8.52	Cleanliness:	8.65
Value:	8.12	Facilities:	8.19
Staff:	8.48	Restaurants:	8.57
Location:	9.31	Families:	7.61

The Dorchester

Park Lane, London, W1K 1QA, England
T: +44 20 7629 8888 **F:** +44 20 7629 8080
www.HotelClub.com/hotels/Dorchester_Hotel_London_The

It's unlikely that the Sultan of Brunei's hotel collection will ever be as extensive as his legendary fleet of classic cars, but when it comes to quality The Dorchester remains well and truly in pole position.

The 1930s are popularly supposed to have been a decade of unease and dispossession; however The Dorchester's opening, in April 1931, was a moment of unparalleled confidence. Stacked high with the (then) avant-garde material concrete, and sound-proofed with cork and seaweed (!), The Dorchester was a class apart from the very beginning.

While some of its original innovations are equally welcome today (many of its 250 rooms and suites have interconnecting doors) the property has not lagged when it comes to re-inventing itself according to the dictates of time. The butlers of the new Millennium are just as obliging as those of three quarters of a century back, but nowadays they can set up an intranet between the hotel and New Zealand, as they helpfully did for the composers of the *Lord of the Rings* movie trilogy.

Gourmet wining and dining has always been a part of life at The Dorchester, however this most pleasurable of necessary pastimes is best indulged in the Krug Room, one of very few such edifices scattered about the world's more discerning hotels. With just a dozen red leather chairs set around a glass table, it's designed to satisfy both the epicure and the voyeur as it's right next to the main kitchen, where master chef Henry Brosi works his particular brand of magic, popping in between courses to explain what's what, as if your

tastebuds weren't already singing several arias all at once.

While the Krug Room is - obvious pun here - the crème-de-la-crème, other parts of the property are equally poised to pay tribute to the culinary arts. China Tang's dim sum should make much of Gerrard Street, and even places in Hong Kong, blush, while the Crystal Suite is a lovely Art Deco private dining area. Alain Ducasse, who arrived in October 2007, needs little in the way of introduction, and The Promenade - always the hub of this hotel - fairly glistens after being given a very superior makeover by Thierry Despont: and its cocktails scintillate.

Of all the glorious parade of Technicolor characters who have stepped in and out of The Dorchester over the years, Oliver Messel - theatrical designer extraordinaire - remains one of the most alluring, and it's fitting that the suite that's the acme of the hotel's accommodation should bear his name. Happy to relate, the other 249 rooms and suites echo his marvellous vision, though none are quite as amazing in either style or size.

Naturally, there's plenty in the way of relaxation here, be it in the spa and gym or the utterly traditional gentlemen's barbers.

Time to leave? There's no finer exit than bowling away down Park Lane in the hotel's Rolls-Royce Phantom, though one of the BMW 7 series limos will do at a pinch. His Majesty would surely approve of either conveyance.

Rates from: 🕭🕭🕭🕭🕭
Star rating: ★★★★★
Overall rating: 🐾🐾🐾🐾

Ambience :	8.96	Cleanliness:	9.22
Value:	7.49	Facilities:	8.57
Staff:	8.83	Restaurants:	9.00
Location:	9.41	Families:	7.86

The Grosvenor House

Park Lane, London, W1K 7TN, England
T: +44 20 7499 6363 **F:** +44 20 7493 3341
www.HotelClub.com/hotels/Grosvenor_House_Hotel_London

The multi-million pound renovation due to finish in mid 2008 will put Marriott's Park Lane property very much back in the forefront of the capital's accommodation. And that's exactly where it should be. The hotel opened in 1929, chiefly notable for an imposing forecourt framed by wrought iron gates designed by Sir Edward Lutyens. The newly-groovy Grosvenor takes its historical antecedents in its stride, but now boasts 494 very hi-tech rooms, equally adaptable to both business and leisure. Wine lovers will be pleased to learn of a new F&B outlet named Bord'Eaux, while fans of the hotel in its former incarnation will be relieved to hear that the service and staff remain exemplary throughout. And The Park Room, setting for many a splendid breakfast, lunch and dinner, continues to serve up much of the same.

Rates from: 𝔅𝔅𝔅𝔅𝔅
Star rating: ★★★★★
Overall rating: 𝔅𝔅𝔅𝔅 ½

Ambience :	9.13	Cleanliness:	9.53
Value:	8.03	Facilities:	8.50
Staff:	9.00	Restaurants:	8.93
Location:	9.53	Families:	8.65

The Hempel

31-35 Craven Hill Gardens, London W2 3EA, England
T: +44 20 7298 9000 **F:** +44 20 7402 4666
www.HotelClub.com/hotels/Hempel_Hotel_The

With a restaurant menu boasting an Avocado Caterpillar Set, and rooms claiming to have their own specially designed oxygen, it may come as a surprise to find The Hempel located on a street in Bayswater, and not attached to a Space Shuttle package tour. The eponymous Ms Anouska H launched her Zen-like establishment when minimalism was at the height of fashion, and guests still clear their thoughts by suspending themselves in "time and place" - literally if you choose the room with a bed that hangs above the lounge. If it all sounds a bit too *Clockwork Orange*, then rest assured it's more Bali than Burgess and rest is what you'll get in this anything but average design hotel. But if you do want to reconnect with the world there's Wi-Fi access throughout.

Rates from: 𝔅𝔅𝔅𝔅
Star rating: ★★★★★
Overall rating: 𝔅𝔅𝔅𝔅

Ambience :	9.40	Cleanliness:	9.47
Value:	7.80	Facilities:	7.59
Staff:	8.60	Restaurants:	8.92
Location:	8.53	Families:	6.88

Hilton London Hyde Park

129 Bayswater Road, London, W2 4RJ, England
T: +44 207 221 2217 **F:** +44 207 229 0557
www.HotelClub.com/hotels/Hilton_Hyde_Park_Hotel_London

Centrally located in the heart of London yet opposite the tranquil sanctuaries of Hyde Park and Kensington Gardens, this branch of the Hilton is just the right mix of practical and pleasurable. Executives will delight in the location of the hotel and its proximity to the West End or the city centre, plus the readily available business facilities; on a more pleasurable aspect, the hotel is a leisurely stroll away from many high street retailers and cultural highlights of London. The hotel features a restaurant and a lounge bar; despite the lack of a fitness centre, this can be readily arranged with a sister Hilton which is only minutes' walk away. There are also 129 stylish rooms - well equipped with all necessities, cosy, compact and yet spacious enough to relax in.

Rates from: 🏵 🏵 🏵
Star rating: ★★★★
Overall rating: 🏩 🏩 🏩 🏩

Ambience :	8.44	Cleanliness:	8.88
Value:	7.88	Facilities:	8.01
Staff:	8.38	Restaurants:	8.50
Location:	8.63	Families:	7.69

Hilton London Kensington

179-199 Holland Park Avenue, London, W11 4UL, England
T: +44 20 7603 3355 **F:** +44 20 7602 9397
www.HotelClub.com/hotels/Hilton_Kensington_Hotel_London

The Kensington Hilton stands on the aesthetically pleasing tree-lined Holland Park Avenue, and only a short distance from the bustling Portobello Road Market as well as the many other local attractions London has on offer. With facilities galore this hotel is in an ideal location for those seeking either a business-related or pleasurable stay. This is a Hilton, after all! The 601 rooms are spacious, light, modern and equipped to meet one's every need - if you're lucky, a room with a view of the Avenue is an additional bonus in such a grand city. As another plus the staff are particularly cheerful, adding welcome hospitality to a grand establishment. A fitness centre, restaurant and lounge bar also feature within the hotel, however a short stroll along Holland Park Avenue leads to many boutique and lively cafes, bars and restaurants.

Rates from: 🏵 🏵 🏵
Star rating: ★★★★
Overall rating: 🏩 🏩 🏩 🏩

Ambience :	7.50	Cleanliness:	8.43
Value:	7.86	Facilities:	8.00
Staff:	8.23	Restaurants:	8.25
Location:	8.71	Families:	8.14

Hilton London Metropole

225 Edgware Road, London, W2 1JU, England
T: +44 20 7402 4141 **F:** +44 20 7262 2921
www.HotelClub.com/hotels/Hilton_Metropole_Hotel_London

For those in the "bigger is better" camp this will be considered the Hummer of London hotels. The slightly cheesy but nevertheless impressive mantra is "Three to 3,000 can meet, two to 2,000 can eat, one to 1,000 can sleep" which gives you an idea about its vitals. It's really three hotels in one which, bundled together, provide a whopping 1,054 bedrooms split across the Tower, East and West Wings. Popular rooms are those on the higher floors with far-reaching, rooftop views over to Big Ben and the London Eye, and the Executive rooms which give access to a private lounge where you can spend all day grazing on complimentary nibbles, and of course working your way through the bar. For fitness fans the health club's 12.5-metre indoor pool is definitely worth bringing your swimmers for and there's a sauna and steam room for those who like to take things more easy. There are plenty of places to get sustenance but for the most panoramic views try the Asian Fusion restaurant, Nippon Tuk, on the 23rd floor. There's something about the hotel's main areas on the ground floor that stirs up thoughts of an airport departure terminal - the vast amount of space dedicated to eating and drinking, the number of staff on hand to offer assistance and the general hum of the place that's exacerbated by TVs broadcasting Sky news. Whatever the reason, it results in a familiar London feel - that of a place being alive.

Rates from: 🏠🏠🏠
Star rating: ★ ★ ★ ★
Overall rating: 🏠🏠🏠🏠

Ambience :	8.31	Cleanliness:	8.97
Value:	7.91	Facilities:	8.56
Staff:	8.33	Restaurants:	8.69
Location:	8.94	Families:	8.53

Hotel Russell

Russell Square, London, WC1B 5BE, England
T: +44 20 7837 6470 **F:** +44 20 7837 2857
www.HotelClub.com/hotels/Hotel_Russell_London

Standard, Ambassador or Contemporary - give the Standard rooms a miss if you don't like chintz. In the public areas the lobby sparkles with Pyrenean marble and the pièce-de-resistance is a restored mosaic floor depicting the signs of the Zodiac, on show for the first time since the second world war.

Check in to the Hotel Russell and you'll be doing so under the auspices of four British queens, whose life-size statues peer down from the hotel's main front entrance. Occupying an enviable location at the heart of Bloomsbury, this redbrick turreted stunner dominates the entire east side of

Russell Square and serves as a spectacular example of Victorian Renaissance revival architecture.

A recent £20 million restoration of the Russell's 373 bedrooms and public areas has brought the hotel's interior in line with its imposing Victorian façade. Rooms adopt three different styles:

Rates from: 🛏🛏🛏🛏🛏
Star rating: ★★★★
Overall rating: 🌐🌐🌐🌐

Ambience :	8.30	Cleanliness:	8.93
Value:	7.52	Facilities:	7.02
Staff:	8.37	Restaurants:	7.86
Location:	8.74	Families:	7.00

The Hoxton Hotel

81 Great Eastern Street, London, EC2A 3HU, England
T: +44 20 7550 1000 **F:** +44 20 7550 1090
www.HotelClub.com/hotels/The_Hoxton_Hotel

Media types bustle about the lobby by day and at night beautiful people sip Rhubarbellinis before hitting the bars and clubs of Shoreditch (London's equivalent of New York's Meatpacking district). Forget about pillow chocolates and mini-bars and snuggle into Frette sheets and duck down for a song.

Sleek, high-quality, no fuss, value-for-money, a Blackberry throw from so-hip-it-hiccups Hoxton, London's first luxury budget hotel is a self-proclaimed pret accompli. Sinclair Beecham (half the brains behind the Pret sandwich revolution) launched this Square Mile stunner in September 2006 under the

mantra "budget needn't be boring". Quite so. With its statement lobby, trendy Grille restaurant, dead cheap phone rates, free WiFi for everyone, everywhere, inexpensive day room rental and Pret breakfast bag delivery - this is urban hotel living for the Noughties generation.

Rates from: 🛏🛏
Star rating: ★★★★
Overall rating: 🌐🌐🌐🌐

Ambience :	8.83	Cleanliness:	9.33
Value:	9.08	Facilities:	7.22
Staff:	8.71	Restaurants:	7.76
Location:	7.79	Families:	6.87

The Hyde Park Towers Hotel

41-51 Inverness Terrace, London, W2 3JN, England
T: +44 20 7221 8484 **F:** +44 20 7221 3901
www.HotelClub.com/hotels/Hyde_Park_Towers_Hotel_London

There can be no better way to get a proper feel for a city than to immerse oneself into local life as much as possible, and what better way to do that than to stay in one of the most desirable residential areas in London? Notting Hill and its surrounding areas have hosted many a film unit - and with good reason. It is home to some of the most quaint streets and lively restaurants and bars in London, and the Hyde Park Towers is mere minutes away from many of the best spots. Tucked away down a quiet leafy terrace in the neighbouring area of Bayswater this property is an elegant early Victorian building located a short stroll from Kensington Palace and its once private 105-hectare gardens. The 115 rooms may err on the small side, but they're comfortable, equipped with Wi-Fi, all ensuite and offer peerless value for money. In the spacious reception area you'll find free

magazines (*Time Out*, *Homes & Antiques*), newspapers and even a vast bowl of mouth-watering Fox's Glacier mints for guests to devour at will. Visit in the summer and you will be able to take advantage of the charming garden where you can order from the hotel bar or restaurant. The amiable hotel staff are on hand to offer a full concierge service and will happily give the low-down on the most popular local hangouts in the area. With

celebrity inhabitants aplenty you'll want to make sure you're headed for the hottest places.

Rates from: 🐚🐚🐚
Star rating: ★ ★ ★
Overall rating: 🐾🐾🐾🐾

Ambience :	8.45	Cleanliness:	8.55
Value:	8.20	Facilities:	8.12
Staff:	8.70	Restaurants:	8.12
Location:	9.05	Families:	8.07

InterContinental London Park Lane

1 Hamilton Place, Park Lane, London, W1J 7QY, England
T: +44 20 74093131 **F:** +44 20 74933476
www.HotelClub.com/hotels/InterContinental_Hotel_London

You'd naturally expect a £76 million facelift to result in a younger, more vibrant version of the original specimen so it's no wonder the Intercon is looking more sparkly than ever. The hotel certainly benefits from its Mayfair address overlooking two Royal parks and with its refurbished interior is set to become the brand's flagship property - praise indeed. They're hot on promoting local culture and brands here so the lobby is hung with etchings of London landmarks, you can order Martin Miller's Gin Martini Afternoon Tea and, whenever possible, they use products from chic London partners like The Tea Palace and Melt Chocolatiers. The 387-bedrooms, stocked with Elemis (British) miniatures, have all the 21st-century comforts you could wish for including rain showers, Bang & Olufsen TVs and Bose sound systems. If you want super-lux book into one of the suites, the flashiest of which have canopy beds, floating staircases and there's even one with a private cinema. Eating is big here. Theo Randall, former head chef at the ground-breaking River Café, (Jamie Oliver is a fellow alumni) has his debut restaurant here serving regional Italian cooking. The more casual Cookbook Café is designed so customers can interact with the chefs for a more personal style of cooking - breakfast is extraordinary with smoothie bar, egg chef *et al*. As for the Elemis Spa - well, it's out of this world. Embellished with Italian marble, Bisazza mosaic tiles, quartz and modern chandeliers you only need to walk in to the place to feel rejuvenated. A bit like the hotel itself.

Rates from: 🏨🏨🏨🏨🏨
Star rating: ★★★★★
Overall rating: 👍👍👍👍

Ambience :	8.41	Cleanliness:	8.72
Value:	6.90	Facilities:	8.34
Staff:	8.31	Restaurants:	8.32
Location:	8.86	Families:	8.00

Jurys Kensington Hotel

109-113 Queen's Gate, South Kensington, London, SW7 5LR, England
T: +44 20 7589 6300 **F:** +44 20 7581 1492
www.HotelClub.com/hotels/Jurys_Kensington_Hotel_London

The late lamented comedian Marty Feldman used to sing: "Kensington High Street is my street for good, it's a luv-er-lee neighbourhood." The ditty ended there, but Kensington's all-round goodness lives on. Of the seven Jurys properties in London, this enjoys perhaps the choicest location, with an imposing frontage which sets the scene for the hotel within.

The guest rooms are straightforward, well laid-out and business like, with duck down duvets and Judith Jackson aromatherapy amenities. The bulk of the accommodation is contained in 133 Classic Rooms; there's more space in the 40 Executive Rooms and suites, which come with extras

like an evening newspaper and mineral water. The décor might be tagged as slightly dated, but remains tasteful.

Back in the public areas, the most lively space is Kavanagh's, featuring the sort of traditional music that might be expected in a themed Irish bar plus accompanying beers and something to soak them up with. The menus at two other outlets, The Cocktail Bar and Il Barista, should provoke little surprise but much in the way of appreciation. Jurys' main restaurant, Copplestone, verges on haute cuisine while maintaining an informal and intimate atmosphere.

Apart from a selection of meeting rooms, Jurys is bed and

board pure and simple, with no further facilities. However there's plenty in the way of exercise and fresh air to be had in nearby Hyde Park, and more commercially-inclined entertainment in the immediate, and luv-er-lee, neighbourhood. A very commendable and unpretentious city hotel.

Rates from: 💰💰💰💰💰
Star rating: ★★★★
Overall rating: 👣👣👣👣

Ambience :	8.65	Cleanliness:	9.24
Value:	7.82	Facilities:	7.54
Staff:	8.35	Restaurants:	7.81
Location:	9.24	Families:	8.33

The Landmark London Hotel

222 Marylebone Road, London NW1 6JQ, England
T: +44 20 7631 8000 **F:** +44 20 7631 8080
www.HotelClub.com/hotels/Landmark_Hotel_London

Grazing on champagne and strawberries in the Winter Garden of what was one of London's finest Victorian railway hotels, you can almost smell the golden age of steam.

The Landmark's soaring eight-storey, glass-roofed central atrium - previously an uncovered courtyard used for horse-drawn carriages - is a focal point of this Gothic, Grade II listed building a ticket's throw from Marylebone station. It has now been transformed into the atmospheric Winter Garden Restaurant where, over afternoon tea, one can almost imagine the flappers of yesteryear Charleston-ing on the former dance floor while their suitors sipped Highballs and Whisky Macs in the sexy and discrete Mirror Bar.

Generous-sized rooms - the hotel's complement of 299 includes some of the largest in the capital - are one of the Landmark's selling points and the "bag will be with you in five minutes policy" impresses, as does the free mobile phone rental (though calls are charged).

But the hotel's trump card can now be found in the bowels of the hotel, where the wrapping has just come off a sleek new £2 million Spa & Health Club. With a generous nod to contemporary Asia, the calm, mood-lit space is all dark wood and muted tones brightened with occasional flashes of colour. A large poolside Sanarium - designed for longer periods of relaxation than that offered by a traditional sauna, Jacuzzi and steam, hi-tech gym and ESPA treatment rooms complete the package, but lapping in the absinthe-green pool to the calming strains of Moby, it's hard to believe the maelstrom of Madame Tussauds and Sherlock Holmes' Baker Street are just down the road.

Rates from: 🛏🛏🛏🛏
Star rating: ★★★★★
Overall rating: 🐻🐻🐻🐻

Ambience :	9.39	Cleanliness:	9.45
Value:	8.00	Facilities:	8.69
Staff:	8.93	Restaurants:	9.17
Location:	8.90	Families:	8.03

The Lanesborough

Hyde Park Corner, London, SW1X 7TA, England
T: +44 20 7259 5599 **F:** +44 20 7259 5606
www.HotelClub.com/hotels/Lanesborough_Hotel_London

If home was The Lanesborough no-one would ever leave. It is the epitome of opulence and oozes class. Who would have thought an old hospital could scrub up so well? The original restoration was supervised by the finest preservation societies - the Georgian Society, the Victorian Society, the Royal Fine Arts Commission and even English Heritage, so as you can imagine, they've hardly scrimped on the décor. The interior is as classically British as scones and cream. The 95 guest rooms are spacious and luxurious, filled with 1820s furnishings which conceal 21st-century technology. Open the armoire and you'll find decanters of spirits, while bathrooms brim with products presented in cut-glass bottles that are far too big to steal. The hotel maintains such a loyal following that the doorman appears to know everyone by name.

The key could well be the hotel's unerring attention to residential-style service. Every guest is allocated a personal butler to assist with unpacking, packing and the co-ordination of social and business itineraries. Personal business cards and stationery are printed and presented to your room on arrival. Should you be tempted to go walkabout you'll find yourself in the heart of Knightsbridge and directly opposite Hyde Park. Stay in, however, and you can't fail to pay a visit to the much-lauded Library Bar. There you'll find a collection of the finest vintage cognacs. It's not necessarily somewhere you'd want to get too comfortable mind you - their most recent cognac acquisition sells at a fairly toppy £3,000 a glass.

Rates from: 😊😊😊😊😊
Star rating: ★★★★★
Overall rating: 😊😊😊😊

Ambience :	9.20	Cleanliness:	9.40
Value:	7.80	Facilities:	8.32
Staff:	9.27	Restaurants:	9.00
Location:	9.40	Families:	7.75

The Langham, London

1C Portland Place, Regent Street, London, W1B 1JA, England
T: +44 20 7636 1000 **F:** +44 20 7323 2340
www.HotelClub.com/hotels/Langham_Hotel_London

The Langham has one of the best locations in the city - right in the heart of the West End with a mind-boggling mass of some of the world's best shops, theatres and restaurants just footsteps away. But after 140 years in the business it was, some said, in desperate need of a substantial refurb. Lucky then, that the owners heard the whisperings. At the core of the renovation project is interior-design maestro David Collins; Madonna was in such awe of his Blue Bar at The Berkeley Hotel she asked him to recreate elements of the design in her own home. Put his name to a place and the whole world seems to flock, and his influence on the Langham is already beginning to have the desired effect. The hotel's new and deeply glamorous Artesian cocktail bar bears all the Collins hallmarks. It oozes sophistication but has a sultry, sexy feel to it. If rum is your tipple this is your temple as it has one of the longest rum-menus in London. At the time of going to press the finishing touches were being applied to his new restaurant, The Landau, and the hotel's 425 spacious guestrooms, with beds fit for a princess, are also due for a complete transformation. What is already in tip-top shape is the hotel's immense health club complete with pool. It would be a shame to spend too much of your stay working out in it - but even the A-listers find it hard not to.

Rates from: 🛏🛏🛏🛏🛏
Star rating: ★★★★★
Overall rating: 🕊🕊🕊🕊

Ambience :	8.89	Cleanliness:	9.44
Value:	8.19	Facilities:	8.73
Staff:	9.26	Restaurants:	8.88
Location:	9.41	Families:	8.21

Le Méridien Piccadilly

21 Piccadilly, London, W1J 0BH, England
T: +44 20 7734 8000 **F:** +44 20 7437 3574
www.HotelClub.com/hotels/Le_Meridien_Piccadilly_Hotel_London

A few steps from the brouhaha of Regent Street and the postcard-pretty neon lights of Piccadilly Circus is the Tardis that is Le Méridien. It may be unimposing from the outside, but venture inside and the hotel opens up into a vast expanse of style. This may not appeal to the contemporary-design lovers, but for those in search of the traditional British look, this certainly fits the bill.

The 267 rooms are warmly decorated and amazingly spacious for such a centrally located hotel, and are fitted with all the latest high-tech gadgetry you would expect. Book a room on one of the higher floors and you'll be treated to some of those splendid rooftop views enjoyed by Ms Mary Poppins.

The original outdoor pool on the 2nd floor has been converted into the sunlight strewn, and partially outdoor, Terrace Restaurant. High above Piccadilly and framed by the original stone pillars, it's a charming setting to feast on breakfast, lunch and mouth-watering dinner. Water-babies need not turn the page just yet though - on the lower-ground floor are a couple of real treats! The new indoor pool must be one of the largest in London, and if you're more of a racket and ball fitness fanatic, the two squash courts should keep you busy for a while.

With three London parks, the wonders of West End theatre and shops galore on your doorstep this hotel ticks so many of the boxes you may never want to stay anywhere else.

Rates from: 🏰🏰🏰🏰
Star rating: ★★★★★
Overall rating: 🐦🐦🐦🐦

Ambience :	8.54	Cleanliness:	8.65
Value:	7.27	Facilities:	8.28
Staff:	8.24	Restaurants:	8.48
Location:	9.48	Families:	7.90

London Bridge Hotel

8-18 London Bridge Street, London, SE1 9SG, England
T: +44 20 7855 2200 **F:** +44 20 7855 2233
www.HotelClub.com/hotels/London_Bridge_Hotel_London

The historic borough of Southwark is undoubtedly one of the most trendy and effervescent areas of London. Having been up-and-coming for a while, it's now firmly up and everyone is coming. It has been immortalised in films like *Bridget Jones's Diary* and the gritty *Lock, Stock and Two Smoking Barrels*, and within its perimeter lie some of the city's biggest crowd-pullers - the Young and Old Vic theatres, HMS Belfast, the London Dungeon and, every epicurean's dream, Borough Market. If it wasn't for the super-effective glazing on the hotel's windows you'd be able to smell the market's sublimely fresh produce from your dreamy bed. It's a short walk to the City and also - and, don't let this put you off - located virtually on top of London Bridge Station. And this is a very good thing indeed. It means you have quite possibly the easiest access to Gatwick of any boutique hotel in London, and can be on the tube, and en route to any other area of town you choose to go, within minutes.

Inside, bathrooms are stocked with blissful White Company products, and the hotel's two restaurants and Borough bar are as popular with local office workers as with hotel guests. There is something deeply alluring about stepping through the door of this 141-room hotel. It's bright and cosy, the furniture's un-hotel-like and the staff are, without exception, charming. Perhaps that's the lure of an independent hotel, there are no fixed rules. It produces this calm, soothing feel.

Rates from: 🛏🛏🛏🛏
Star rating: ★★★★
Overall rating: 👍👍👍👍

Ambience :	8.91	Cleanliness:	9.27
Value:	8.32	Facilities:	8.48
Staff:	8.87	Restaurants:	8.56
Location:	8.93	Families:	9.04

London Hilton on Park Lane Hotel
22 Park Lane, London, W1K 1BE, England
T: +44 20 7493 8000 **F:** +44 20 7208 4142
www.HotelClub.com/hotels/London_Hilton_Hotel_on_Park_Lane

views across London. Apparently there are a mighty 453 guestrooms - though with a lack of long corridors you wouldn't know it - all furnished in contemporary, comforting colours and equipped with all the hi-tech wizardry you could need. This is just about everything anyone could want from a hotel.

It may not be palatial from the outside, but that's a good thing. It keeps hoi polloi out, and the royalty and fashionistas in. Leading off from the cavernous reception area are food and drink venues to suit every genre and generation of guest. There's the POP champagne bar, the Polynesian-themed Trader Vic's, the re-launched Podium restaurant and, for late-nighters, the hip, celebrity-filled Zeta Bar. On the 28th floor is the much heralded bar and restaurant, Galvin at Windows with the most awesome, expansive

Rates from: 🏠🏠🏠🏠
Star rating: ★★★★★
Overall rating: 🔑🔑🔑🔑

Ambience :	8.43	Cleanliness:	9.14
Value:	7.32	Facilities:	7.96
Staff:	8.41	Restaurants:	8.67
Location:	9.36	Families:	7.63

The London Marriott Hotel, County Hall
London County Hall, Westminster Bridge Road, London, SE1 7PB, England
T: +44 20 7928 5200 **F:** +44 20 7928 5300
www.HotelClub.com/hotels/London_Marriott_Hotel_County_Hall

sized rooms boast unbeatable views north to Big Ben, while a short meander eastwards is the Tate Modern and the Old Vic. Gorging on the hotel's culinary creations is far too easy - as is, fortunately, the route to the hotel's vast fitness centre and 25-metre pool. This is classic Marriott mastery.

A hop, skip, and large leap across the Thames from the Houses of Parliament is the mighty County Hall. Opened in 1922 by none other than King George V and Queen Mary, it was the seat of London's government for 64 years. The councillors have long since vacated and the building's original striking interior - laden with oak panelling and marble busts of Milton, Shakespeare and other classical figures - is now on show to visitors. Many of the 200 bright and ample-

Rates from: 🏠🏠🏠🏠
Star rating: ★★★★★
Overall rating: 🔑🔑🔑🔑

Ambience :	8.89	Cleanliness:	9.33
Value:	7.89	Facilities:	8.65
Staff:	8.58	Restaurants:	8.88
Location:	9.30	Families:	8.33

Malmaison

18-21 Charterhouse Square, London, EC1M 6AH, England
T: +44 20 7012 3700 F: +44 20 7012 3702
www.HotelClub.com/hotels/Malmaison_London

There is a well-tested formula to Malmaison hotels that never fails to result in a successful outcome, and this is no exception. Decorated in cool dark colours (lots of burgundy and charcoal), the furniture is contemporary and unusual, the background music's up-tempo and with a seriously funky neighbourhood location - this feels every bit a hip hotel. Weekend business is driven by weddings held at intimate churches hidden down nearby cobbled streets, and a party crowd drawn by local nightlife. On weekdays, the City execs and legal-eagles take over, while the basement bar buzzes with locals even on a schoolnight. Being an on-trend kind of place, the restaurant runs a locally-sourced Home Grown Heroes menu alongside its usual à la carte. In fact, this is run throughout the Malmaison group - you can't help imagining that the chef in Edinburgh has a distinctly easier time sourcing than the chef in the London hotel. He's done an extremely good job of it though. Breakfast is particularly sublime - whole vanilla pods float in the yoghurt! It's a simple but great pleasure to find full-sized mugs in the guest rooms rather than the oh-so-small cups and saucers synonymous with many British hotels. Someone's had a great time with the toiletries. "Snog me senseless" reads the label on the breath freshener and free postcards carry headlines like "Suite and not so innocent". Sure there are gimmicks - fun ones at that - but it doesn't detract from the fact that this is a splendidly chic hotel.

Rates from: 🛏🛏🛏🛏
Star rating: n/a
Overall rating: 🛏🛏🛏🛏

Ambience :	8.78	Cleanliness:	9.50
Value:	7.50	Facilities:	7.91
Staff:	8.94	Restaurants:	8.19
Location:	8.72	Families:	6.73

Mandarin Oriental Hyde Park, London

66 Knightsbridge, London, SW1X 7LA, England
T: +44 20 7235 2000 **F:** +44 20 7235 2001
www.HotelClub.com/hotels/Mandarin_Oriental_Hotel_London

Sandwiched between leafy Hyde Park (for joggers and walkers) and Knightsbridge (for very serious shoppers) the Mandarin Oriental is an eclectic fusion of the MO global brand thickly spread over an obviously grand old piece of English architectural history which traces its gentlemen's club beginnings all the way back to 1889.

The Prince of Wales (later Edward VII) was a frequent visitor for society balls and Queen Elizabeth II and her late sister, Princess Margaret, learnt to dance here. Baroness Margaret Thatcher even held her 80th birthday party in the Grand Ballroom.

The public rooms are surprisingly small (and in frequent use for private functions so unavailable to guests) however there's ample space for enjoyment in the Michelin-starred Foliage restaurant and The Park, which showcases all-day contemporary dining. The Mandarin Bar is an exciting modern space, and obviously a popular meeting point, so both busy and noisy, with live jazz every evening.

Prolific and polite staff everywhere (including an escort from the dining table to the door of the ladies' loo) could not be more pleasant or attentive.

The 198 sumptuous bedrooms are well equipped with all the expected technology and with cosseting Irish linen bed sheets on supremely comfortable bed and pillows. And the bathrooms contain Jo Malone toiletries in generous supply to provide the requisite touch of luxury.

The real jewel is the subterranean Spa, dark and mysteriously oriental with an unparalleled level of service and care. Booking is of "time" rather than a specific treatment and the experience of a "Time Ritual" focused on well being, relaxation and revitalisation is an essential part of any stay in this luxurious London hotel.

Rates from: 🪙🪙🪙🪙🪙
Star rating: ★★★★★
Overall rating: 🐾🐾🐾🐾 ½

Ambience :	9.40	Cleanliness:	9.70
Value:	7.87	Facilities:	8.92
Staff:	9.37	Restaurants:	9.00
Location:	9.53	Families:	8.25

The Metropolitan

Old Park Lane, London, W1K 1LB, England
T: +44 20 7447 1000 **F:** +44 20 7447 1100
www.HotelClub.com/hotels/Metropolitan_Hotel_London

and you might revise your shopping wish-list. Nobu, the Michelin-starred Japanese-Peruvian restaurant, is a paean of praise to cosmopolitan fusion, and the Shambhala Urban Escape (ie spa) another east-meets-west triumph. Some say this is the best hotel in London; die-hard fans aver the world.

Coolly contemporary, virus-free trendy and happily hip, the Metropolitan's Bar is one of the most sought-after locales in the capital, particularly after 6pm when it's open to guests and members only. But what about the rest of the hotel? Well, as the bar kicks off, so the 150 rooms follow through.

Whether you're looking over Hyde Park or the city, you're guaranteed a crisp and energising stay, surrounded by natural hardwoods like pear, Egyptian cotton sheets and fresh, muted colours. Experience the in-room multi-faceted, zillion-channel entertainment system just once

Rates from: 💰💰💰
Star rating: ★ ★ ★ ★
Overall rating: 🐸🐸🐸🐸 ½

Ambience :	9.55	Cleanliness:	9.73
Value:	7.30	Facilities:	9.09
Staff:	9.10	Restaurants:	9.71
Location:	9.00	Families:	8.60

The Milestone Hotel and Apartments

1 Kensington Court, London, W8 5DL, England
T: +44 20 7917 1000 **F:** +44 20 7917 1010
www.HotelClub.com/hotels/Milestone_Hotel_and_Apartments_London

stations, plus old-fashioned sweets provided at turn-down); three restaurants with just the right emphasis on modern British cuisine and an accompanying 400-strong wine list; then it's not beyond the bounds of possibility that The Milestone (45 rooms, 12 suites and half a dozen apartments) might tickle your fancy rather.

With Typical British Understatement to the fore: if you quite like being in hailing distance of both Harrods and Kensington Palace; are not averse to a chauffeured Bentley; are moderately partial to a glass of champagne or a cup of green tea on arriving at your Victorian-era hotel

which carries more than a few historical associations; prefer a ratio of two staff to one guest, with butlers on call 24 hours a day; and take to the idea of somewhere that can both host small business meetings while remaining child-friendly (Bose and iPod docking

Rates from: 💰💰💰💰
Star rating: ★ ★ ★ ★ ★
Overall rating: 🐸🐸🐸🐸 ½

Ambience :	9.27	Cleanliness:	9.67
Value:	8.50	Facilities:	8.61
Staff:	9.36	Restaurants:	9.00
Location:	9.27	Families:	8.60

Millennium Hotel London Mayfair

44 Grosvenor Square, London, W1K 2HP, England
T: +44 20 7629 9400 **F:** +44 20 7629 7736
www.HotelClub.com/hotels/Millennium_Hotel_Mayfair_London

This could be one of London's safest hotels, as its neighbour, the American embassy, sprouts all the apparently obligatory paraphernalia needed to protect its staff. Rumour has it that inside, the ambassadorial décor is drab and underground offices stark. Admittedly the Millennium's bright reception area is partially subterranean but that's where the similarities end. This grand 18th-century property is where Wellington's victory over Napoleon was first announced, and it was built as a stately town house for the Duchess of Kendal, mistress of George I.

The hotel retains the charm of a private residence with many original features including the striking Georgian façade still in place. Rooms at the front are marginally less generous than those at the rear but have the benefit of views overlooking the quintessentially English Grosvenor Square. The marvel of Wi-Fi works throughout the 348 bedrooms (and all public areas), bathrooms are small but perfectly formed and the honesty system operated on the mini-bar reflects the hotel's cordial atmosphere. Book a Club room and you'll have free access to the 7th floor lounge with its fabulous roof-top views as well as a shower - handy for those recovering from a red-eye flight and not wanting to pay for an extra night.

Traditional British fare is served in celebrity chef Brian Turner's buzzy restaurant, while those with an appetite for eastern flavours flock to Shogun, which some say serves the best sushi in town. With one of the most exclusive addresses in London, it's little wonder there are so many regulars.

Rates from: 💰💰💰💰
Star rating: ★★★★
Overall rating: 👣👣👣👣

Ambience :	8.53	Cleanliness:	9.07
Value:	8.33	Facilities:	7.65
Staff:	8.71	Restaurants:	8.64
Location:	9.60	Families:	7.64

The Park Lane Hotel

Piccadilly, London, W1J 7BX, England
T: +44 20 7499 6321 **F:** +44 20 7499 1965
www.HotelClub.com

London is replete with hotels that boast interiors smarter than many a private home, and histories as colourful as the city itself, and this is one such example. The renowned hotelier and one-time owner of The Ritz, Sir Bracewell-Smith, opened the property to great acclaim in 1927 and cabbies instantly nicknamed it the American Workhouse - later a generic term used to describe luxury hotels in London. Confusingly the main entrance is now tucked away at the back of the property on Brick Street, the original sweeping carriageway entrance on Piccadilly having been enclosed by a stunning dome. The space has now morphed into Palm Court and this charming lounge is where residents and locals alike now kick back and enjoy cream teas and evening cocktails. The 307 rooms, spread over eight floors, are entered through the original 1920s doors. Inside they're generously sized and full of character with many retaining original features like fireplaces and art deco marble bathrooms. You may have no cause to need it but the hotel is also home to arguably the capital's finest monument to Art Deco in the form of the stunningly restored Ballroom - sneak a peek if you can. It was chosen by Westminster as a replacement venue for the Commons should the Palace of Westminster be damaged, but fortunately it was never required. The hotel has been the setting for films such as *Brideshead Revisited* and *Jeeves and Wooster* and it's easy to see why. The Park Lane oozes vintage charm.

Rates from: 🛏🛏🛏🛏
Star rating: ★ ★ ★ ★ ★
Overall rating: 👌👌👌👌

Ambience :	8.86	Cleanliness:	8.71
Value:	8.00	Facilities:	8.04
Staff:	8.57	Restaurants:	9.00
Location:	9.07	Families:	7.89

Park Plaza Victoria

239 Vauxhall Bridge Road, London, SW1V 1EQ, England
T: +44 20 7769 9999 **F:** +44 20 7769 9841
www.HotelClub.com/hotels/Victoria_Park_Plaza_Hotel_London

Poke and pry where you will around the Park Plaza, the verdict is always going to be the same - pretty damn swish. The dozen apartments (studio, and one- or two-bedroomed) are for long-stayers, but even if you're here for a one-night stand, so to speak, it'll be difficult not to let out a sigh of satisfaction as you flip open your suitcase in any of the accommodation here. The lines are clean and modern, with sufficient tech add-ons to please either travelling exec or simply happy travellers. Excellent eating and drinking is nigh guaranteed in the restaurant and bar, both dubbed jb's, while lighter breakfast, lunch and afternoon tea is showcased at MIX Espresso Gourmet. A health club and a full-on, highly versatile meetings team completes this very sleek all-in-one package.

Rates from: 🛏🛏🛏🛏🛏
Star rating: ★ ★ ★ ★
Overall rating: 🐾🐾🐾🐾

Ambience :	8.29	Cleanliness:	8.94
Value:	8.12	Facilities:	8.41
Staff:	8.88	Restaurants:	7.64
Location:	8.88	Families:	8.50

Radisson Edwardian Hampshire Hotel

Leicester Square, London, WC2H 7LH, England
T: +44 20 7839 9399 **F:** +44 20 7930 8122
www.HotelClub.com/hotels/Radisson_Edwardian_Hampshire_Hotel_London

For those whose Latin goes no further than "etcetera", *rus in urbe* loosely means "country in the city"; and so to this hotel in Leicester Square named for the very rural county an hour's train ride to the west. The Radisson's other moniker neatly indicates the Mediterranean influences. There's a small fitness centre, but plenty of exercise to be had pounding the streets in the surrounding centre of the capital. Whether you're shopping or sightseeing. And of course, if you want to catch a movie, you can join the ticket queues practically outside the front entrance.

Edwardian elegance found in the rooms and suites, and indeed throughout the property. Opportunities for wining and dining are concentrated in the single bar and restaurant, also called the Hampshire, whose menu is a well-judged blend of British and

Rates from: 🛏🛏
Star rating: ★ ★ ★ ★ ★
Overall rating: 🐾🐾🐾🐾

Ambience :	9.00	Cleanliness:	8.76
Value:	7.76	Facilities:	7.79
Staff:	8.71	Restaurants:	8.75
Location:	8.41	Families:	8.15

Renaissance Chancery Court, London

252 High Holborn, London, WC1V 7EN, England
T: +44 20 7829 9888 **F:** +44 20 7829 9889
www.HotelClub.com

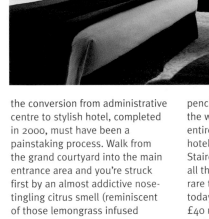

The Renaissance Chancery Court in bustling Holborn has been described as "one of the most exciting hotels in the world", and it's not hard to see why. Formerly the headquarters of Pearl Assurance, the property occupies an imposing Edwardian building in the belle époque style, which was restored under the watchful eye of English Heritage. Much of the interior, from ceilings to floors, is safeguarded by a Grade II listing so

the conversion from administrative centre to stylish hotel, completed in 2000, must have been a painstaking process. Walk from the grand courtyard into the main entrance area and you're struck first by an almost addictive nose-tingling citrus smell (reminiscent of those lemongrass infused hotels in Thailand) and then by the vastness of the place - a theme recurrent throughout. Those insurance executives clearly had a

penchant for marble. Not only are the walls on the first floor almost entirely covered in it but the hotel's tour de force, the Grand Staircase, which rises up through all the floors, is made of marble so rare that building an equivalent today would cost an estimated £40 million. Venture into any one of the 356 bedrooms and you'll notice the size theme continues. Even the very smallest rooms are out-sized and, as you'd expect, all offer five-star comfort and mod-cons. The lively Pearl restaurant and bar on the ground floor serves mouth-watering modern French food while to abstain from a visit to the Espa Spa would certainly be a mistake. This place is a gem.

Rates from: 🛏🛏🛏🛏🛏
Star rating: ★ ★ ★ ★ ★
Overall rating: 🐦🐦🐦🐦

Ambience :	9.50	Cleanliness:	9.31
Value:	8.19	Facilities:	8.84
Staff:	9.25	Restaurants:	9.07
Location:	9.06	Families:	8.33

The Ritz

150 Piccadilly, London, W1J 9BR, England
T: +44 20 7493 8181 **F:** +44 20 7493 2687
www.HotelClub.com/hotels/Ritz_Hotel_London

Happy the hotelier whose name passes into the language! A century on from its opening, The Ritz is putting on pirouettes as gracefully as Fred Astaire while César Ritz must be spinning in his grave with sheer delight. It's typical that a hotel that's regarded by many as quintessentially English should have been conceived by a Swiss, and designed (in part) by a Frenchman in the style of a chateau.

Now owned by that renowned entrepreneurial double act, Barclay Bros, The Ritz has certainly stood the test of time, albeit aided by a hefty recent makeover and the inclusion of the adjacent William Kent House. It's tempting to think that Edward VII, Winston Churchill, Charlie Chaplin, Talullah Bankhead (who apparently gulped Champagne from a slipper during a 1950s press conference) *et al*, could

walk through the main doors and detect very little in the way of change, at least as far as ambience is concerned. Naturally, it almost goes without saying that this is a top hotel for top people. Sumptuousness is given its full measure in the 136 rooms and suites, which adhere to colour schemes of pink, yellow or blue, and manage to meld such modernistic accessories as wireless connectivity quite seamlessly. The Ritz's main restaurant is often lauded as the most beautiful in the world, a claim that is pretty much untainted by hyperbole. Ironically, when it comes to summing up this truly grande dame, "ritzy" seems almost inadequate. Here's to the next century.

Rates from: 🪙🪙🪙🪙
Star rating: ★★★★★
Overall rating: 🌙🌙🌙🌙

Ambience :	9.50	Cleanliness:	9.76
Value:	7.64	Facilities:	8.58
Staff:	9.22	Restaurants:	9.31
Location:	9.42	Families:	8.52

Royal Garden Hotel

2-24 High Street Kensington, London W8 4PT, England
T: +44 20 7937 8000 F: +44 20 7361 1991
www.HotelClub.com/hotels/Royal_Garden_Hotel_London

New arrivals may be forgiven for thinking that jet lag has finally triumphed when they first pull back the curtains. But, no, you are in London and, yes, that really is greensward unrolling before your eyes. Kensington Gardens to be precise, and the hotel is every bit as regal as its surrounds and name suggest. An understated (naturally!) English finish characterises the 396 rooms and suites, which are spread over ten floors. Guests are assured of fine dining, and fronting up to Bertie's Bar is something of a rite of passage for anyone who knows or would like to meet its manager, Luis Cobas, who's been with the hotel for 30 years. And take time out to explore the stellar Soma Spa, run by Carolan Brown, former trainer to the late Princess of Wales.

Rates from: 💰💰💰
Star rating: ★★★★★
Overall rating: 👍👍👍👍

Ambience :	8.67	Cleanliness:	9.17
Value:	8.04	Facilities:	8.28
Staff:	8.54	Restaurants:	8.82
Location:	9.54	Families:	7.87

The Royal Horseguards

2 Whitehall Court, Whitehall, London, SW1A 2EJ, England
T: +44 870 333 9122 F: +44 870 333 9222
www.HotelClub.com/hotels/Royal_Horseguards_Hotel_London

A Grade I listed building on the banks of the Thames, the Royal Horseguards encapsulate all that London does well - Gothic drama, historical intrigue, pomp and Potter. It's frequented by Parliamentarians, dignitaries, peers and the occasional film crew. London regulars will have seen this building, with its landmark chateau-style turrets punctuating the Embankment skyline, scores of times. But it's unlikely they've trodden its grand, spheriform staircase hewn from Sicilian marble, peeked into its cellar-cum-function room with its mysterious staircase that disappears into a wall, or gasped at its magnificent pillared library. The 280 rather frilly and a tad dated rooms won't be to everyone's taste but if the prototype next-generation room is anything to go by, the hotel's phased refurbishment, finishing at the end of 2009, will be worth the wait.

Rates from: 💰💰💰💰
Star rating: ★★★★
Overall rating: 👍👍👍👍

Ambience :	8.96	Cleanliness:	9.29
Value:	8.38	Facilities:	8.26
Staff:	9.26	Restaurants:	8.68
Location:	9.58	Families:	8.67

The Rubens at The Palace

39 Buckingham Palace Road, SW1W 0PS, England
T: +44 20 7834 6600 **F:** +44 20 7233 6037
www.HotelClub.com/hotels/Rubens_At_The_Palace_Hotel_London

Possibly one of the only hotels in London to offer a pet concierge, The Rubens makes the most of its enviable location, and then some. While locals and no-nonsense business travellers might balk at the fluff of tradition (no prizes for guessing the target market) it's the attention to detail and consistently good service that wins out here. In the 161 rooms, padded silk hangers, a foot spa in the bathroom, telephone message pads embossed with essential hotel extension numbers, a list of sample UK telephone charges and an extensive pet menu (Woof Waffles, anyone?) are thoughtful touches. The atmospheric Library - straight from the pages of a Famous Five novel - serves up watercress and sorrel soup and Gressingham Duck plus a display cabinet showcasing, among other delights, a 1950s trout-fishing license. Final hurrah? Fresh pomegranate juice with organic pumpkin seeds at breakfast. Dig deep and above all enjoy yourself or this city stunner.

Rates from: 🛏🛏🛏🛏
Star rating: ★ ★ ★ ★
Overall rating: 🕊🕊🕊🕊

Ambience :	9.24	Cleanliness:	9.59
Value:	8.65	Facilities:	8.28
Staff:	9.18	Restaurants:	9.27
Location:	9.71	Families:	8.36

Sanderson

50 Berners Street, London, W1T 3NG, England
T: +44 20 7300 1400 **F:** +44 20 7300 1401
www.HotelClub.com/hotels/Sanderson_Hotel_London

world that constantly delights with design features that include an ornamental Billiard Room straight out of a Peter Greenaway film, a minimalist spa and gym for puritan workouts and chef Zak Pelaccio's dramatic black-and-white, canteen-like Anglo Malaysian Suka restaurant.

The truly surprising thing about Ian Schrager's Sanderson is just how far from London's bruising Oxford Street it feels once you're ensconced in one of the 150 baroque guestrooms, notably designed minus the presence of interior walls. Guests are invited to create their own space via electronic layers of sheer white that open and close off spaces, and to lie back on silver-leaf sleigh beds or take tuition from the silk screened images of exercise positions.

This is a fantasy world, completely at odds with the drab 1950s office block exterior that announces its presence, but it's a

Rates from: 🛏🛏🛏🛏🛏
Star rating: n/a
Overall rating: 🕊🕊🕊🕊

Ambience :	9.43	Cleanliness:	9.48
Value:	7.30	Facilities:	8.67
Staff:	8.72	Restaurants:	9.03
Location:	9.20	Families:	6.38

The Selfridge Hotel

Orchard Street, Central London, W1H 6JS, England
T: +44 870 333 9117 **F:** +44 870 333 9217
www.HotelClub.com/hotels/Selfridge_Hotel_London

If location is a priority then you can't beat The Selfridge. Owned by its eponymous and substantial retail neighbour, stay here and you'll be mere seconds away from Oxford Street with some of the best shopping in the capital, and within a short stroll of Hyde Park, home to the Serpentine Gallery and Speaker's Corner. As a member of the dependable Thistle Hotel group the property bears all the trimmings you'd expect. Hanging over the reception desk are two grand 18th-century portraits of a Lord and Lady Overstone. Their relationship with the hotel isn't clear, but their appearance definitely sets the scene for the rest of the property. The hotel describes the décor as "country cottage style", but given the size of the main areas, traditional English country mansion would seem more appropriate. The lounge is dotted with antique furniture and is understandably a popular place to pop in for afternoon tea. If bitter is more your tipple then you can't beat the Old English Selfridge Bar, whose exposed open beams and wood panelling make it feel just like a good pub should. There are 294 bedrooms, spread over seven floors, all a decent size. The select group overlooking the quiet inner courtyard are the ones to request. If the weather's bad and you want to eat in (with the plethora of dining establishments on your doorstep that can be the only reason) you'll find the hotel's two restaurants will more than fit the bill.

Rates from: 💰💰💰💰💰
Star rating: ★★★★
Overall rating: 🦋🦋🦋🦋

Ambience:	8.38	Cleanliness:	9.05
Value:	7.90	Facilities:	7.90
Staff:	7.95	Restaurants:	8.35
Location:	9.67	Families:	8.46

The Sheraton Park Tower

101 Knightsbridge, London, W1T 3NG, England
T: +44 207 2358050 **F:** +44 20 72358231
www.HotelClub.com/hotels/Sheraton_Park_Tower_Hotel_London

The address is 101 Knightsbridge, not something that's likely to slip your memory after a meal at One-O-One, remarkable for its fish and in particular the signature seabass encrusted in Brittany rock salt, a dish which executive chef Pascal Proyart is a dab hand (small pun intended) at preparing.

Taken as a metaphor for the hotel as a whole, the seabass works pretty well. The Park Tower is exclusive and handles just about everything it does to perfection. On the accommodation side, head for the Butler Rooms, with the closest thing imaginable to a Wi-Fi'd Jeeves on 24-hour call. Occupying a slightly loftier echelon, the wood-panelled Penthouse Suites include such enticing goodies as a free-standing bathtub and a personal dining room.

The Park Tower numbers the intimate Piano Bar, with a cigar humidor and daily live entertainment, and a glistening fitness centre among its other delights. While the temptations of Knightsbridge, retail and otherwise,

are only a short hop away, there is ample reason to linger in the hotel, not least the Terrace, which is open from April to October, and a fine locale to sip and survey the local scene. Staff throughout the hotel are exceptional, blending hospitality with efficiency to a degree not often found in Britain's capital city.

Incidentally, for those who find simply dining at One-O-One insufficient, M Proyart also conducts Cook & Eat evenings,

imparting tips with his customary culinary flair, which conclude with a five-course feast. Proof of the pudding, and all that...

Rates from: 🏨🏨🏨🏨🏨
Star rating: ★★★★★
Overall rating: 🏨🏨🏨🏨

Ambience :	8.20	Cleanliness:	9.07
Value:	7.87	Facilities:	8.33
Staff:	8.53	Restaurants:	8.64
Location:	8.87	Families:	8.00

Sheraton Skyline Hotel & Conference Center

Bath Road, Hayes, Middlesex, London, UB3 5BP, England
T: ++44 20 87592535 **F:** +44 20 87509150
www.HotelClub.com/hotels/Sheraton_Skyline_Hotel_London

The Sheraton Skyline has thrown away the rulebook for airport hotels to come up with something a bit clubbier. Forget the Terminal-like exterior; it's the only thing to indicate that you're close to a runway. The adventure begins at the efficient check-in, which is more akin to arriving at a top-notch private function than a bustling 350-room hotel, and then continues once you feast your eyes on the size of the beds. Even in the standard Classic Rooms they are King Size in the sense of kings being the size of Henry VIII. Although far from cutting-edge, rooms are tastefully decked out in contemporary creams and blues (ask for one overlooking the Atrium). Guests who opt for one of the 36 Club Rooms will find warm wood sleigh beds with complimentary Internet access in the private Club Lounge. But if that all sounds too much like an extension of the airport lounge experience here's what you do; check into the Italian Al Dente restaurant where chef Marco di Tulio will cook up a treat Mamma would be proud of, then head for the Sky Bar topped off with a soaring glass canopy. Here the blueprint is decidedly tropical and you'll feel like you've gone from Bologna to Bali in a matter of minutes. If your visit falls on a Friday night you'll even be treated to the sound of bangra at one of London's more unusual club events, Mumbai Nights. Then flop back to one of the Sheraton's much vaunted Sweet Sleeper beds for a perfect night's rest.

Rates from: 💰💰💰💰
Star rating: ★★★★
Overall rating: 👍👍👍👍

Ambience :	8.48	Cleanliness:	8.76
Value:	7.62	Facilities:	8.15
Staff:	8.52	Restaurants:	8.30
Location:	8.67	Families:	8.31

Sofitel St James London

101 Knightsbridge, London, SW1y 4AN, England
T: +44 20 7747 2200 **F:** +44 20 7747 2210
www.HotelClub.com/hotels/Sofitel_St_James_London

Pall Mall, on the doorstep of the Sofitel, takes its name from a now defunct form of croquet and is highly suggestive of the pell-mell pace of life in the capital. So it's a relief to step inside the hotel's doors and enter a haven of calm and order.

Central to the success of this stunning property is the Brasserie Roux, inspired by the celebrated Albert and thoroughly, evocatively French while contained in a soaring grandiose hall. Dining here is naturally not cheap, but worth every sou.

From the acme of cuisine, to the pinnacle of the hotel's sleeping arrangements, fittingly - considering Buckingham Palace is just down the road - called The Royal Suite. As might be expected, the bed's a king-sized four-poster and there's a separate dining room and a fully fitted kitchen. A panoply of slightly less expansive rooms and suites complete the accommodation picture, each with stylish chrome and marble bathrooms backed up by Roger & Gallet unguents.

Pall Mall is of course club land, and the St James Bar - dark blue carpets, mahogany parquet floors, black leather armchairs, pin-stripe walls - dovetails perfectly, while supplying an extensive menu of champagnes. The Rose Lounge offers a rather more feminine counterpoint.

This is a hotel very much aimed at the corporate market, so there are also extensive meeting facilities, able to cater from a mere two up to 170.

Speaking of business, the Sofitel was formerly the headquarters of Cox & Kings. There can be few better uses for a boring old bank.

Rates from: 🛏🛏🛏🛏🛏
Star rating: ★★★★★
Overall rating: 🐾🐾🐾🐾

Ambience :	9.06	Cleanliness:	9.50
Value:	8.06	Facilities:	8.39
Staff:	9.35	Restaurants:	8.43
Location:	9.39	Families:	7.89

The Soho Hotel

4 Richmond Mews, London, W1D 3DH, England
T: +44 20 7559 3000 **F:** +44 20 7559 3003
www.HotelClub.com

In just a few short years the 91-room Soho Hotel has become as much of a London icon as Changing the Guard. A favourite activity of the media-savvy clients who crowd the long pewter ReFuel bar is spotting whatever A-list celebrity is thought to be in town; if they're not actually in residence, they'll probably be popping in for a bite at the restaurant or for an exclusive party in one of the hotel's four rooms reserved for private events. It all began in 2004 when the Soho opened to an inferno of publicity and it's hard to believe the area had nothing like this before. Designer Kit Kemp did wonders with the site of an old car park tucked down a dead-end street, but it does mean that the most fabulous aesthetic treats are reserved for inside; a three-metre-high bronze Botero cat in the lobby, cow-print seats in the private cinema, and efficient staff stylishly decked out in outfits by Paul Smith, John Smedley and Mark Powell. And that's before you make it to your room which, chances are, will be one of the largest you'll find anywhere in the capital. Each one is individually designed with a seamless mix of sleek, modern furniture and rococo fixtures. There is no such thing as a standard room here, but if someone else is paying get them to book the Terrace Suite with wrap-around balconies and floor-to-ceiling-windows. Then slip on the hotel's CD soundtrack and pretend you're one of the bling-loving, rock-star, regular guests.

Rates from: 🐾🐾🐾🐾🐾
Star rating: ★★★★★
Overall rating: 🐾🐾🐾🐾

Ambience :	9.31	Cleanliness:	9.38
Value:	7.56	Facilities:	8.60
Staff:	8.21	Restaurants:	9.00
Location:	9.44	Families:	6.33

St George's Hotel

115 St Georges Drive, Pimlico-Victoria, Westminister, London, SW1V 4DA, England
T: +44 20 7834 0210 **F:** +44 20 7931 0704
www.HotelClub.com/hotels/St_Georges_Hotel_London

It may just do bed and breakfast - but what class! You'll need to take lunch and dinner elsewhere (or carry back some spoils from Pret a Manger in Buckingham Palace Road), likewise find another venue to spa or gym it. By way of compensation the George offers practically the next best thing to staying in a friend's house, and an imposing Victorian pile at that. Best of all, beyond the obvious choices of singles or doubles, are family-style triples and quads. The last can be set up either as combination of king-sized bed plus two singles, or simply a quartet of solos. The rates mean that this property is very competitively priced, especially if Mum and Dad are doing the sights (Changing the Guard etc) with the sprogs on a budget.

Rates from: 🛏️🛏️
Star rating: ★★★
Overall rating: 🌀🌀🌀

Ambience :	8.43	Cleanliness:	9.23
Value:	8.43	Facilities:	7.27
Staff:	8.36	Restaurants:	8.29
Location:	7.75	Families:	7.46

St Martins Lane

45 St Martin's Lane, London, WC2N 4HX, England
T: +44 20 7300 5500 **F:** +44 20 7300 5501
www.HotelClub.com/hotels/St_Martins_Lane_Hotel_London

As the property that arguably started London's hotel renaissance in 2000, the St Martins Lane has much to compete with seven years on. But if it fails to make the glossy magazine hip lists quite so frequently then that is an oversight. It was always designed to be as fluid as a theatre stage, appropriate enough given its theatre-land location. The 204 rooms and suites are simplicity itself, Zen-like in their rejection of fussy décor in favour of guest-controlled mood lights. The vast atrium lobby opens out onto no fewer than six public bars and restaurants, the most impressive of which is the arty Asia de Cuba where colonnades divide the space with ever-changing installations. Stop at the Rum Bar for pre-theatre cocktails, where intriguing lean-to tables resemble a field of flat-topped aluminium mushrooms.

Rates from: 🛏️🛏️🛏️🛏️
Star rating: ★★★★★
Overall rating: 🌀🌀🌀🌀

Ambience :	8.94	Cleanliness:	9.57
Value:	7.06	Facilities:	8.14
Staff:	8.51	Restaurants:	8.69
Location:	9.40	Families:	5.89

St Giles Hotel London

49 Gloucester Place, London, W1U 8JE, England
T: +44 20 7300 3000 **F:** +44 20 7300 3001
www.HotelClub.com/hotels/St_Giles_Hotel_Central_London

There is something of a young, vibrant feel to the St Giles. The cause may very well be its supreme West End location. A few minutes away is Oxford Street, one of Europe's largest high streets, while across the tourist-laden Tottenham Court Road is the area recently dubbed Noho. This is one of the hippest neighbourhoods in town - it throbs with a heady choice of bars and restaurants. But the real root of the hotel's energy is that it started life as a YMCA. These days, visitors are spoilt by a laid-back but dutiful staff who recognise that their guests need to be welcomed without being over-whelmed. Divided across four towers that rise up to 12 storeys high, the 670 rooms (with another 30 coming on line in 2008) are simple but spacey and many are drowned in natural daylight thanks to floor-to-ceiling windows. Of the four room categories to choose from, the newly refurbished executive rooms seem to offer the most bang-for-your-buck and come complete with broadband and flat screen TVs. But here it would be such a shame to stay room-bound. Not only are there the usual outdoor touristy activities to pursue, but deep down underneath St Giles is what must arguably be the largest hotel gym in the city. This is really more of a fully-fledged sports centre complete with 25-metre indoor pool, squash, badminton and basketball courts and the requisite workout suites. It's no wonder the hotel feels so alive.

Rates from: 🛏🛏🛏
Star rating: ★ ★ ★
Overall rating: 👍👍👍👍

Ambience :	8.03	Cleanliness:	8.19
Value:	8.72	Facilities:	8.30
Staff:	8.26	Restaurants:	7.61
Location:	9.53	Families:	8.00

Strand Palace Hotel

372 Strand, London, WC2R 0S5, England
T: +44 20 7836 8080 **F:** +44 20 7836 2077
www.HotelClub.com/hotels/Strand_Palace_Hotel_London

Very much on the larger side of things, with getting on for 800 rooms, the much modernised Art Deco Strand Palace avoids the dreaded pitfall of anonymity with two trump cards: a clutch of exciting restaurants and bars, and a whiz of a concierge service. The former includes 372, an English carvery buffet, and Hops! - a sports bar where the clink of raised glasses vies with the mega screens for decibel count. And the golden keys brigade are past masters at sorting VIP entrance to the capital's top attractions, be it the London Dungeon or a box at the opera, as well as chauffeur driven-excursions about town or further afield. Plus the hotel's smack dab central: as the legendary Dr Johnson so pithily put it: tired of London, tired of life.

Rates from: 🪙🪙🪙
Star rating: ★★★
Overall rating: 🦋🦋🦋🦋

Ambience :	7.88	Cleanliness:	8.58
Value:	8.26	Facilities:	7.55
Staff:	8.31	Restaurants:	8.27
Location:	9.33	Families:	7.95

Swissôtel The Howard, London

Temple Place, London, WC2R 2PC, England
T: +44 20 7836 3555 **F:** +44 20 7379 4547
www.HotelClub.com/hotels/Swissotel_The_Howard_London

Whether you go for a view of the Thames, or overlooking the courtyard, you're pretty much assured a good night's rest chez Howard. Each of the 189 rooms and suites has a sizeable desk for those here on business, but which can be more or less disregarded by anyone here to sample London's multifarious pleasures, while everyone can enjoy the commodious bathroom and Body Logic products. Exercising a similar universal appeal is the modern French menu at JAAN (wild pigeon and foie gras, lobster and rabbit roulade) and the cosy confines of the Temple Bar adjacent to the garden courtyard (meals served in summer), while Mauve falls into the see-and-be-seen category of lounges. For exercise, take your pick of jogging or pottering along the river, or a complimentary off-site health club.

Rates from: 🪙🪙🪙🪙
Star rating: ★★★★★
Overall rating: 🦋🦋🦋🦋

Ambience :	8.36	Cleanliness:	9.44
Value:	8.04	Facilities:	7.97
Staff:	8.32	Restaurants:	8.06
Location:	9.28	Families:	7.50

The Tower

St Katharine's Way, London, E1W 1LD, England
T: +44 870 333 9106 **F:** +44 870 333 9206
www.HotelClub.com/hotels/Thistle_Tower_Hotel_London

As the old saying goes: "close your eyes and think of England" - the outside of this hotel falls somewhat short of architectural pulchritude - but reopen them once you've gained the interior. As might be expected, The Tower is right next to the Tower of London and ditto Bridge, with splendid views of both and much of the rest of the city. Hard by London's financial district, this 801-roomer is primarily a business hotel (and an exceptionally well-run one) with its sights set firmly on the corporate side of things, be it providing venues to dine, exercise, meet or simply pound the laptop (the entire property is Wireless). Even if you're not staying, dropping by Xi Bar - dusk over the Thames can evoke the best images of Joseph Turner - means you can skip queuing up for the London Eye.

Rates from: ₤₤₤₤₤
Star rating: ★★★★★
Overall rating: 👍👍👍👍

Ambience :	8.50	Cleanliness:	8.88
Value:	7.80	Facilities:	8.27
Staff:	8.60	Restaurants:	8.88
Location:	9.38	Families:	7.78

The Waldorf Hilton Hotel

Aldwych, London, WC2B 4DD, England
T: +44 20 7836 2400 **F:** +44 20 7836 7244
www.HotelClub.com/hotels/Waldorf_Hilton_Hotel_London

The half price tickets booth in Leicester Square is the capital's most economical entrée to its many theatres, and - a few streets distant - the Waldorf Hilton one of the best places to stay if you're here to take in *No Sex Please, We're British* and similar cultural offerings. Expect the full Hilton treatment from the moment you are greeted by the doormen on arrival. There's a grand choice of rooms and suites, with an executive lounge for those staying in the upper echelons. The patisserie (truly scrumptious), bar and main restaurant are all dubbed Homage, no understatement when it comes to praising the chefs' abilities. There's also a very cool pool; and of course the concierge desk knows exactly where to get those invisible theatre tickets for the most popular shows, but probably not at 50 per cent off.

Rates from: ₤₤₤₤₤
Star rating: ★★★★★
Overall rating: 👍👍👍👍

Ambience :	9.00	Cleanliness:	9.41
Value:	8.04	Facilities:	8.97
Staff:	8.98	Restaurants:	9.05
Location:	9.50	Families:	8.43

The Westbury Hotel, Mayfair, London

Bond Street, Mayfair, London, W1S 2YF, England
T: +44 20 7629 7755 F: +44 20 7499 1270
www.HotelClub.com/hotels/Westbury_Mayfair_Hotel_London

To not exactly unknown names such as Versace, Tiffany, Armani, Sotheby and Burberry, add the Westbury, the only hotel on Bond Street and very much in keeping with its band of retail neighbours. Some half a century on from its opening - when its stated aim was to "combine American standards of comfort and service with the best of English tradition" - this 249-room hotel is succeeding on all counts.

King of the accommodation hill is very definitely the penthouse suite, tucked away on the seventh floor with grandstanding views of Mayfair and a dining room seating eight in a conservatory next to the terrace. One step down, so to speak, the Deluxe Terrace suite is only marginally less impressive, while the remaining rooms are solid mines of comfort and amenities, to say nothing of a welcome and healthy dose of style.

Many patrons come to the Westbury even when they aren't actually staying, for two very good reasons, the first of which is Artisan, the modestly named modern European restaurant which is undoubtedly the apple of chef Daniel Hillier's eye. It's refreshingly unpretentious yet packed with surprises, not least of which are the sautéed breakfast mushrooms.

Artisan is boldly supported by the Polo Bar, aglitter with Swarovski crystal and swish Gucci furnishings which adapt themselves equally to afternoon tea or cocktails once the sun's over the yardarm.

Incidentally, despite the address, the main entrance faces Conduit Street, which the cockney cognoscenti pronounce Cundit. Black-cab drivers will have no trouble finding it, however you enunciate.

Rates from: 🛏🛏🛏🛏🛏
Star rating: ★ ★ ★ ★
Overall rating: 👍👍👍👍

Ambience :	9.00	Cleanliness:	9.24
Value:	8.41	Facilities:	7.49
Staff:	9.00	Restaurants:	9.00
Location:	9.12	Families:	8.10

Britannia Hotel

Portland Street, Manchester M1 3LA, England
T: +44 161 228 2288 **F:** +44 161 236 9154
www.HotelClub.com/hotels/Britannia_Hotel_Manchester

As good an example of Victorian Manchester as you're likely to see, this Grade II listed building's facade is peppered with extravagant detail. Each storey has been constructed in a classical style with Elizabethan, Italian and French influences.

Once a textile warehouse, it was the world's first cash and carry. Today, wholesale changes may not be required but the interior does deserve a little TLC. The balconied staircase and huge chandelier that greet you on entry are majestic, and a once grand dining room, now a French restaurant, is looking a touch down-at-heel. Some of the rooms and communal areas are also suffering from slight fatigue, although new carpets throughout add a little bounce.

While the hotel's status among the glitterati may have waned in the wake of newer, funkier, more contemporary alternatives, there's a healthy selection of suites (the four-poster version is certainly good value) and superior rooms among the 363 on offer. And plenty for the budget traveller to admire, not least inexpensive standard rooms and a three-course carvery in Jenny's Restaurant for just a fiver. The bustling location in the heart of the transit zone that is Piccadilly Gardens will excite visitors looking for a slice of real city centre life. The Gay Village and China Town are right on the doorstep, but if all that's a leap too far, the in-house bars are a lively mix of locals, students and bemused travellers, while the DJ's in the two on-site nightclubs will assault your ears, and make no apologies for it.

Rates from: 🛏🛏
Star rating: ★ ★ ★
Overall rating: 👍👍👍👍

Ambience :	8.60	Cleanliness:	8.70
Value:	8.85	Facilities:	7.73
Staff:	8.45	Restaurants:	8.32
Location:	9.00	Families:	8.33

Hilton Manchester Deansgate

303 Deansgate, Manchester, M3 4LQ, England
T: +44 161 870 1600 **F:** +44 161 870 1650
www.HotelClub.com/hotels/Hilton_Manchester_Deansgate

Manchester's first skyscraper lords it over the city skyline and as well as being seen, can often be heard. The blade design feature at the top of the 48 floors (the first 23 of which belong to Hilton - the rest are private apartments) often creates a humming noise when the wind picks up. During construction some locals were convinced the UFOs had landed.

And there is something other-worldly about this sleek, ultra-stylish venue built on the site of a car dealership in a handy location close to theatres, museums, the metro and Coronation Street.

Take the express lift for a drink in the Cloud 23 bar where you'll get the very best views of the city and beyond through floor-to-ceiling windows. Order an Ena Sparkles cocktail and look down through the glass portal at your feet and watch the earthlings scurry about their business on Deansgate below. But if you'd rather relax on ground level, the Podium bar and restaurant offers intimate booth dining or casual al fresco on the patio.

Attention to detail isn't lost on any of the 279 bedrooms. Again the floor-to-ceiling windows allow light to spill through, and all rooms boast plasma screen TVs and broadband, while the furnishings focus on wood and natural materials.

A trip to the health club is a must for even the laziest of guests. The 20-metre swimming pool is suspended from the side of the tower, and like the rest of the building, is surrounded by glass. Beautifully lit at night, you can glide (or thrash) through the water while looking up at the stars above.

Rates from: 🏠🏠🏠
Star rating: ★ ★ ★ ★
Overall rating: 👍👍👍👍

Ambience :	8.40	Cleanliness:	8.60
Value:	7.60	Facilities:	6.81
Staff:	8.67	Restaurants:	7.80
Location:	8.50	Families:	8.00

The Lowry Hotel, Manchester

50 Dearmans Place, Chapel Wharf, Manchester, M3 5LH, England
T: +44 161 827 4000 **F:** +44 161 827 4001
www.HotelClub.com/hotels/Lowry_Hotel_Manchester

No wonder this place is the first pick of every Manchester-bound A-lister. Savvy not snotty, discreet yet bursting with northern hospitality.

It knows it's cool, but wants everyone to enjoy the party. Mr LS Lowry himself would surely approve.

And not surprisingly, there's a small detail from a work of Salford's finest artist to be found in every sizeable room. Big working desks and comfy chairs are found in all 165 rooms - each one a sweet-smelling balance of style and content. The "simple art of luxury", and all designed by Sir Rocco Forte's sister.

If it's sheer opulence you're after, then book into the Charles Forte Suite. If you're not too busy playing the baby grand piano, have your butler prepare dinner in the pantry - one of many rooms in the largest hotel suite in Manchester. Who would have thought a view of the mucky River Irwell or the grey city skyline could work so well?

A new-build, the Lowry lies on the site of a printing factory that was once responsible for the Beano and Dandy comics. The cartoon cowboy Desperate Dan himself would no doubt love to tuck into the locally-sourced, seasonal menu. No cow pie maybe, but

simply tremendous fare just the same all year round. Finish the evening with a cocktail at the River Bar. Local pride jumps out from the drinks list where you can choose to box clever with a Ricky Hatton Punch, or maybe roll with an Oasis and just go mad for it.

Rates from: 🛏🛏🛏🛏🛏
Star rating: ★ ★ ★ ★ ★
Overall rating: 🐻🐻🐻🐻

Ambience :	8.95	Cleanliness:	9.65
Value:	7.84	Facilities:	8.56
Staff:	9.06	Restaurants:	9.03
Location:	8.54	Families:	8.38

Malmaison Manchester

1-3 Piccadilly, Manchester, M1 1L2, England
T: +44 161 278 1000 **F:** +44 161 278 1002
www.HotelClub.com

blingery. Too big to be dubbed boutique at 167 rooms, the feel is nevertheless intimate, and the place swaggers to a Mancunian beat that the five-stars of the city wouldn't understand. The Piccadilly location adds up-and-coming edginess with the northern quarter's bars and clubs a mere goal-kick away.

Whilst *Moulin Rouge* is the décor theme, the deep red and black colours throughout this refurbished cotton factory are wholly apt considering its claim that the world's most famous football club was founded here. A meeting at the Imperial Pub (now a five-storey red-

brick extension) decided the new name for Newton Heath FC was to be Manchester United. That obsession with local talent continues, from the hearty north-west sourced menu to the Theatre of Dreams - a wow suite of pure decadence and utter

Rates from: 🏠🏠🏠
Star rating: n/a
Overall rating: 👍👍👍👍

Ambience :	9.07	Cleanliness:	9.43
Value:	8.29	Facilities:	8.86
Staff:	8.96	Restaurants:	8.88
Location:	9.46	Families:	7.82

The Midland Hotel

Peter Street, Manchester, M60 2DS, England
T: +44 161 236 3333 **F:** +44 161 932 4100
www.HotelClub.com/hotels/The_Midland_Hotel_Manchester

place doesn't feel the need to compete with the trendy upstarts. It's still regarded as a special place among locals - an institution where you could be treated to afternoon tea on the Octagon Terrace. You still can, although the star-spotting ain't what it used to be. This is certainly somewhere to enjoy to the fullest.

As you sit at the walnut desk in one the vast presidential suites facing Central Library, you can smell the history and imagine Sir Winston Churchill penning a speech on one of his many visits here. A true railway hotel, unlike most Victorian factory refurbs, the Midland was

built to accommodate. Marble and Mancunian memorabilia adorn the corridor walls, the 312 rooms a comfortable mix of traditional and contemporary. The high ceilings, trouser presses and irons make easy bedfellows with the multi-channel TVs and broadband. This

Rates from: 🏠🏠🏠
Star rating: ★★★★
Overall rating: 👍👍👍👍

Ambience :	9.11	Cleanliness:	9.43
Value:	8.26	Facilities:	8.55
Staff:	9.22	Restaurants:	8.81
Location:	9.38	Families:	8.74

The Palace Hotel

Oxford Street, Manchester, M60 7HA, England
T: +44 161 288 1111　**F:** +44 161 288 2222
www.HotelClub.com/hotels/Palace_Hotel_Manchester_The

elegant, recline on a crème leather sofa and listen as the grand piano in the corner plays itself.

No two bedrooms (of which there are 257) are the same, all have high-ceilings and have been refurbished in a traditional style with modern comforts such as Wi-Fi.

This is a hotel that's making the best use of what it's been given. From the 70-metre tall clock tower to the colourful tiles throughout the terracotta building, the former Refuge Assurance HQ can rightly take its place among the city's top-end hotel market. Located in the heart of Manchester's theatre land, on first entry the large, open and airy foyer has the feel of a museum or cathedral with its marble floors and stained glass ceiling. Space is the key word here. The Tempus bar and restaurant area is casual and

Rates from: 🐾🐾
Star rating: ★★★★
Overall rating: 🐾🐾🐾🐾

Ambience :	9.14	Cleanliness:	9.05
Value:	8.81	Facilities:	7.94
Staff:	9.24	Restaurants:	9.53
Location:	9.43	Families:	8.00

Radisson Edwardian Manchester Hotel

Free Trade Hall, Peter Street, Manchester, M2 5GP, England
T: +44 161 835 9929　**F:** +44 161 835 9979
www.HotelClub.com/hotels/Radisson_Edwardian_Hotel_Manchester

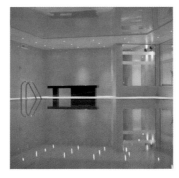

Every one of the 263 bedrooms is at the very least king-sized, with the flattest of TV screens, complimentary Wi-Fi and enough room to swing a cat with each arm. As for the Penthouse suites...well there isn't a member of the cat family big enough or sophisticated enough for the analogy.

From the Peterloo Massacre of 1819 to the Sex Pistols of the late 1970s, this site has seen it all. But with the passing of the Free Trade Hall, a new working piece of art has developed in its place. The original Victorian façade has been incorporated into a 14-storey glass and chrome structure. Artefacts from the original building can be found, perched easily alongside Buddhas shipped in to give a calming *feng shui* aura about the place.

Rates from: 🐾🐾🐾
Star rating: ★★★★★
Overall rating: 🐾🐾🐾🐾

Ambience :	8.82	Cleanliness:	9.30
Value:	8.18	Facilities:	8.72
Staff:	9.03	Restaurants:	8.52
Location:	9.30	Families:	8.13

The Best Western Three Swans Hotel

High Street, Market Harborough, Leicestershire, LE16 7NJ, England
T: +44 1858 466644 **F:** +44 1858 433101
www.HotelClub.com

It's sometimes been said that the comedy series *Fawlty Towers* plays better as a documentary of the British hotel industry; certainly, no more eccentric proprietor could be imagined than John Fothergill, who ran The Three Swans in the 1930s, repelling outsiders from his lavatories and ever vigilant for suspected adulterers.

His name lives on in the main bar of this charming 500-year-old

coaching inn, and while his portrait still hangs above the fireplace his "customer is always a right nuisance" philosophy has long gone. And behind the glossy white High Street exterior with its bay windows and distinguished wrought iron gallows sign lies a surprisingly large number of attractions, from a trio of four-poster rooms to the Cromwell Suite which can seat around 170 for events and private dinners.

There's another 58 guestrooms of varying size but all sympathetically decorated and blessed with accessories both hi- and lo-tech. Apart from Fothergills, there's a choice of the ultra posh Swans or the rather more relaxed Bistro, while lunch at the Conservatory in the sunny courtyard in summer pulls in a select crowd of regulars on balmier days. Relaxed yet attentive staff complete the picture of a very well run country hotel, where (thanks to recently introduced regulations that in fact hark back to the Middle Ages) couples may also plight their troth.

"Am in Market Harborough; where should I be?" ran GK Chesterton's classic telegram to his wife. If you're in, or going anywhere near this thoroughly picturesque market town, you should be at The Three Swans.

Rates from: 💰💰
Star rating: ★★★
Overall rating: 🦢🦢🦢

Ambience :	9.00	Cleanliness:	9.50
Value:	7.50	Facilities:	7.50
Staff:	8.50	Restaurants:	9.00
Location:	7.50	Families:	7.50

Rookery Hall

Worleston, Nantwich, Cheshire CW5 6DQ, England
T: +44 845 072 7533 **F:** +44 845 072 7534
www.HotelClub.com

William Cooke, who had this now-chateau-styled country pile built for him in 1816, was the owner of a Jamaican sugar plantation and was therefore probably implicit in the slave trade, while Baron Von Schroder, who bought it from him in 1867, founded the merchant bank called ...

Yes, yes, but did you know that Becks and Posh stayed here when they got engaged?

History aside, this 70-room property must have one of the loveliest settings in the country - 15 hectares of gardens and wooded parkland on the banks of the River Weaver. Having just undergone a £10-million rejuvenation, it now also offers a luxurious health club and spa, with an 18-metre, glass-roofed swimming pool, hydrotherapy and massage facilities, sauna and treatment rooms, as well as its own brasserie and bar.

The fare in the mahogany-panelled dining room has been rosetted and be-ribboned by numerous institutions; rooms - which include the four-poster-bed variety - have flat-screen TVs embedded in the wall at the foot of the bathtub; you can play croquet on the lawn; and there are even a couple of tame ghosts haunting its corridors - The Grey Lady, a former maid, and Young Master Schroder, who can sometimes be heard crying for his lost dog.

Why would you want to go to Nantwich? The Trentham Monkey Forest, the Blue Planet Aquarium (Britain's largest), Chester Zoo, Oulton Park race track, Jodrell Bank and Snugbury's ice-cream factory are all nearby. Nuff said?

Rates from: 🐾🐾🐾
Star rating: ★★★★
Overall rating: 🐾🐾🐾🐾🐾

Ambience :	9.50	Cleanliness:	9.50
Value:	9.00	Facilities:	9.00
Staff:	10.0	Restaurants:	10.0
Location:	10.0	Families:	950

Chewton Glen

Hampshire, New Milton, BH25 6QS, England
T: +44 1425 275341 **F:** +44 1425 272310
www.HotelClub.com

Chewton Glen combines stunning contemporary design and colour with a country house feel and the result is both stylish and welcoming. The lounge areas have been extensively refurbished; the colour combination of charcoal, chartreuse, bitter chocolate and Granny Smith apple green may be unusual but certainly achieves a sensational new look without detracting in the slightest from the relaxing atmosphere.

Attention to detail is the key at Chewton Glen, and the staff are unfailingly attentive and friendly without being obtrusive.

Bedrooms are large (even the least expensive bronze rooms) and all have top notch bathrooms with spacious power showers and Molton Brown toiletries.

Tucked away towards the bottom of the New Forest and only 20 minutes' walk from the sea, the wooded grounds are a real bonus with a croquet lawn, putting green and nine-hole golf course, outdoor pool, tennis centre with indoor courts, and sweeping lawns bordering a natural stream. Outdoor terraces abound for al fresco dining and lolling during the summer months.

Fish features large at The Marryat Restaurant. Perfectly yummy cold buffet and cooked breakfasts with New Forest mushrooms and organic sausages are a particular treat.

The spa and health club offer the ultimate in relaxation and luxury, showcasing indoor pool, refurbished gym, hydrotherapy spa pool, outdoor whirlpool, dance studio, aromatherapy, saunas and crystal steam rooms and a full programme of power walks and exercise classes. Do book well in advance for the treatments.

Few guests check out without a tinge of reluctance; but a gift of homemade flapjacks and bottled water provides some compensation for the journey home.

Rates from: 🛏🛏🛏🛏🛏
Star rating: ★ ★ ★ ★ ★
Overall rating: 🐾🐾🐾🐾

Ambience :	9.30	Cleanliness:	9.56
Value:	7.41	Facilities:	8.93
Staff:	9.31	Restaurants:	9.56
Location:	9.22	Families:	7.69

Malmaison Newcastle

Quayside, Newcastle Upon Tyne, NE1 3DX, England
T: +44 191 245 5000 **F:** +44 191 245 4545
www.HotelClub.com/hotels/Malmaison_Newcastle

The Malmaison hotels make a strong appeal to couples looking for a romantic break, and this one in Newcastle is ideal for what might be termed a snog on the Tyne. The group's CEO, who was once GM here, personally oversaw a revamp of the 19th-century cooperative warehouse to put it back on top in the city's most happening area - Quayside, where the Winking Eye Millennium Bridge connects Newcastle with revitalised Gateshead - and the result has been universally applauded by customers, critics and colleagues alike.

Prince is probably more of a musical inspiration than the northern folk group Lindisfarne given the hotel's preponderance of purple, but whether you regard it as pretentious or ironically Post Modern, there is no gainsaying this property's swaggering style. And tellingly, the locals - who are now knee-deep in cutting-edge bars and restaurants - are big fans of the Brasserie, with its leather banquettes nestled in candlelit bays; the Bar, with up-to-the-minute music by an in-house DJ and fashion frolics on its plasma TV screens; and the Café Mal's paninis, salads, coffee and smoothies - and riverside views (without the chill winds that all too often accompany them).

Add to all this the Gymtonic work-out space and the basement's Petit Spa - the biggest facility of its kind in the city centre, complete with massage, beauty treatment and tanning rooms - and you have a thoroughly modern concept that is about as far from the city's old *Likely Lads* and brown ale image as you could get.

Rates from: 💰💰💰💰
Star rating: n/a
Overall rating: 💰💰💰💰

Ambience :	8.97	Cleanliness:	9.26
Value:	7.85	Facilities:	8.02
Staff:	8.88	Restaurants:	8.60
Location:	9.29	Families:	8.00

Headland Hotel

Headland Road, Newquay, Cornwall, TR7 1EW, England
T: +44 1637 872 211 **F:** +44 1637 872 212
www.HotelClub.com

Early eco-warriors in the shape of local farmers and fishermen nearly prevented construction of this hotel in the Newquay Riots of 1897. Thankfully, they didn't succeed because it is a classic of its kind. Owned for nigh on three decades by John and Carolyn Armstrong, who have sunk many millions into its refurbishment, it would certainly have impressed poor old Silvanus Trevail, who suffered such vituperation giving birth to it that he shot himself on a train just three years after it opened.

That year, 1900, you could have booked the best room for £5 and one for your servant for £1.50. Royalty stayed here, the BBC broadcast Palm Court music from its ballroom, it was turned into an RAF hospital during World War II (uniformed ghosts are said to walk the corridors at night), and more recently, the movie *The Witches* was filmed here.

Its wonderful location overlooking the World Surfing Championship's Fistral Beach is the main attraction of this Grade II listed building.

Added to this, the service is superb (it is a major hotel staff training centre), the food in The Restaurant and various cosy private dining rooms, as well as the Sand Brasserie (with a view out over the breakers), is excellent, and the oil paintings and open fires give it a country-house feel.

Two heated pools and a sauna, plus golf, tennis, croquet and snooker facilities (and a games room for teenagers) offer activities other than glorious swimming, surfing and walking. And it's dog-friendly!

Rates from: 🌸 🌸 🌸
Star rating: ★ ★ ★ ★
Overall rating: 🐾 🐾 🐾 🐾

Ambience :	9.25	Cleanliness:	9.06
Value:	8.63	Facilities:	8.13
Staff:	9.31	Restaurants:	9.06
Location:	9.69	Families:	9.00

Lace Market Hotel

19 31 High Pavement, The Lace Market, Nottingham, NG1 1HE, England
T: +44 115 852 3232 **F:** +44 115 852 3233
www.HotelClub.com

Most people have heard of Robin Hood's adversary, the Sheriff of Nottingham, and Boots the Chemist (founded here in 1849) is almost as well known. But the city really made its name (and fortunes) in lace. Hence the Lace Market, although the industry has declined sharply, so the mart's old buildings have been turned into boutique bistros and hotels. Hence - with a modest drum roll - the Lace Market Hotel.

And it's a cracker. Cream of the crop of 42 rooms are the split-level studios, with enticing views of the afore-mentioned market; however all the (quietly minimalist) guestrooms are well set out and come equipped with hypo-allergenic bedding and Aveda toiletries.

There's nothing remotely slimmed down about the hotel's very British brasserie, Merchants, which was designed by David Collins and rejoices in solid, hearty fare. The Best of British ethos is echoed in the Cock & Hoop next door, which is several notches above "pub grub" while retaining all the cheery ambience of a Victorian alehouse. The Saint Bar leans more toward modernity, and rocks until the early hours for those guests who fancy a night on the town without having to look for a cab at the end of it.

Anyone in search of a health club to round out the hotel won't find such on the premises, however guests get in free at the Virgin joint just down the road.

Endnote: any dogs ("clean, leashed, lap or miniature") reading this should be aware they're charged 15 quid a night, and come accordingly cashed up.

Rates from: 🐾🐾
Star rating: ★ ★ ★ ★
Overall rating: 🐾 🐾 🐾 🐾

Ambience :	8.67	Cleanliness:	9.00
Value:	7.33	Facilities:	7.50
Staff:	7.67	Restaurants:	9.00
Location:	9.00	Families:	8.35

Whipper-In Hotel

The Market Place, Oakham, Rutland, LE15 6DT, England
T: +44 1572 756 971 F: +44 1572 757 759
www.HotelClub.com/hotels/Whipper_In_Hotel_Oakham

Now that fox-hunting is banned in Britain, how long will it be before the PC brigade starts hounding hotels such as this to change their names?

Brook Hotels, which specialises in seeking out olde worlde gems and equipping them for the 21st century without sacrificing any of their character, must hope that it's still okay to be nostalgic about blood sports, at least where this 17th-century coaching inn with its tally-ho connotations is concerned.

For now, you can still stand in the courtyard and conjure up visions of men in scarlet livery sipping sherry on horseback to a chorus of baying dogs being brought to heel by the whipper-in. You will be rested from a night in one of the 22 comfortably furnished rooms, ranging from singles and doubles to four-posters, and equipped with all you would expect from a modern-day hostelry, from TV to trouser press, plus 24-hour room service and Wi-Fi Internet access.

You will also be well fed, having dined in the St George Restaurant (which includes vegetarian dishes and a children's menu) or the more informal Bistro. To say nothing of having slaked your thirst at the two pub bars. There is free parking and the hotel is wheelchair-friendly.

And all the reasons why the Red Queen urged Alice to visit Rutland, England's smallest county, still apply: Burghley House, Britain's grandest Elizabethan-era dwelling and the setting for part of The Da Vinci Code, Belvoir Castle, dating back in different incarnations to Norman times, and the quaint old village of Uppingham, are all within easy reach of this classic country inn.

Rates from: 🛏 🛏 🛏
Star rating: ★ ★ ★
Overall rating: 🐾 🐾 🐾 🐾

Ambience :	9.00	Cleanliness:	9.00
Value:	8.00	Facilities:	9.00
Staff:	10.0	Restaurants:	9.00
Location:	9.00	Families:	9.00

Le Manoir aux Quat' Saisons

Church Road, Great Milton, Oxford, OX44 7PD, England
T: +44 1844 278 881 F: +44 1844 278 847
www.HotelClub.com

This 15th-century manor house exudes French ooh la la seduction. Chefpatron Raymond Blanc uses sensuality to tempt guests with silks, laces, flowers, private gardens themed to room décor and blissful comfort. Blanc was the Brit hotelier who brought bathrooms into bedrooms. Come clean à deux in double tubs with taps in the middle for comfortable toe-to-toe wallowing. The bath's surrounds hold champagne buckets, and

there's relayed music, dimmer lights and huge church candles. The 32 rooms in the main house and around garden courtyards are, as Blanc puts it, "warm and cosy like a lemon soufflé". As a single example, Opium oozes sex with scarlet drapes, dark wood, moongate door, Chinese bed, and a bamboo and water walled garden. With fresh flowers, fruit, Madeira, and newspaper provided, guests won't want to get out of bed for

anything less than Michelin-starred meals. Blanc has held two Michelin stars for 22 years and showcases his specialities in set menus comprising five large or ten small dishes. Stroll the intake off in the surrounding 11 hectares which embrace a wild flower meadow, a Japanese tea garden, Britain's first wild mushroom valley, a spice-scented Malaysian garden and an organic kitchen garden that sprouts 70 herbs and 90 vegetables. Learn what to do with them on one of Manoir's cookery courses - extremely hands-on and lasting up to four days. Blanc is by no means an absentee landlord; you may well find him at your elbow gently demonstrating how to beat egg white without wrist strain.

Rates from: 💰💰💰💰💰
Star rating: ★★★★★
Overall rating: 👍👍👍👍

Ambience :	9.50	Cleanliness:	9.81
Value:	7.38	Facilities:	6.84
Staff:	8.69	Restaurants:	9.44
Location:	8.56	Families:	7.50

Macdonald Randolph Hotel

Beaumont Street, Oxford, Oxfordshire, OX1 2LN, England
T: +44 870 400 8200 **F**: +44 1865 791 678
www.HotelClub.com/hotels/Randolph_Hotel_Oxford

The Randolph is both Town and Gown (Oxford's traditional social divide) befitting its role as *the* grand dame hotel hereabouts. Its imposing yellow brick 1864 Victorian Gothic exterior leads to a wooden and glass concierge desk reminiscent of an eagle-eyed college porter's office beyond which a massive staircase sails upwards, edged with stained glass, pointed gothic windows and plaster statuary. The hotel took its name and logo from Dr Francis Randolph who endowed the gallery in the Ashmolean museum opposite. The recently renovated 151 rooms mix ancient and modern: four-posters, heavily draped bedheads, and chandeliers in the suites contrast with 40 new executive rooms in soothing beiges and whites. The stately restaurant's huge windows frame the Martyrs' Memorial and tables are spaced so Town may not hear what Gown is debating and vice versa. The comfort food menu is the stuff of high table: sirloin of beef, lamb chops, trifle. In the intimate Drawing Room, students celebrating exam successes and American visitors take afternoon cream teas (bookings are a necessity) cosseted in pale yellow armchairs. The Randolph does not blink at fame and fortune; seen it, done it and been in the movies. On which subject, The Morse Bar is where film casts and crews hang out; Colin Dexter, the author of the Inspector Morse novels, drinks his whisky; and now Lewis - Morse's TV Sidekick - also drops in. Below stairs in the old cellar, a smart Spa blots out Oxford's competitive traffic with lantern-lit walkways, vaulted ceilings and candlelit treatment rooms.

Rates from: 💰💰💰💰💰
Star rating: ★★★★★
Overall rating: 🏰🏰🏰🏰

Ambience :	9.32	Cleanliness:	9.47
Value:	8.42	Facilities:	8.53
Staff:	9.42	Restaurants:	9.37
Location:	9.68	Families:	8.25

Malmaison Oxford

3 Oxford Castle, New Road, Oxford, OX1 1LD, England
T: +44 1865 268 400 **F:** +44 1865 268 402
www.HotelClub.com/hotels/Malmaison_Oxford

AKA HM Prison Oxford until 1995, this Victorian Gothic pile has been airily transformed into the 94-roomed Malmaison, with ample play made of its antecedents.

A path of ever-lit candles leads past purple plush, bishop's throne-sized chairs to Reception which is decorated with Oxford rowing caps. The bedrooms are spread over five wings including the House of Correction, formerly for solitary confinement but now favoured by groups. The elite stay in the Governor's former living quarters with balconies, light-enhancing glass expanses and iPod speakers. The main A-wing atrium is pure prison with metal staircases leading to narrow, open-sided corridors. Both *Bad Girls* and Michael Caine's *The Italian Job* were filmed here. Today's inmates - the brochure's coy term - sleep behind original heavy metal doors, with the peepholes

happily reversed. Once up to five men shared a cell; now two cells make up the bedroom under high barred windows. Plasma TVs, CD/DVD players, free broadband and internet access while away the time inside. A third cell forms the bathroom with a simple rolltop bath, separate rain shower, clinical square white basin and underfloor heating. Guests are encouraged to 'steal' the branded toiletries, while the Visitor's Room provides afternoon tea, evening drinks and billiards. The exercise yard (the gym is in the basement) hosts summer Shakespeare performances with free tickets for hotel guests. Solitary confinement cells have become intimate private dining rooms off the Brasserie that details local ingredient suppliers on the table d'hote menu; the hamburgers and Oxford Blue pancakes are particularly notable.

Rates from: 🏰🏰🏰
Star rating: ★★★
Overall rating: ✋✋✋✋

Ambience :	9.54	Cleanliness:	9.83
Value:	8.42	Facilities:	8.29
Staff:	9.21	Restaurants:	9.05
Location:	9.08	Families:	7.36

The Royal Oak Hotel

5 Upper High Street, Sevenoaks, Kent, TN13 1HY, England
T: +44 1732 451 109 **F:** +44 1732 740 187
www.HotelClub.com/hotels/Royal_Oak_Hotel_Sevenoaks

Many of England's Royal Oaks claim to have sheltered a fugitive King Charles - this one plumps for Queen Victoria, who was paying a visit to the Renaissance pile called Knole House rather than absconding.

Indeed, a stroll through Knole's extensive nearby grounds (home to a herd of free-roaming fallow deer) makes a marvellous start to the day, especially if followed by "the works" at breakfast in the hotel's No 5 Bistro.

Set away from the business end of the High Street, The Royal Oak is a traditional market town hotel, susceptible to guests' needs and providing hospitality, good food and a place to relax in equal measure.

There are 41 rooms, divided between the main block and a separate one at the back of the property. The solitary four-poster room lends itself to a romantic break, and the remaining crop of doubles, twins and singles should suit guests with other objectives in mind. The décor is restrained, overwhelmingly comfortable, and satellite TV and room service both operate 24 hours a day.

Three meeting rooms cater to business types; the garden is on the small side - though still a very pleasant spot for lunch or evening drinks - however there is ample (and free) parking. Kent's known as the Garden of England, and there are few better home bases in the whole county.

While the seven oak trees that gave the town its name are long gone, The Royal Oak blossoms and flourishes more strongly than ever.

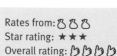

Rates from: 🛏🛏🛏
Star rating: ★★★
Overall rating: 🐾🐾🐾🐾

Ambience :	10.0	Cleanliness:	10.0
Value:	9.00	Facilities:	6.00
Staff:	10.0	Restaurants:	8.00
Location:	10.0	Families:	10.0

Hotel du Vin & Bistro, Tunbridge Wells

Crescent Road, Tunbridge Wells, Kent, TN1 2LY, England
T: +44 1892 526455 **F:** +44 1892 512044
www.HotelClub.com

Referred to as *Royal* Tunbridge Wells by its more pedantic residents, this attractive spa town was a logical choice for a Hotel du Vin, and a Georgian mansion just the right structure to house it. The details are as immaculate as always, with antiques and memorabilia dotted about the 34 bedrooms, while the cellar and kitchen complement each other to perfection. It takes little sleuthing to deduce the contents of the wine list in the Burgundy Bar, and a logical process of deduction will answer the question of why meals on the garden terrace, overlooking Calverley Park, tend to get drawn out. In-room spa treatments, and outdoor games of boules, round out the hotel, while the staff - even by this group's exacting standards - meld professionalism with amicability seamlessly. This Hotel du Vin is much more of a bonus than any regal moniker.

Rates from: ☻☻☻
Star rating: ★★★★
Overall rating: ♫♫♫♫

Ambience :	8.79	Cleanliness:	9.36
Value:	8.15	Facilities:	7.07
Staff:	8.57	Restaurants:	9.00
Location:	8.50	Families:	7.56

Miller's at Glencot House

Glencot Lane, Wells, Somerset, BA5 1BH, England
T: +44 1749 677 160 **F:** +44 1749 670 210
www.HotelClub.com

Quirky and oozing character, this fabulous mock-Jacobean mansion close to historic Wells, the smallest cathedral city in England, is hotel heaven for those who loathe mainstream and minimalism and purr with delight at antiques and the unexpected. Surreal touches (and candles) abound: an audience of slightly creepy porcelain dolls lines the walls in the bijou cinema; stuffed peacocks flash their tails in the drawing room and gilt mirrors loll against trees in the pretty garden alongside the River Axe. Individual and intriguing, it's quite literally a gin palace - the owner responsible for recently transforming this eclectic, eccentric 15-bedroomed hotel is the man behind Miller's London Dry Gin - and Miller's Antiques Price Guide. Hence the cram-packing of old curiosities, and gin on the breakfast menu. But a toot'n tonic is probably better enjoyed in the ravishingly romantic bathroom of Room Three. All in all, this is a splendidly imaginative and well run property, thoroughly worth a lengthy visit.

Rates from: ☻☻☻☻☻
Star rating: ★★★
Overall rating: **Editors' Pick**

Ambience :	n/a	Cleanliness:	n/a
Value:	n/a	Facilities:	n/a
Staff:	n/a	Restaurants:	n/a
Location:	n/a	Families:	n/a

Estbek House

East Row, Sandsend, Whitby, North Yorkshire, YO21 3SU, England
T: +44 1947 893 424 **F:** +44 1947 893 625
www.HotelClub.com

When Tim Lawrence and David Cross bought Estbek House in Sandsend, just north of Whitby, they set out to make it "somewhere we would like to eat and stay". Would that this were the motto of the entire hospitality industry.

While Estbek is more a restaurant with rooms than hotel proper, it delights on both counts. Above all, the personal touch is evident everywhere, from the quartet of rooms named Alum, Florence, Nora and Eva, to the obvious concern for guests' welfare evidenced by every member of staff, right down to Maddie and Scottie, a brace of Scottish Terriers who take their security duties ultra seriously.

The rooms are packed with charm, with extra touches like patchwork quilts, shutters, ship's timbers and "half-height" windows which start at the floor. It all feels very much like a family home, rather than a hotel.

Mealtimes come with a sense of occasion, overseen by co-owner Tim Lawrence from the ground floor open kitchen whose granite walls are festooned with copper pans. The restaurant itself is upstairs, and the menus concentrate on fresh wild fish and moorland meat complemented by a range of Antipodean wines. The rhubarb and stem ginger trifle makes for a classic finish.

Sandsend itself is one of the most picturesque villages on this part of the coast, little changed over the past half century and with pretty lanes and a broad beach that invite gentle exploration. Estbek's owners have done a magnificent job. England - indeed most countries - could do with rather more hotels like this.

Rates from: 🛏 🛏
Star rating: ★ ★ ★ ★
Overall rating: **Editors' Pick**

Ambience :	n/a	Cleanliness:	n/a
Value:	n/a	Facilities:	n/a
Staff:	n/a	Restaurants:	n/a
Location:	n/a	Families:	n/a

Hilton York

1 Tower Street, York, Y01 9WD, England
T: +44 1904 648111 **F:** +44 1904 610317
www.HotelClub.com/hotels/Hilton_Hotel_York

All roads lead to Rome or in this case York - Eboracum as it was known during the time when it developed from a small camp site set up by the Roman Governor of Britain, Quintus Petillius Cerialis, into one of the leading cities of the Roman Empire. And today York is still a leading city and ranks as Great Britain's third top tourist destination.

History is alive and well in the Hilton York, a solid red brick building in the city centre. Both Tower's Restaurant serving local and European fare and Tower's Bar offer views of Cliffords Tower, built by William the Conqueror and so named because Roger de Clifford was hanged there in 1322. Even a bit of US history is thrown in with the bar and grill offering Tex Mex classics taking its name from Henry J. Bean, a Chief Justice of the Oregon Supreme Court and at the time of his death one of the longest serving justices in the state of Oregon.

Entranced by the view? Then be sure to book a deluxe room with balconies overlooking the tower. Décor in the 130 rooms and eight meeting rooms, as throughout most of the hotel, is in bright yellow and blue.

The Minster (which attracts two million people annually, both pilgrims and tourists), Mulberry Hall, The Walls, The Bars and Treasurer's House all beckon guests to come and have a look and the Hilton York adds an extra inducement by offering free or reduced rates to these and other local places of interest.

Rates from: 🪙🪙🪙
Star rating: ★★★★
Overall rating: 🦢🦢🦢🦢

Ambience :	8.64	Cleanliness:	9.29
Value:	8.60	Facilities:	8.60
Staff:	8.80	Restaurants:	9.07
Location:	9.47	Families:	9.00

Ireland

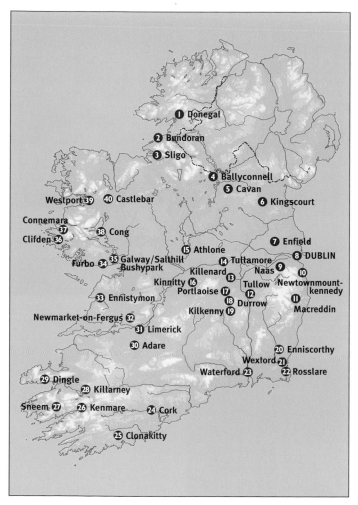

Anyone looking for a more lengthy introduction to Ireland need only dip into *McCarthy's Bar*, a hilarious yet thoughtful vignette by the eponymous Pete whose enduring primary rule of travel enshrined the principle of never passing a bar with your name on it. As might be imagined, he was spoilt for choice as he roamed around the country variously known as The Land of Saints and Scholars, The Poor Old Woman, Silk of the Kine and The Old Sod.

More pertinently, Ireland now enjoys an enviable reputation as The Celtic Tiger, with rather more in the way of exports than just Guinness. A surge of investment in high-end industries and services and a low rate of taxation in the 1990s kicked things off faster than the start of a Gaelic football match, and favourable interest rates from the European Central Bank greased the economic wheels even more swiftly. By 2006, Ireland was rated the second wealthiest country in the world per capita (Euro150,000)

just a short way behind Japan.

It wasn't always so. Famines in the 19th century caused widespread devastation, and spurred waves of immigration to the United States. A bloody struggle for independence (catch Liam Neeson as *Michael Collins* for the celluloid version of events) finally ended in 1921, but a civil war dragged on for another two years. While remaining officially neutral during the second world war, thousands of volunteers sign up to join the fight against Nazi Germany.

Half a century on, Ireland has been transformed, and Dublin, the capital, is the centre of the country's cultural offerings, which extend far beyond stags and hens romping around Temple Bar. Around ten per cent of the republic's six million or so residents are foreign nationals (including many Poles and Lithuanians), with the majority concentrated here.

Secondary cities, such as Cork, Waterford, Limerick and Galway are less ethnically diverse, but each offers a lively menu of diversions. The Roman Catholic church continues to exert a certain influence on daily life, particularly on Sundays, and Ireland is similarly bound together by its passion for sport, with the locally devised game of hurling (played with an axe-shaped stick and minimal protective clothing) enjoying an especially strong following. Even if the very mention of the Eurovision Song Contest causes a certain curling of the toes, it's significant that Ireland has won it seven times. Dublin and other cities host numerous musical events - after all this is the country that nurtured Clannad, U2 and The Corrs among numerous other musical artistes. Most importantly, if you can time a visit here for 17th March, the country erupts for St Patrick's Day, a bibulous celebration that brings out the Irish in everyone, whatever passport they may hold.

Perhaps Ireland's best-known sobriquet is The Emerald Isle, and the interior, both mountainous and beautifully lush, is easily explored given the well-developed transport network, though some rural signposting needs to be interpreted carefully. Hiking, angling, cycling and similar activities are the obvious choices for anyone who wants to experience the beauties of the

country at first hand. Golf courses abound, while at the other end of the scale a sizeable amount of visitors come here to take part in religious retreats and pilgrimages. Sites of worship include not simply cathedrals, but rings of standing stones which may not even be marked on the map.

Rather as Irish Bars, festooned with shamrock emblems and flowing with craic, have spread out to colonise much of the known world, so the descendants of former emigrants have returned to Ireland to trace their roots, most notably the late US President Ronald Reagan. A dig through genealogical records, followed by a trek to a remote village or town, has proved to be a highly satisfying holiday for more than a few Boston residents, and indeed many folk from other parts of the planet.

It's fair to say that nothing exemplifies Ireland's resurgence better than its hotels. From grand old castles to the new breed that might be classified as Electric Eclectic (the g hotel in Galway being the prime example) there's something to suit all tastes and pockets, and the country has taken to resort spas like proverbial ducks to water.

On which point, the weather is about the one thing that hasn't changed drastically of late (annual rainfall in some districts is 200 centimetres a year) but neither, for that matter, has the country's traditional cheery brand of hospitality, which is dispensed as easily and naturally in the very best five-star hotels as it is in any of McCarthy's many bars. Good luck to you now.

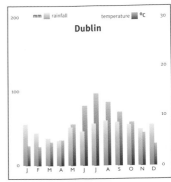

Adare Manor Hotel & Golf Resort

Adare, Co. Limerick, Ireland
T: +353 61 396 566 **F:** +353 61 396 124
www.HotelClub.com

The Second Earl may have done raving when gout restricted him to this crenellated folly in 1832, but there have been plenty of high jinks at the magnificent manor since American Thomas Kane turned it into one of Europe's leading luxury hotels a century and a half later, incorporating the last golf course designed by Robert Trent Jones Sr. in 1995 (host to the Irish Open in 2008 and featuring an 18th hole that the maestro modestly rated the best in the world).

Set in 340 hectares of park and gardens, the 63-room resort (with adjoining townhouses) offers all the huntin', shootin' and fishin' that the poor old peer had to forgo, with its own Equestrian Centre, and the River Maigue winding lazily through the estate. The formal, French-style gardens are made for moonlight strolling - preferably after having dined regally on venison, suckling pig or fresh salmon under the Waterford crystal chandeliers in the Oakroom Restaurant, or more casually at The Carriage House. Drinks in the Tack Room basement bar, serenaded by Irish folk singers, will round off a romantic evening to remember.

Rooms vary from gigantic to huge, some with four-poster beds, some with log fires and chaises longues in the marble bathrooms! There are no fewer than 75 open fireplaces in the entire property - and a leaded-glass window for every day of the week. The Minstrels' Gallery is modelled on the Hall of Mirrors at Versailles. Ironic footnote: you can fox-hunt, but you can't smoke here (or anywhere else in Ireland).

Rates from: 💰💰💰💰
Star rating: ★ ★ ★ ★ ★
Overall rating: 🐾🐾🐾🐾

Ambience :	9.31	Cleanliness:	9.00
Value:	8.38	Facilities:	8.42
Staff:	8.83	Restaurants:	9.03
Location:	8.62	Families:	7.76

Dunraven Arms Hotel

Adare, Co. Limerick, Ireland
T: +353 61 605 900 **F:** +353 61 396 541
www.HotelClub.com/hotels/Dunraven_Arms_Hotel_Adare

Adare owes its reputation as "Ireland's prettiest village" to the Earl of Dunraven, who in keeping with his Conservative philosophy, refused to bow to the early 19th-century trend for replacing thatched roofs with slate. Though many of these quaint dwellings now house designer boutiques and souvenir shops, the place is still a living picture-postcard.

And the late-18th-century Dunraven Arms, a former coaching inn, fits right into the olde-worlde scheme of things. An enticing establishment, it has been playing host to celebrities since aviation pioneer Charles Lindbergh stayed there while advising on the design of nearby Shannon Airport.

Its 86 generously sized rooms include half-a-dozen suites and 24 junior suites, some with four-poster beds, and for all their antique charm (literally - the place is stuffed with them), they have most of the modern facilities, including flatscreen TVs and free Wi-Fi Internet access. And there is an extensive Leisure Centre, with a 17-metre pool, eucalyptus steam room, computerised gym with on-site instructors, and all the beauty and massage therapy you can handle.

Classic Irish cuisine "with a twist" tops the bill of fare at the Maigue Restaurant (named after the local river) - the roast pheasant is a must during the game season -

while for more informal dining, simply pop across the road to The Inn Between, which operates out of one of the original thatched cottages. The oak-panelled walls and leather banquettes in the aptly named Hunters' Bar - this is the assembly point for the Limerick Hunt - give it a comfortingly clubby feel.

Rates from: 🛏🛏🛏🛏
Star rating: n/a
Overall rating: 🐚🐚🐚🐚

Ambience :	9.19	Cleanliness:	9.62
Value:	8.62	Facilities:	7.63
Staff:	9.00	Restaurants:	8.95
Location:	8.90	Families:	8.75

Hodson Bay Hotel

Athlone, Co. Westmeath, Ireland
T: +353 90 6442000 **F:** +353 90 6442020
www.HotelClub.com

No, not the famous body of freezing Canadian water as pronounced by an Irishman, but a beauty spot on the banks of Lough Ree, just outside Athlone in the heart of Ireland's Lake District. And this 182-room hotel has some spectacular views of it, as well as its own cruise boat in which to explore it. It also adjoins Athlone Golf Club.

Built in 1992 and recently refurbished, this property tries - and largely succeeds - to be all things to all people: business travellers, conference groups, couples on honeymoon or getting married, families, pensioners. It is very child-friendly, with a great activities camp, but if you want to avoid the ankle-biters, book a room in the new Retreat wing (which is a better bet anyway).

This also houses the state-of-the-art Spa, the only one in Ireland to feature "watsu", which is shiatsu massage performed in water and an experience not to be missed according to connoisseurs. The huge heated pool is breathtaking and looks as if it is an extension of the lake.

Fare at L'Escale - a member of the Feile Bia Charter, committed to quality ingredients - is unusual to say the least, ranging from fresh local lobster and Roscommon lamb to ostrich, springbok, kangaroo, crocodile and rattlesnake (all,

presumably, authentically sourced). The Octagon, with views over the lake, offers steak-on-a-stone or fish-on-a-skewer, and there is day-long casual dining at the Waterfront Carvery. A Juice Bar does snacks and salads and the Waterfront Bar has live music at weekends. As we said, something for everyone.

Rates from: 🛏🛏🛏
Star rating: ★★★★
Overall rating: 🛎🛎🛎🛎

Ambience :	9.13	Cleanliness:	9.29
Value:	8.42	Facilities:	8.80
Staff:	9.03	Restaurants:	9.03
Location:	8.82	Families:	8.84

Radisson SAS Hotel, Athlone

Northgate Street, Athlone, Co. Westmeath, Ireland
T: +353 90 644 2600 **F:** +353 90 644 2655
www.HotelClub.com

What is always referred to as the "Mighty" River Shannon - Ireland's longest - divides the country and also the town of Athlone, and the Radisson perches right beside it, overlooking the marina. It's just around the corner from the railway station and the town centre, dominated by the iconic Castle (which opera fans may be interested to learn houses an exhibition on the life of Ireland's greatest tenor, John McCormack).

This riverside location is key to the 127-room hotel's appeal. Its Synergy Health & Leisure Club, for example, which includes a 16.5-metre heated indoor pool, sauna and steamroom, is at water level -

so guests working out in the gym can relieve the treadmill boredom by gazing out at the goings-on on the busy river. Likewise, the Quayside Bar & Lounge has a heated outdoor terrace where you can sip a cocktail or a coffee while watching the boats cruise by.

The rooms (including a couple of dozen suites) are divided into "Ocean" and "Urban" in terms of décor, and all run the gamut of Radisson's standard high-class amenities, which these days encompass free broadband Internet access.

Contemporary cuisine at Elements Restaurant is excellent, but the place would be worth a visit

even if the grub wasn't that great just to admire the cleverly themed ambience, based on water, fire, earth and air. All four are also present in Europe's, if not the world's oldest pub, Sean's Bar, just a short walk away. Go there for a post-prandial snifter and enjoy the contrast.

Rates from: 🏠 🏠 🏠
Star rating: ★★★★
Overall rating: 🏠 🏠 🏠 🏠

Ambience :	8.20	Cleanliness:	9.20
Value:	8.07	Facilities:	8.88
Staff:	8.31	Restaurants:	8.50
Location:	9.47	Families:	7.90

Shamrock Lodge Country House Hotel & Conference Centre

Clonown Road, Athlone, Co. Westmeath, Ireland
T: +353 90 649 2601 **F:** +353 90 649 2737
www.HotelClub.com

Three years on from opening after an extensive refurbishment, "hale and hearty" pretty much sums up the Shamrock Lodge, which stands less than five minutes' walk from the town centre. Back at the start of the 19th century, this was the home of one Mr Michael Monks, who may or may not have been a Freemason, hence (one theory runs) the property's current name.

Converted into a hotel in 1951, the Shamrock's current owner - Paddy McCaul - appeared on the scene in the early 1990s. Its stately corridors now lead to some 40 deluxe bedrooms and a dozen family suites, as well as a conference and banqueting room.

Whether you're staying for a conference, a wedding, or simply taking in the sights of this historic city, being well fed and watered is pretty much guaranteed. The Iona Bar also serves lunch, and makes for a pleasant spot to have a drink at any time of day with views out over the well-tended gardens. For a more intimate midday (or evening, for that matter) repast, book the conservatory of the An Luain restaurant; local produce is a given, as is the passion of the chef's brigade.

Sundays see the function room opened for a splendid carvery lunch. Friendly and proactive staff set the seal on this very acceptable hotel.

Of the Shamrock's many well-known guests over the years, Queen Salote of Tonga is of particular note; not exactly a featherweight, if she passed a comfortable night here, then so must just about everyone else!

Rates from: 🐾🐾
Star rating: ★★★★
Overall rating: 🐾🐾🐾🐾

Ambience :	8.75	Cleanliness:	10.0
Value:	9.75	Facilities:	5.75
Staff:	9.75	Restaurants:	7.67
Location:	9.75	Families:	10.0

Slieve Russell Hotel Golf & Country Club

Ballyconnell, Co. Cavan, Ireland
T: +353 49 952 6444 **F:** +353 49 952 6046
www.HotelClub.com

Singing: *"Come all without, come all within, you'll not see nothing like the mighty Quinn"...*

One of the most prepossessing of the fast expanding Quinn hotel group, the Slieve Russell is possibly the furthest imaginable antithesis of an Eskimo igloo. This is one of the new generation of Ireland's super hotels, a veritable circus of business and leisure piled one atop the other a couple of hours' drive away from Dublin and as tigerishly Celtic as they come. Fittingly, the Slieve Russell's owned

by squillionaire Sean Quinn, very much a local boy made good as he lives just down the road.

Few socio-economic groupings fall outside the hotel's welcoming embrace. The combination of a lady and gentleman who run their own company hosting a conference prior to their wedding banquet and a honeymoon which they intend to split between being pampered in the spa and playing golf might seem a little far-fetched, but it would certainly encompass the main attractions at

this impressive 219-room property, which sits in 120 hectares of beautifully manicured grounds.

To start with what many visitors regard as the most important part of the Slieve Russell, the par-72, 18-hole championship course weaves its way about a series of lakes, with some devilishly tricky greens. An academy provides a wealth of tuition and a five-bay floodlit driving range fills in for anyone unsure of how to occupy themselves in the evenings.

Non golfers puzzled about how to pass the time after dusk need only head to The Kells Bar, which takes its name from the eponymous ornately illustrated gospels that were produced by Celtic monks around 800 AD; a copy is housed in the bar, which is a repository of traditional Irish bonhomie.

Dining is concentrated in two main restaurants: the traditional Conall Cearnach, and the rather more modern Setanta. Both display an exemplary wine list,

and the whole culinary scene is helmed by the inspirational chef Peter Denny.

The meetings and conference arrangements pretty much speak for themselves, able to accommodate up to 1,200 in the larger venues, with a host of techno gizmos to make presentations go with a bang.

Rather as the Slieve Russell attracts international conference delegates, the hotel's spa and wellness centre - dubbed Ciuin - has drawn in treatments from the four corners of the earth to provide a dose of rest and relaxation. There's also a 20-metre pool and a fully-equipped fitness suite. On a parallel theme, the great outdoors beckons with clay pigeon shooting, archery, horse riding and leisurely cruises on Lough Earne.

And so, finally, to bed. A recent refurbishment added 60 rooms to the total complement. In general, the décor is bright and airy, and suggestive of the Noughties rather than the Irish countryside, with digital TV and Internet access as standard. Ask for a corner room if one's available, as their balconies sport the best views of the surrounding parkland, and - like this hotel in its entirety - they are well worth taking some time to absorb.

Rates from: 🐾🐾🐾
Star rating: ★★★★
Overall rating: 🐾🐾🐾🐾

Ambience :	8.86	Cleanliness:	9.33
Value:	8.27	Facilities:	9.00
Staff:	8.83	Restaurants:	9.06
Location:	7.64	Families:	8.91

The Great Northern Hotel

Bundoran, Co. Donegal, Ireland
T: +353 71 9841 204 **F**: +353 71 9841 114
www.HotelClub.com/hotels/Great_Northern_Hotel

A true family atmosphere is The Great Northern Hotel's speciality. Each of the 112 rooms is decorated to create a "home away from home." With water sports, angling, horse riding and one of Ireland's largest indoor heated aqua adventure centres nearby, it's easy to keep the whole family happy. For those kids and adults who want to pursue their own interests, there are plenty of facilities on hand at the hotel. Go! Kids! keeps the younger ones happy with bunny hunts and story telling; the adrenalin rush teenagers often crave is satisfied with adventure trips and water sports. All this is contained in an environment that still lingers with memories of yesteryear. Head to the Atlantic Ballroom and experience the old world feel of what it was like in the days when hotels were designed for the gentry.

Rates from: 🐚 🐚
Star rating: ★ ★ ★ ★
Overall rating: 🐚 🐚 🐚 🐚

Ambience :	8.93	Cleanliness:	9.21
Value:	8.36	Facilities:	8.35
Staff:	9.21	Restaurants:	8.85
Location:	9.29	Families:	9.45

Glenlo Abbey Hotel

Bushypark, Co. Galway, Ireland
T: +353 91 526 666 **F**: +353 91 527 800
www.HotelClub.com

If you ever go across the sea to Ireland ... you could watch the sun go down on a genuine 1927 Pullman train carriage that once plied the Monaco/Istanbul/St. Petersburg route. Today, it is the fine-dining restaurant of the Glenlo Abbey and specialises in a succulent mix of Irish and Oriental fare. But that is just the most recent slice of history attaching to this family-owned hotel that dates back to 1740. Bags of atmosphere, then, and some dramatic views over the 56-hectare estate, which includes a nine-hole golf course. The property is crammed with Irish art and antiques, but its 46 rooms have cable TV and Wi-Fi Internet access. The all-day-dining Oak Cellar Bar & Lounge is the Big House's converted kitchen, while the Kentfield Cocktail Lounge does afternoon tea and before- and after-dinner drinks.

Rates from: 🐚 🐚 🐚 🐚 🐚
Star rating: ★ ★ ★ ★ ★
Overall rating: 🐚 🐚 🐚 🐚 ½

Ambience :	9.46	Cleanliness:	9.69
Value:	8.08	Facilities:	8.76
Staff:	9.54	Restaurants:	9.25
Location:	9.62	Families:	9.00

Breaffy House Hotel & Spa

Castlebar, Co. Mayo, Ireland
T: +353 94 902 2033 **F**: +353 94 902 2276
www.HotelClub.com/hotels/Lynch_Breaffy_House_Resort

The hotel's exterior is that typical Irish country estate look and dates back to 1890, but step inside Breaffy House and you'll see that its buzzing Life Spa has gone far beyond the borders of Ireland for its 150 treatments.

Built along the classic lines of a Roman Spa, Life employs the marine therapies of the French and the brightness of the Mediterranean in the Sabbia Med sun suite. Also on offer are Moorish traditions in what was Ireland's first Rasul room - which for novices is a mud exfoliation and herbal steam chamber.

The soothing feeling continues after the treatments. With their light pastel coloured walls contrasting with rich fabrics on warm wood and stone, the hotel's 125 rooms smack of relaxation. The selection of family rooms and suites grant much more space for youngsters to spread themselves and their paraphernalia. A special children's club - hosted by Sammy the Squirrel no less - aims to give parents some time to themselves as well as provide much in the way of entertainment for younger guests.

When a hungry tummy beckons after all that relaxation, head to Garden Restaurant for some tasty wholesome food. Alternatively, there's fine dining in the Mulberry Restaurant, which espouses the thoroughly commendable philosophy of using only the freshest regional ingredients, combined with international cooking methods to create succulent cuisine to suit all palates.

Should all this sound like a cool location for a stag night, take note that such frolics are frowned upon here, and revellers of this ilk can expect to be turned away at the door.

Rates from: 🪙🪙🪙
Star rating: ★★★
Overall rating: 🦋🦋🦋🦋

Ambience :	8.71	Cleanliness:	9.10
Value:	9.14	Facilities:	8.90
Staff:	8.62	Restaurants:	8.40
Location:	8.67	Families:	8.82

Cavan Crystal Hotel

Dublin Road, Co. Cavan, Ireland
T: +353 49 436 0600 **F:** +353 49 436 0699
www.HotelClub.com

The Cavan Crystal - whose relationship with the celebrated glass makers is best expressed in the hotel's glorious chandeliers - is a contemporary bolt-hole in the very heart of the countryside.

There are many reasons to come here - principally the proximity to leading golf courses and a top notch equestrian centre, and then there's the Crystal's health and beauty clinic: yin to the Zest Health & Fitness Club's yang.

Rather more noisily and physically, go-karting and bowling are also within striking distance.

However you pass your time, it's a pleasure at day's end to return to the hotel, which sports a fair amount of handcrafted brick and rich native Irish wood to go with those glittering crystals.

There's just 85 rooms, including three suites, all of them following the general ethos of contemporary design but not skimping when it comes to luxury.

It's a similar theme in Opus One, which specialises in modern Irish cuisine which is supported by an extensive and intriguing wine list. The Atrium bar is an inspiring spot to drop by for a drink.

The Crystal makes a fairly strong pitch toward the corporate market, with two large suites which can accommodate up to 600, and a dedicated conference centre with adjoining syndicate rooms.

The hotel's staff seem to take their cue from their surrounds, dishing up a bright and efficient brand of hospitality that's especially refreshing. And if you're looking for a souvenir of your stay here, would suggesting a couple of pieces of Cavan Crystal be too blindingly obvious?

Rates from: 🏵 🏵
Star rating: ★ ★ ★ ★
Overall rating: 👍 👍 👍 👍 ½

Ambience :	9.36	Cleanliness:	9.93
Value:	8.79	Facilities:	8.84
Staff:	9.36	Restaurants:	9.21
Location:	7.64	Families:	9.50

Radisson SAS Farnham Estate Hotel

Farnham Estate, Cavan, Ireland
T: +353 49 437 7700 **F:** +353 49 437 7701
www.HotelClub.com

It's one of the biggest spas in Ireland, but - as the old saying goes - size isn't important. However what definitely is significant is the rave reviews the Farnham gets from its visitors.

"A mixture of classic and funky, fusing a Georgian house with a sleek modern wing - the perfect place to spend a spa break, a wonderful little interlude to rebalance body, mind and soul" pretty much sums up the chorus of approval.

The 158 rooms here are split between the new wing and the 400-year-old Farnham House, which contains eight of the total of 12 suites. The interior design was inspired by the estate's natural surrounds, with a combination of subtle and dramatic patterns and colours.

And so to the spa. Rightly reckoned as the Rolls-Royce of such facilities in Ireland, it sports a plethora of holistic whistles and bells from a water mint thermal suite to an ice fountain to Amethyst, the salt inhalation room. Caviar facial anyone?

The wit and exuberance of the Farnham Estate continues at meal times. The Botanica restaurant overlooks the lawn, and contains a more intimate space, The Lemon Tree Room, with direct access to the courtyard. The Pear Tree serves healthy cuisine throughout the day, and there's also a private dining room which can host up to 12. Ask for The Potting Shed if you want to make a reservation.

And more good news; the championship golf course, designed by Jeff Howes, is due to open mid 2008.

Rates from: 💰💰💰💰💰
Star rating: ★★★★
Overall rating: 🛏🛏🛏🛏 ½

Ambience :	9.33	Cleanliness:	9.80
Value:	9.20	Facilities:	9.47
Staff:	9.47	Restaurants:	8.79
Location:	8.27	Families:	8.43

Abbeyglen Castle Hotel

Sky Road, Clifden, Co. Galway, Ireland
T: +353 95 21201 **F:** +353 95 21797
www.HotelClub.com/hotels/Abbeyglen_Castle_Hotel_Clifden

Overlooking the sea and the village of Clifden - which often invites comparison with Switzerland - the Abbeyglen is the classic example of an Irish castle hotel.

And of course, its history is as chequered as they come. It was built in 1832 by John D'Arcy, a local powerbroker whose son sold the property to the Irish Church Mission Society. But with the famines in the mid 19th century, the castle fell derelict, and it wasn't until 1969 that the new owners, the Hughes family, were able to start on a full scale restoration.

Their labours have been rewarded over the years, and it's hard to credit that Abbeyglen was once a near ruin. Light floods in through the wide windows of the rooms and suites, which are spacious and tastefully decorated.

And guests are free to roam about the hotel, to take their ease in the study, catch up on the papers in the lounge, or join in the spontaneous sing-songs in the bar.

Abbeyglen's restaurant more than verges on the gourmet; successful anglers can ask for their catch to be cooked to taste, and - in the event of one-that-got-away syndrome - there's an aquarium richly stocked with shellfish. Connemara lamb is another speciality, and the wine list is truly excellent.

The hotel's surrounds are renowned as great walking country, so there'll be no problem working up an appetite.

Best of all, as a family-run hotel, the Abbeyglen has that welcoming atmosphere that's akin to staying in a friend of a friend's home.

Rates from: 🛏🛏🛏🛏
Star rating: ★★★★
Overall rating: 👜👜👜👜 ½

Ambience :	9.67	Cleanliness:	9.54
Value:	9.50	Facilities:	7.51
Staff:	9.70	Restaurants:	9.58
Location:	9.46	Families:	9.31

Inchydoney Island Lodge & Spa

Clonakilty, West Cork, Ireland
T: +353 23 33143 **F:** +353 23 35229
www.HotelClub.com

Many hotels trumpet their location, and rightly so, but Inchydoney is the full works of Henry Purcell. Overlooking two incredible beaches and with complimentary ocean panoramas, it's an endearing retreat made more so by a spa that's the last word in bliss.

The lodge is made more remarkable by seeming to double as an art gallery. Arresting pieces by Terry Bradley, Kevin Sharkey, Graham Nuttel, Majella Collins O'Neill and many other vibrant artists are hung throughout Inchydoney, making for a provocative as well as a decorative atmosphere.

Both regular rooms and self-catering apartments are on offer; whichever you choose, you'll have unlimited use of the heated seawater pool, sauna, steam room, gym and relaxation area.

This invokes mention of the spa, which apart from the regular treatments and amenities, includes a private sanctuary with its own hydrotherapy bath that's ideal for couples planning to spend some time to - well - get to know each other is a good, all-encompassing term. And if you're looking for an unusual treatment, the Chocolat Sensualité Ritual is as tasty as it sounds.

Dining at Inchydoney takes in both the Gulfstream - harking back to the lodge's splendid location - and Dunes Bar & Bistro, which has a similarly nautical theme. The general concept is based on modern French and light Mediterranean, employing the very best available oils, pestos, salads and herbs. Chef Adam Medcalf puts a strong emphasis on fresh coastal seafood - in particular turbot, sole and shell fish - accompanied by low fat sauces and dressings. It's all utterly delicious, like Inchydoney itself.

Rates from: 🛏🛏🛏🛏🛏
Star rating: ★ ★ ★ ★
Overall rating: 👣 👣 👣 👣 ½

Ambience :	9.42	Cleanliness:	9.42
Value:	7.92	Facilities:	9.13
Staff:	9.17	Restaurants:	9.33
Location:	9.75	Families:	8.88

Ashford Castle

Cong, Co. Mayo, Ireland
T: +353 94 9546003 **F:** +353 94 9546 260
www.HotelClub.com/hotels/Ashford_Castle

The Guinness family are perhaps Ireland's quintessential protestant aristocrats, well known in the field of diplomacy, banking, politics and yes, brewing too. For a long time Ashford Castle was their country seat, and Benjamin G refurbished it extensively in the mid 19th century. But country seats rarely come cheap, no matter how many pints of the black stuff you sell, and shortly before the outbreak of the second world war, with perhaps not the greatest commercial timing, Ashford became a hotel.

In a country with more than its fair share of crenallated accommodation, Ashford is particularly remarkable. It's now owned by a group of Irish American entrepreneurs, and understandably wildly popular with a rather wider ethnic grouping. What's really amazing it that what is essentially a 13th century shell (built by the Anglo-Norman de Burgo family) has gradually metamorphosed into somewhere that's so incredibly and luxuriously comfortable.

The rooms and suites are uniformly gorgeous, smartly upholstered and lacking almost nothing unless you're looking for Guinness on tap. The requisite interactive TVs and broadband connectivity are there if you need them, but can safely be ignored by anyone who's had enough of the outside world and simply

wants to concentrate on the Ashford Experience.

Wander where you will among the castle's corridors, staircases and imposing public rooms, and it's almost overwhelming. Chef Stefan Matz oversees operations in the four dining rooms - the George V room which does breakfast, the Connaught Room (significant for a local produce tasting menu), the Drawing Room - best for afternoon tea - and the charismatic thatched Cullens Cottage, a more informal bistro across the River Cong, named for a former maitre d who worked at the hotel for 25 years. There are also two bars, one emphasising the art of the cocktail shaker and the Dungeon Bar, which comes alive in the evenings with ballads and story telling.

The matter of pastimes at Ashford is a tale in itself, and it's possible to indulge in just about every sort of country pursuit, mimicking the grand old days of the past. The nine-hole golf course integrates beautifully with the surrounding countryside. Ghillie Frank Costello knows the angling on Lough Corrib like the back of his hand, and there's also falconry (already established in Ireland when the castle was built in 1228), clay pigeon shooting, archery, and horse riding. And there are few better ways to absorb the majesty of this area than a cruise on the lake, puttering out to Inchagoill island to see the church built by St Patrick in 450AD, and Europe's second oldest Christian inscription which dates from just a few years later. Suffice to say that wherever you roam here, and whatever you do, it's a blissful experience.

As an end note, and as any movie buff can tell you, when John Ford wanted a location to shoot the lush Irish countryside for his 1952 biopic, *The Quiet Man*, Ashford Castle and nearby Cong were the obvious choices. John Wayne and Maureen O'Hara starred; and just like Ashford Castle, it's a classic.

Rates from: 👜👜👜👜👜
Star rating: ★ ★ ★ ★ ★
Overall rating: 👜👜👜👜

Ambience :	9.49	Cleanliness:	9.49
Value:	8.13	Facilities:	8.30
Staff:	9.10	Restaurants:	9.28
Location:	9.24	Families:	8.33

Ballynahinch Castle Hotel

Recess, Connemara, Co. Galway, Ireland
T: +353 95 31006 **F:** +353 95 31085
www.HotelClub.com/hotels/Ballynahinch_Castle_Hotel

Few Irish castle hotels come without a very good tale attached, and that's certainly the case with Ballynahinch, whose one time owner Richard Martin (known as Trigger Dick thanks to a fondness for duelling) was instrumental in founding the Society for Prevention of Cruelty to Animals.

Regrettably, he subsequently lost much of his fortune and died in straitened circumstances in France in 1834. But his former estate lives on - nearly 200 hectares of beautiful gardens, lakes, rivers and woodland that are home to foxes, teal, mallard, kestrels and pine martins, with Ballynahinch Castle at its centre.

There are some 40 guestrooms, of which the riverside suites are the most attractive, with separate bed and living rooms and luxurious bathrooms. Four-poster bed fans will have to settle for a Superior room, and if you don't like courtyard views, aim higher than the Standard Rooms.

Perhaps the hotel's centrepiece is the Owenmore restaurant, guided by the careful hand of head chef Robert Webster. As many ingredients as possible are drawn from local sources, and after a brief period in the kitchen are served up as chilled Atlantic oysters with shallot and red wine vinegar, oven roasted rack of Connemara lamb or poached wild salmon with spinach and lemon beurre blanc. The wine list is drawn from both Old and New World vineyards, and there are some very reasonable House selections.

Working up an appetite should present few problems, as there are plenty of outdoor pursuits, including shooting, but it's grouse, woodcock and pheasant rather than the Trigger Dick variety.

Rates from: 🛏🛏
Star rating: ★ ★ ★ ★
Overall rating: 🐚🐚🐚🐚

Ambience :	9.74	Cleanliness:	9.44
Value:	7.89	Facilities:	6.90
Staff:	9.24	Restaurants:	9.15
Location:	9.48	Families:	8.13

Ambassador Best Western Hotel

Military Hill, St. Lukes, Cork City, Ireland
T: +353 21 453 9000 **F**: +353 21 455 1997
www.HotelClub.com/hotels/Ambassador_Hotel_Best_Western_Cork

If you don't mind stretching your legs, the bulk of Cork city's attractions are within walking distance of the Ambassador. Located on a hilltop, you will work off any local treat you indulge in by the time you reach the hotel's charming entrance. The stunning view of Cork city and the River Lee is probably the hotel's biggest selling point. Be sure to request a bedroom with a balcony.

The hotel's toasty with authentic Irish charm. It dates back to 1872 when it was built as a Military Hospital and then later used as a nursing home, before opening as the Ambassador Hotel in June 1997.

It is particularly good for crashing after a hard day's sightseeing and unless you are travelling to attractions out of the city, you won't need a car.

The rooms are clean and spacious and well insulated from the hustle and bustle outside. The staff are friendly and helpful and it has the feeling of a family-run business rather then the nameless faces of a large hotel.

Although the décor is dated in parts, it has a modern health centre complete with gym, Jacuzzi, steam room and sauna. The gym can sometimes be overly busy because it is also used by local members.

The hotel's Embassy Bar can be just as packed after dusk, especially at weekends, but if you want to mingle with the 'Corkonians' you would be hard pressed to find a better place to enjoy a pint or two of Murphy's.

Rates from: 🛏🛏
Star rating: ★ ★ ★ ★
Overall rating: 🛏🛏🛏🛏 ½

Ambience :	9.20	Cleanliness:	9.73
Value:	9.33	Facilities:	8.03
Staff:	9.57	Restaurants:	9.29
Location:	9.07	Families:	9.17

Hayfield Manor

Perrott Avenue, College Road, Cork, Ireland
T: +353 21 4845900 **F:** +353 21 4316839
www.HotelClub.com/hotels/Hayfield_Manor_Hotel

Champagne breakfasts, sumptuous afternoon tea, and after-dinner gatherings are a daily ritual at Hayfield Manor.

Expect the charm and character of an inviting manor house, but without the pretentiousness of a typical five-star hotel. Those who want to experience everything that Cork has to offer before shutting the door and soaking in a long bath will love this central abode.

Although the hotel is but a short way from the city centre, it is discreetly tucked away in a leafy cul de sac. Start the morning with a swim in the palatial swimming pool followed by a hot dip in the outdoor Jacuzzi, which overlooks the private walled garden.

The bedrooms offer the finest creature comforts of flat-screen TVs, Internet access and antique furnishings, combined with a warm, earthy colour scheme, luxurious toiletries and soft bathrobes that are perfect for cuddling up in.

You need not venture out to discover Cork's restaurant scene. Local fish, meat and sweet treats are on the menu in the hotel's main dining room, Orchids. To the front of the hotel, Perrotts offers more casual food combined with striking views of the aviary. End the night with a visit to their lively bar where you can sit by the fire and choose from an impressive selection of whiskeys, champagnes and cocktails. Though the romantic setting of the hotel is more suited for a couple, the hotel is surprisingly welcoming to young children with cookies and milk available before bedtime.

Rates from: 🛏🛏🛏🛏🛏
Star rating: ★ ★ ★ ★ ★
Overall rating: 🌸🌸🌸🌸 ½

Ambience :	9.52	Cleanliness:	9.55
Value:	8.11	Facilities:	8.88
Staff:	8.57	Restaurants:	9.32
Location:	8.97	Families:	9.00

Jurys Inn Cork

Anderson's Quay, Cork, Ireland
T: +353 21 494 3000 **F**: +353 21 427 6144
www.HotelClub.com/hotels/Jurys_Inn_Cork

Living up to its reputation as a reliable budget hotel, Jury's Inn is a handy base for a one or two night stopover in Cork. Don't expect any luxury frills, but the accommodation is clean and there is a friendly and relaxed atmosphere. Step outside the hotel, turn left and much of the city is on thedoorstep. Located within a shilelagh throw of St Patrick's Street, this is where high-end boutiques and department stores tempt in all types of shoppers.

A rather banal entrance to the hotel is offset by a selection of pleasant dining areas - including the relaxed Infusion Restaurant, the more informal Inntro Bar or Il Barista café (great for a quick snack or coffee to go). The hotel is only a brisk walk from Cork's energetic social scene so there is no need to bother with taxis. It is relatively easy to reserve one of the 133 bedrooms all year round (except for the weekend of the Jazz festival in late October when the hotel is booked out well in advance).

All of the bedrooms are well furnished with full en-suite facilities, coffee/ tea maker and TV and can accommodate up to two adults and two children, or the slightly unusual combination of three adults sharing. Nobody is ever going to wax lyrical about the stylistic marvels of Jury's, but the joint's easy on the plastic and if you're here simply to enjoy Cork, what more can you ask?

Rates from: ☽☽
Star rating: ★★★
Overall rating: ☽☽☽☽

Ambience :	8.43	Cleanliness:	9.14
Value:	8.71	Facilities:	8.25
Staff:	8.37	Restaurants:	8.60
Location:	8.93	Families:	8.62

Maryborough Hotel and Spa

Maryborough Hill, Douglas, Cork, Ireland
T: +353 21 436 5555 **F:** +353 21 436 5662
www.HotelClub.com/hotels/The_Maryborough_House_Hotel

The expectation of being well fed and massaged into a wonderful slumber comes with good reason - after all Maryborough Hotel boasts a renowned spa, plush accommodation and a top notch restaurant. Even if you take luxury in your stride, prepare for a very Irish experience with all the lavish trimmings. Tucked away in one of Cork's most chic suburbs, the Georgian residence is just a five-minute drive from the city and in a pleasant location if you want to explore the outskirts.

The glamour of the original building seeps into the modern part of the hotel where the bedrooms and Spa facilities are located. When the most basic type of room looks like a superior, it doesn't take a detective to work out that luxury is a priority. The bedrooms are so spacious they could hold dinner parties while it is hard to resist diving between the creamy sheets. Everything is in warm colours, from the wooden floors to the extravagant curtains. Some of the rooms have inspiring views of the picture perfect gardens - a setting that would rival any tropical beach scene.

If you need a reminder that you are on holiday, the Spa is there to while away those relaxing evenings. This cocoon of sophistication has a range of treatments that conjure images of awe-inspiring results. While the Spa offers every invitation to be lazy, there is a gym on site for the more energetic guests. There is also the chance to get the gladrags on and revel in the restaurant's refined dining. An especially extensive cellar allows you to choose something to match whatever your favourite dish may be. Bon appétit.

Rates from: 🏰🏰🏰🏰🏰
Star rating: ★★★★
Overall rating: 🌀🌀🌀🌀

Ambience :	8.00	Cleanliness:	9.00
Value:	8.00	Facilities:	8.50
Staff:	9.00	Restaurants:	10.0
Location:	8.00	Families:	9.00

The Rochestown Park Hotel

Rochestown Road, Douglas, Cork, Ireland
T: +353 21 489 0800 **F:** +353 21 489 2178
www.HotelClub.com/hotels/Rochestown_Lodge_Hotel

Avoid the chaotic humdrum of Cork city by staying ten minutes' drive away in the sprawling Rochestown Park Hotel. This pleasant abode is highly regarded for family holidays - its winning formula includes impressive leisure facilities, spa treatments and a reliable babysitting service. The 163-bedroom hotel may hold as many

weddings and conferences as it serves hot dinners, but don't let that put you off. The staff will meet and greet you as gregariously as they treat their bridal parties.

Formerly home to the Lord Mayor of Cork, the attractive hotel stands in lovely grounds and the original parts of the building feature elegant and well-proportioned rooms. Guests can enjoy large beds, power showers, cable TV and impressive buffet breakfasts. If you want to indulge in some of Cork's finest food take advantage of their hearty Irish breakfast or their popular pub grub served at the Douglas Tavern. Long-staying guests might consider taking one of the eight executive townhouses or those who want to indulge can book a deluxe or presidential suite. If in need of a mid-day pick-me-up, the hotel has a thalasso therapy clinic with a mammoth list of treatments to pick and choose from.

The hotel is in a pleasantly secluded location - adding appeal for parents with young children. Although there is a regular bus service into Cork city, it is worthwhile to rent a car to explore the attractions in the surrounding area. Nearby Douglas is a trendy quarter with an array of reliable restaurants and lively pubs.

Rates from: 🐚🐚
Star rating: ★ ★ ★ ★
Overall rating: 🐚 🐚 🐚 🐚

Ambience :	8.73	Cleanliness:	9.15
Value:	8.54	Facilities:	9.13
Staff:	8.56	Restaurants:	8.88
Location:	8.42	Families:	8.56

Dingle Skellig Hotel

Dingle, Co. Kerry, Ireland
T: +353 66 915 0200 F: +353 66 915 1501
www.HotelClub.com/hotels/Dingle_Skellig_Hotel

You don't have to be an ace cartographer to know that Dingle is the most westerly town in Ireland, and Europe too for that matter, and the whole of the Skellig Hotel is invigorated by the breezes off the Atlantic.

Fresh pretty much sums up this 113-room property, sitting a short walk from the town centre which manages to combine the cosmopolitan with the traditional.

To get a taste of what's in store, slip into the Coastguard restaurant, whose menus blend magnificently with the panoramas of the Dingle Peninsula. And the Gallarus Lounge provides similarly inspiring views.

The Skellig's no simple bed-and-boarder. Guests who don't want to venture further afield can dip into the indoor pool or the Peninsula Spa. Families are well catered for - there's a changing room, crèche (discounts for multiple occupancy), a free kids' club and even a Junior Evening Meal starting at the very sensible time of 5.30pm.

On the accommodation side there's 13 suites and 98 regular rooms to choose from. The bulk of the rooms have been refurbished recently, tricked out in combinations of chocolate brown, cream, russet and gold. The overall effect is of chic comfort, and many rooms inter-connect making them ideal for families.

Perhaps the best aspect of the Skellig is the staff, who are companionable and informative, and will happily spout ideas about what to see and do locally.

And yes, Fungie the Dingle Dophin (first spotted in 1984 by the harbour lighthouse keeper) is alive and well and currently renegotiating his contract with the tourism board.

Rates from: 🐚🐚
Star rating: ★ ★ ★ ★
Overall rating: 🐚 🐚 🐚 🐚

Ambience :	8.86	Cleanliness:	9.14
Value:	8.54	Facilities:	8.38
Staff:	8.81	Restaurants:	8.96
Location:	9.46	Families:	9.04

Harvey's Point Country Hotel

Lough Eske, Donegal Town, Co. Donegal, Ireland
T: +353 74 972 2208 **F:** +353 74 972 2352
www.HotelClub.com/hotels/Harveys_Point_Country_Hotel

A touch of Switzerland by Lough Eske in Donegal - that's Harvey's Point Country Hotel. What was once an old Irish cottage has been replaced over the years by chalet-style buildings linked by covered walkways. The abundance of wood - from the pillars in the lobby to the beds in all 60 rooms - creates an atmosphere of warmth. And what rooms they are! Plush and lavish is the best way to describe them with king-sized beds, roaming space, wall-to-ceiling Italian marble in the bathrooms and a sunken bath fit for two. The choice ranges from not-exactly basic Courtyard rooms up to the Penthouse suites which include their own jet pool.

Include a Wednesday or Friday in your stay and you can partake of the Celtic Menu in the a la carte restaurant followed by rousing Celtic Harmonies in the cocktail lounge.

Guests can join in these performances by Irish entertainers and maybe even realise that they missed their true vocation.

In what might be described as a fairly sharply defined contrast, Harvey's Point also puts on special de-tox programmes, packaging yoga sessions, bike rides, four-hour hikes, full body massages and a low-calorie diet into a few action-packed days that are guaranteed to give both body and soul a thorough work-out.

As success stories go, Harvey's Point is exemplary. Owned and managed by the Gysling family, who hail from Switzerland, the hotel marries Continental efficiency with Irish charm in a stunning location.

Rates from: 🪑🪑🪑🪑🪑
Star rating: ★★★★
Overall rating: 🐶🐶🐶🐶🐶

Ambience :	9.57	Cleanliness:	9.77
Value:	8.79	Facilities:	8.43
Staff:	9.38	Restaurants:	9.79
Location:	9.64	Families:	9.58

Arlington Hotel, Dublin

Bachelors Walk, O'Connell Bridge, Dublin 1, Ireland
T: +353 1 804 9100 **F:** +353 1 804 9152
www.HotelClub.com/hotels/Arlington_Hotel_Dublin

Poised between Dublin's landmark O'Connell and Ha'penny bridges, The Arlington Hotel straddles the gap between tourist hospitality and amusement for locals with its Knightsbridge bar now a well established watering hole for Dubliners. Priding itself on "knightly" entertainment, The Arlington doles out knees-up diversion alongside a traditional Irish welcome. The imposing dark mahogany reception area is guarded by knights in shining armour. But fear not, the staff is far from medieval and guests can feel secure about service standards. Pleasantries aside, the staff indulgently identifies Dublin's delights for curious guests. Décor in the 115 bedrooms is unfussy and homely, clean and convivial. Mini-suites in the Georgian wing boast modem lines and trouser presses, and vie for unrestricted views over the River Liffey and beyond. Parking facilities are a welcome, rare commodity in the hotel's prime city centre location. Feeling famished? Choose from candle-lit round tables at Knights Bistro, before demolishing a nourishing Irish beef stew. Join late-night punters in the aforementioned Knightsbridge bar and boogie to live bands belting out all-time-favourites. The Arlington embraces Excalibur entertainment, something that too-cool-for-school Dubliners have historically up-turned their noses at. But Celtic is newly cool. Enjoy a traditional Irish dancing show in the Arlington's dedicated basement banquet room; long tables and beer swilling locals set the scene. Feast your eyes on the lads and lasses from the Celtic Rhythm dancing troupe kicking up their heels and diddly-eyeing across the stage. Gentlemen dust down your chivalrous ways and treat your lady to a knight to remember.

Rates from: 🐗🐗🐗🐗
Star rating: ★★★
Overall rating: 🐾🐾🐾🐾

Ambience :	8.47	Cleanliness:	8.53
Value:	8.43	Facilities:	6.85
Staff:	8.63	Restaurants:	8.40
Location:	9.57	Families:	8.47

The Beacon

Beacon Court, Sandyford, Dublin 18, Ireland
T: +353 1 291 5000 **F:** +353 1 291 5005
www.HotelClub.com/hotels/Beacon_Hotel_Dublin

The snow queen palace of The Beacon Hotel in Sandyford is a real cool place to stay. Ice white interiors and subtle lighting effects encourage maximum chill out in this chic hotel. Surrounded by busy Sandyford Industrial Estate, the hotel benefits from good infrastructure. Glide swiftly into the city centre on board the Luas, Dublin's light rail system. Slap on some walking boots and explore Wicklow Way which wends its way through nearby Dublin Mountains, or tramp down to Dundrum Shopping Centre for some superior shoe shopping. The 88 guestrooms and suites are a wonderland. Melt into snowball soft beds or bubble-filled Philippe Starck baths. For an optimal slumber, be sure to book a room far from ground level where trendy disco tunes emanate. Business apartments with kitchen facilities provide a welcoming, temporary home for those on the move. Chill out with packages such as "Suite Dreams" or "Shopping Delight", aimed at pamper seekers and shopaholics. Brian McDonald is the brain behind the interiors and has created a slick space maximising natural light. A quirky four-poster bed in the lobby invites curiosity cats while glass chandeliers up the ante on the elegance stakes. At night The Beacon truly twinkles in candlelight. Flake out at the Crystal Bar, an über trendy watering hole and be sure to ask for extra ice in your cocktail glass. Chow down on flavoursome Asian cuisine at My Thai restaurant and "chillax" to a jazz brunch on Sundays. There's oodles to do on the fringes of Dublin city.

Rates from: 💰💰
Star rating: ★ ★ ★ ★
Overall rating: 🏆🏆🏆🏆

Ambience :	8.67	Cleanliness:	9.50
Value:	7.83	Facilities:	7.83
Staff:	8.83	Restaurants:	7.67
Location:	7.33	Families:	5.50

Bewleys Hotel Ballsbridge

Merrion Road, Ballsbridge, Dublin 4, Ireland
T: +353 1 668 1111 **F**: +53 1 668 1999
www.HotelClub.com/hotels/Bewleys_Hotel_Ballsbridge

Go back to school with Bewleys. This imposing 19th century Masonic school has been restored to its former glory, only now it's far from hard desks and the dog days of homework. Pop up to the top floor for panoramic views of Dublin Bay. Slip around the corner and explore the elegant show grounds of The Royal Dublin Society, or hop on a bus into the city centre (quiet down the back!). The 304 rooms are not particularly fancy, but are diligently cleaned, decidedly comfortable and very reasonably priced. Select spacious suites for that extra bit of class. Dossing is encouraged with free Internet access. O'Connells restaurant receives top marks for its quality food and its links to renowned Ballymaloe House. Home-baked breads compliment fresh Irish food, and not a dinner lady in sight. This is a studiously good hotel.

Rates from: 🐚🐚
Star rating: ★ ★ ★
Overall rating: 👍 👍 👍 👍

Ambience :	8.23	Cleanliness:	9.00
Value:	8.80	Facilities:	7.38
Staff:	8.58	Restaurants:	8.51
Location:	8.16	Families:	8.59

Photo: David Toase - Killiney Bay, Ireland

Brooks Hotel

Drury Street, Dublin 2, Ireland
T: +353 1 6704 000 **F**: +353 1 6704 455
www.HotelClub.com/hotels/Brooks_Hotel_Dublin

For scrupulous time-keepers on a strict schedule, Brooks fits the bill perfectly. Tucked away on a side alley near Grafton Street, this contemporary, compact hotel is a marvellous base for dipping your toes into the Dublin scene. While a smack-bang-in-the-middle of the city location means that views are not the most inspired, the hotel's merits balance out upon calculation. Ponder over a menu of plump pillows for maximum snoozability in plush plum-toned rooms. The 98 bedrooms equipped with plasma screen TVs are generously sized, and budding Elvis impersonators can get all shook up in the shower with piped radio. Start your day the healthy way with Brooks' deliciously wholesome breakfast or alternatively, try a fry, it'll set you up! Save the leftovers (if any) and follow tradition, feeding the plump ducks in St Stephen's Green after enjoying a stroll in this mini oasis in the city. A fitness dock is available for the most eager fitness fanatics, or you may prefer to patiently thaw in the sauna after exploring Dublin on a chilly winter's day. VIP it up at the resident's lounge, secluded and sleek. Enjoy the perks of free Internet and an extensive library. Begin your night on the right note accompanied by Brook's resident pianist in Jasmine Bar. Muted tones and nooks and crannies aplenty make this a pleasant place for passing the hours. Francesca's restaurant delivers delish dishes. Keep eyes peeled for celebs wolfing down food, pre-appearance at the Gaiety Theatre around the corner.

Rates from: 🪙🪙🪙
Star rating: ★★★★
Overall rating: 🎸🎸🎸🎸 ½

Ambience :	9.06	Cleanliness:	9.35
Value:	8.47	Facilities:	9.28
Staff:	9.56	Restaurants:	9.00
Location:	9.29	Families:	9.00

Cassidys Hotel

Cavendish Row, Upper O'Connell Street, Dublin 1, Ireland
T: +353 1 878 0555   **F:** +353 1 878 0687
www.HotelClub.com/hotels/Cassidys_Hotel_Dublin

Family-run Cassidy's Hotel bestows a welcome not dissimilar to an Irish mammy's hug. The staff are genuinely amiable, the rooms curiously cosy and there's always time for a cuppa. This snug hotel is tucked away in the corner of a city quarter that was once the *choix du jour* of Dublin's elite. Row upon row of regal Georgian houses recall the brief, bygone era of BCBG attributed to this, the north side of the city. Since then, the area underwent a republican makeover.

Cassidy's sits in nationalistic Parnell Square, overlooking the Garden of Remembrance - a park dedicated to the noble cause of the Republic's freedom. This locale is a fierce blend of national identity and cultural hedonism. Drop by the lovely little Hugh Lane Art Gallery, the not-so-touristy James Joyce Museum and the richly historic Gate Theatre to sample some alternative entertainment. The hotel's 113 standard rooms have been given more than a lick of paint

and are well appointed with the usual facilities, while executive rooms supply ampler creature comforts. Black-out curtains are a welcome addition in this effervescent capital. Reasonably priced, homely grub is served at Restaurant Six. Grab a seat near the fake flickering fire on the flat-screen for a contemporary twist on a twee Irish feel. Flake out in Grooms Bar, the kind of place Orson Welles could have sipped a cool, creamy Guinness after a fiery performance at the Gate. A short slink up the stairs and you'll soon slip into a snug slumber at Cassidy's.

Rates from: 💰💰💰💰💰
Star rating: ★ ★ ★
Overall rating: 🏠 🏠 🏠 🏠 ½

Ambience :	8.24	Cleanliness:	9.12
Value:	8.71	Facilities:	7.29
Staff:	9.13	Restaurants:	8.35
Location:	9.06	Families:	9.13

Citywest Hotel

Saggart, Co. Dublin, Ireland
T: +353 1 401 0500 **F:** +353 1 401 0945
www.HotelClub.com/hotels/Citywest_Hotel_Dublin

For golfers and scenery addicts, The Citywest Hotel is exactly right. At the foot of the western reaches of the Dublin Mountains, this massive hotel isn't immediately apparent owing to its impressively expansive grounds. The lobby area's glistening bottled glass windows, roaring fire and ruby red wall furnishings attract patrons aplenty so the hotel always appears abuzz with activity. A staggering tally of 1,314 classically styled and comfortably cosy rooms compete for clientele in maroon and cream. Play at being Christy O'Connor Junior on the championship golf course or be pampered in the Health and Leisure Club. Snug (or smug) after-links drinks and post-pampering snacks can be relished in the hideaway Hibernian Bar. Alternatively, chow down on Thai cuisine at Lemongrass restaurant. This is a grand halfway house in the not-so-wild west.

Rates from: 💰💰💰
Star rating: ★★★★
Overall rating: 👣👣👣

Ambience :	8.73	Cleanliness:	9.30
Value:	9.23	Facilities:	8.84
Staff:	9.10	Restaurants:	8.87
Location:	8.27	Families:	8.50

The Clarence

6-8 Wellington Quay, Dublin 2, Ireland
T: +353 1 407 0800 **F:** +353 1 407 0820
www.HotelClub.com/hotels/The_Clarence_Hotel_Dublin

Rather like its owners, the Clarence is at once classy and grungy. When Bono and the boys redeveloped this fringes-of-Temple Bar establishment, they became property pioneers. Maintaining an austere art deco aesthetic and an iconic industrial image, this hotel simply rocks. Each of its 47 rooms is an individual, varying from comfortable industrial balconied rooms speckled with Guggi Art to a rock god's playhouse. The two-storey pad perched on the roof is kitted out with A-List essentials: hot tub, baby grand and cocktail bar. The Tea Room keeps it simple with a "Market Menu" that's great for a speedy lunch. Once the place to be seen in this city of blinding lights, the Octagon Bar is now ideal for quietly quaffing cocktails; while the residents' lounge, The Study, is even more peaceful.

Rates from: 💰💰💰💰
Star rating: ★★★★★
Overall rating: 👣👣👣

Ambience :	9.18	Cleanliness:	9.47
Value:	8.02	Facilities:	7.83
Staff:	9.25	Restaurants:	8.88
Location:	9.60	Families:	7.70

Clontarf Castle Hotel

Castle Avenue, Clontarf, Dublin 3, Ireland
T: +353 1 833 2321 F: +353 1 833 0418
www.HotelClub.com/hotels/Clontarf_Castle_Hotel_Dublin

Clontarf Castle crowns the eponymous Dublin suburb with a spectacularly spooky history. Not only does Dracula's author, Bram Stoker, hail from Clontarf, but the area itself has a bloody history dating back to 1014. Brian Boru, an old Irish high king, was murdered by Vikings in the Battle of Clontarf, while praying in his tent. Some 100 years later, Hugh de Lacy (the first Lord of Meath and a man fond of infrastructure) built Clontarf Castle as a line of defence for his demesne. The original building was demolished in 1835 to make way for the dignified digs that exist today. Recent restoration has tugged the castle into modern times, although its past is omnipresent in its aesthetics: the property is bedecked in tapestries and turrets.

All elegantly appointed 111 guest rooms use richly Gothic tones of red and dark mahogany wood. Dramatic four-poster beds in the suites amplify palatial aspirations. Specify your preference for a Victorian free-standing bath, for an extra bit of bubbly luxury. Temperatures soar at the Fahrenheit Grill, where flaming steak is a speciality. The Indigo Bar is saturated with colour; bright red chandeliers and modern quirky furnishings add to its comfort factor. Knights Bar is true to its roots and remains mainly medieval. Snuggle up beside an enormous open fire and wonder at the kaleidoscopic stained glass windows. If staying in an ancient castle isn't enough to thrill you, head for the broodingly bloody Bram Stoker Museum in Clontarf or clamber along the coast: Bull Island is known for satisfying avian spotting. This hotel on the northern reaches of Dublin town is scarily good.

Rates from: 💰💰💰💰
Star rating: ★★★★
Overall rating: 👣👣👣👣 ½

Ambience :	9.00	Cleanliness:	9.52
Value:	8.48	Facilities:	8.25
Staff:	9.14	Restaurants:	9.09
Location:	8.52	Families:	9.13

Conrad Dublin

Earlsfort Terrace, Dublin 2, Ireland
T: +353 1 602 8900 **F:** +353 1 676 5424
www.HotelClub.com/hotels/Conrad_Hotel_Dublin

Get tuned up for a stay at The Conrad. This hotel's premier position facing Ireland's National Concert Hall deserves an encore. Step into its expansive foyer and listen as the buzz crescendos, with concert goers partaking of refreshments pre-show. At weekends jazz evenings are a "saxy" event for Dublin's musically astute in the Alex Cocktail Bar, where succulent seafood is also a speciality. Below stairs overlooking a contemporary corporate plaza, Alfie Byrnes is a firm favourite with commercial creatures sneaking a few scoops, après work. Catch the last rays of evening sun on the terrace cocooned between tall corporate buildings while drinking in views of the nation's classic

theatre and the erudite environs of University College Dublin.

Interior design at the Conrad has been given a decisive update and its moderately-sized 191 bedrooms are comfortably contemporary. Trimmings in the bedrooms are tasteful. Molton Brown toiletries accessorise the marbled bathrooms. Sculpt your silhouette in the gym or opt for environmentally friendly exercise by strolling through nearby Stephen's Green. However, if your visit is one with a policy of indulgence, stay at the Presidential Suite; your constitution will be greatly improved by slumbers in these fine chambers. A large arched window frames views of Greater Dublin, stretching as far as the

moody Dublin Mountains. Tremendously roomy living quarters and a cosy kitchen stretch into an expansive bedroom. The hotel's location in a busy commercial district means the area's bustling during business but is calm after hours. An assiduous concierge will be pleased to advise on all delicious diversions, whether musical or otherwise.

Rates from: ☾☾☾☾
Star rating: ★★★★★
Overall rating: ☾☾☾☾

Ambience :	9.27	Cleanliness:	9.73
Value:	8.05	Facilities:	8.70
Staff:	9.18	Restaurants:	8.95
Location:	9.27	Families:	8.41

Fitzpatrick Castle Hotel, Dublin

Killiney, Co. Dublin, Ireland
T: +353 1 230 5400 **F:** +353 1 230 5430
www.HotelClub.com/hotels/Fitzpatrick_Castle_Hotel_Dublin

Fitzpatrick's Hotel has a noble history, harking back to feudal days in Ireland. The original building was built in 1740 by Colonel John Mapas. A century later the house was extended and renamed Killiney Castle. It's more of a stately manor house but its situation in the upper reaches of the most fashionable district of South County Dublin is enviable. Nod to celeb neighbours like U2s front-men and Enya. In earlier times bohemian residents such as George Bernard Shaw chose to live here. Take on the steep challenge of a climb up Killiney Hill. Its spectacular slopes embrace the curve of Killiney Bay and the view is guaranteed to chase the cobwebs away, whatever the weather. Get studious beside the fire in the Library Bar or visit PJ's Restaurant. Although heavy with floral patterns, it serves up tasty Irish victuals. The Dungeon Bar and Grill in the oldest part of the castle serves tasty, local treats that are far from grim. Feel ladylike in the lovely bedrooms: all 113 maintain a soothing ambience. Splashes of pattern provide relief in an otherwise morosely maroon hotel. Specify your preference for front of house deluxe rooms where you will truly have a room with a view. The most pleasurable aspect of the hotel is the lavish leisure centre, added in latter days. You'll be lapping in luxury in the 20-metre indoor pool, whirlpool or the Scandinavian sauna. The hotel's salon teases out any extra tensions with masterful massages. Lord it up with a stay at Fitzpatricks.

Rates from: 💰💰💰💰💰
Star rating: ★★★★
Overall rating: 👍👍👍👍

Ambience :	9.21	Cleanliness:	9.36
Value:	8.43	Facilities:	8.73
Staff:	9.08	Restaurants:	9.36
Location:	9.07	Families:	9.00

Fitzwilliam Hotel

St. Stephen's Green, Dublin 2, Ireland
T: +353 1 478 7000 **F:** +353 1 478 7878
www.HotelClub.com/hotels/Fitzwilliam_Hotel_Dublin

A hotel positioned in the posh part of town allowing access in a moment to the city's prime retail parade and permitting views over a verdant park... too good to be true? It seems not at The Fitzwilliam. This contemporary cache is in a unique position in Dublin's city centre. Perch, pint in hand, on Ireland's largest roof garden and gaze over both St Stephen's Green and Grafton Street. Further scenes of crowds hurtling towards the shopping Mecca can be glimpsed through glistening panoramic glass at the hotel entrance. Purple-tuxedoed staff usher guests into a spacious, Starck(-esque) lobby. Upon entering, a chessboard marble foyer floor invites guests to make further moves within. Check mate and self in to stay at the welcoming reception. Later, sneak into the cosy library corner, stacked with tempting novels for devouring on a wet Dublin day. Dine at the zesty Citron restaurant which teeters on a mezzanine level overlooking reception. Exceptional Michelin starred food is served at Thornton's Restaurant, a firm favourite with gastronomes. Excellent refreshments are enjoyed at dusk by Dublin's trendy at the chic Inn on the Green. On the siesta side, the 139 bedrooms at the Fitzwilliam vary from sufficiently sized, minimalist rooms with plush furnishings to a peculiarly posh penthouse. Submerge into a quirky pod-shaped bath, tinkle on a grand piano or let padded leather walls in the sitting area test your sanity. Such a large, open suite in such a prime Dublin location is unparalleled. Indulge in pampering at The Fitzwilliam's Free Spirit Hair and Beauty Salon. Because you're worth it.

Rates from: 🏵🏵🏵🏵🏵
Star rating: ★★★★★
Overall rating: 🏵🏵🏵🏵

Ambience :	8.90	Cleanliness :	9.50
Value :	8.00	Facilities :	7.87
Staff :	9.10	Restaurants :	8.71
Location :	9.50	Families :	8.60

Four Seasons Hotel Dublin

Simmonscourt Road, Dublin 4, Ireland
T: +353 1 665 4000 **F:** +353 1 665 4099
www.HotelClub.com/hotels/Four_Seasons_Hotel_Dublin

Positioned along Dublin's Embassy Row, the Four Seasons is a popular spot for prominent personalities. Internally, its opulence caters to a more traditional palate. A heavily marbled lobby leads through to the (un)originally labelled Lobby Lounge and the Bar where guests are lulled into a state of relaxation as ivories are tinkled on a baby grand. Take afternoon tea inside or out, overlooking a formal courtyard garden. Much recommended is the speciality hot chocolate served in mini silver teapots with homemade Irish chocolates; delicious for dunking. What would the Seasons Restaurant be if it didn't offer seasonal fayre? The resident chef puts a spring into contemporary European food and reworks popular Irish classics. Unusual specialities grace menu pages with scallops, fowl and red chard featuring. The Café serves more casual cuisine. A winter wonderland atmosphere enthrals at The Ice Bar, renowned for serious society manoeuvring and celebrity spotting. Frozen Margaritas are order of the day when the heat is on and the lights go down. The hotel's selection of 197 blissfully quiet guestrooms rises from the standard to the downright sumptuous. Employees are experts in personalisation: if you're on the guest list everybody knows your name: cheers to that! House policy dictates that children will always be tolerated, even treated kindly. Mention you're staying for a special occasion, and you'll be bestowed with gifts of fresh fruit or personalised cookies. A thoughtful concierge is at beck and call, attending deftly to the minutiae of guest requests. The Four Seasons does service with a super smile.

Rates from: 💰💰💰💰💰
Star rating: ★★★★★
Overall rating: 🏵🏵🏵🏵

Ambience :	9.23	Cleanliness:	9.60
Value:	7.50	Facilities:	8.91
Staff:	9.08	Restaurants:	9.21
Location:	8.70	Families:	8.39

The Gresham Hotel

23 Upper O'Connell Street, Dublin 1, Ireland
T: +353 1 874 6881 **F:** +353 1 878 7175
www.HotelClub.com/hotels/Gresham_Hotel_Dublin

Ireland's obsession with celebrity means that The Gresham Hotel now hosts a remarkably decadent penthouse suite named after Joan Collins. This is somewhat surprising in a hotel that's inextricably linked to recent Irish historical events. The core of the Irish rebellion occurred around O'Connell Street in 1916. Controversially, another suite, the Ian Ritchie, is named after the architect responsible for the lump of metal which now divides O'Connell Street in two. If nothing else, The Spire provides fuel with

which to start a conversation in any Dublin pub. Mention the 'Spike' and you'll ignite sparks of Dublin wit: a lively list of alternative nicknames is likely to flow. The hotel has christened some of its other rooms after Irish writers, including Swift and Wilde. Leaving aside the intricacies of naming names and name calling, the Gresham is old world class and one of a kind. It's an enormous hotel and with staff that demonstrates an enthusiasm to match. A recent upgrade has done plenty to improve the interior of what has long been a Dublin institution. Long time favourite dinner dance destination for Dublin's well heeled social set, it has of late reinvented itself. Thick, royal blue carpets and glittering chandeliers add to its latter day class. A true to life rags to riches story lies behind the history of the Gresham. As a baby, Thomas Gresham was abandoned on the steps of the Royal Exchange in London. He travelled to Ireland and gained employment as a butler to a

well-to-do family, before eventually doing good himself and opening a hotel on what was then called Sackville Street. Following Ireland's long struggle for independence, the street was renamed O'Connell Street post-1916. When selecting accommodation from the standard 288 rooms, opt for those with rather dull views towards the back of the hotel. Rooms facing bustling O'Connell Street suffer from decibel overload, despite double glazing. Feel like a princess in the Grace Kelly Suite or glitzy in the aforementioned flash and fabulous Joan Collins. Nothing has been spared in catering for VIPs. The hotel's penthouses are plush and luxurious with enormous balconies. Views from these vertiginous suites are something special. Survey historical statues paying homage to the founding fathers of modern day Ireland; Parnell and Larkin now stand tall on O'Connell Street. Smart, old-school doormen flank the heavy glass doors and deftly usher guests to the appropriate

dining area. Put on your lace gloves for Sunday style, old Irish afternoon tea at The Writers Bar. Warm up on hot toddies of whiskey in Toddy's Bar, a favourite for sports supporters. Whet your appetite for art in The Gallery Restaurant, where a display of tempting art is for sale or dine out on a large selection of dishes at No. 23 Restaurant. Take in a play at the Gate Theatre (almost on The Gresham's doorstep), enjoy some art at The Hugh Lane Gallery or brush up on literary history at James Joyce Gallery. The Gresham is great - central location combined with class service.

Rates from: 🐚🐚
Star rating: ★ ★ ★ ★
Overall rating: 🐚🐚🐚🐚

Ambience :	8.88	Cleanliness:	9.24
Value:	8.41	Facilities:	8.09
Staff:	8.94	Restaurants:	8.72
Location:	9.63	Families:	8.62

The Merrion

Upper Merrion Street, Dublin 2, Ireland
T: +353 1 603 0600 **F:** +353 1 603 0700
www.HotelClub.com/hotels/Merrion_Hotel_Dublin

In the heart of the right honourable government district, The Merrion has evolved with the superb conversion of some of Dublin's finest Georgian townhouses. Once the home of the Earl of Mornington, its interiors pay homage to an aristocratic history. All 142 chambers are beautifully appointed, particularly in the Main House, while rooms in an elegant extension peer over immaculate box gardens. Obliterate all ounces of tension in the Tethra Spa before scuttling below stairs to the scullery (now The Cellar Restaurant), enjoying an eyeful of The Merrion's renowned art collection along the way. Restaurant Patrick Guilbaud tempts with French finesse, while No. 23 bar contrives spiffing cocktails. Enjoy afternoon tea in the courtyard or as evening closes in, withdraw to the drawing rooms to toast by a crackling fire.

Rates from: 👹👹👹👹
Star rating: ★★★★★
Overall rating: 👹👹👹👹

Ambience :	9.26	Cleanliness:	9.53
Value:	8.19	Facilities:	8.67
Staff:	9.26	Restaurants:	9.18
Location:	9.60	Families:	8.23

The Morgan Hotel

Fleet Street, Temple Bar, Dublin 2, Ireland
T: +353 1 6437 000 **F:** +353 1 6437 060
www.HotelClub.com/hotels/Morgan_Hotel_Dublin

The Morgan Hotel holds fort in Dublin's once forgotten, now pulsating Temple Bar district. Centrally situated, it's perfect should you wish to experience the merits of this tourist-thronged melee. It's a crisp, bijou hotel that sparkles with originality and quirky furnishings abound. The 121 rooms range from smartly dressed standard bedrooms to designer apartment suites, which are kitted out with full kitchen accoutrements. Rooms to the rear of the hotel are recommended if sound slumber is on your agenda, post-playtime. Downstairs, the bar serves up tangy mojitos and tasty tapas to a satisfied clientele while a laid-back house DJ with bongo accompaniment entertains. Respite from the urban rumble can be found early or late in an outdoor courtyard that's bedecked with an array of iron beds, dressing tables and chandeliers.

Rates from: 👹👹👹
Star rating: ★★★★
Overall rating: 👹👹👹👹

Ambience :	9.00	Cleanliness:	9.29
Value:	7.29	Facilities:	6.85
Staff:	8.50	Restaurants:	7.92
Location:	9.36	Families:	6.17

Morrison

Ormond Quay, Dublin 1, Ireland
T: +353 1 887 2400 **F:** +353 1 874 4039
www.HotelClub.com

The ancient art of *feng shui* is employed at The Morrison with calm precision and attributable to Hong Kong-born, Irish-based designer, John Rocha. Wandering through these sumptuous lodgings, aesthetically astute guests can quickly gather evidence of this long-revered Chinese practice. Feng shui translates as "air and water", both of which flow freely through the hotel. High ceilings and the waters of the River Liffey outside allude to calmness. Entering this cathedral of calm, guests leave bustling Dublin traffic at the threshold and achieve a position of perfect *qi* in no time. A calming black and white, *ying* and *yang* reception area renders a balanced first impression. Low lighting, soothing jazz tones and the hushed whispers of unhurried patrons pervade during waking hours. As day wanes the music is grooved up and the restaurant is chic-ed out with a host of hip and happening patrons just hanging. Sink into vibrant velvet chairs at Halo Restaurant; seafood lovers will be in heaven. Silk throws designed by Mr Rocha are fancily flung in each of the 138 rooms, together with umbrellas geared towards the "soft" Irish weather. Decorated in dark colours with plump pillows and magic mattresses, the superior rooms are just that. Studio rooms and suites are kitted for the future, with GHD straighteners, iPod stations and Apple Mac LCD screens. For a tech-free moment, ease into a warm bath and lull on a leather headrest. Close your eyes. Relax. You are feeling sleepy... A spell in the Morrison should harmonise your centre. Far out, man.

Rates from: 🛏🛏🛏🛏🛏
Star rating: ★★★★
Overall rating: 🪔🪔🪔🪔

Ambience :	8.54	Cleanliness:	9.23
Value:	7.86	Facilities:	7.31
Staff:	8.41	Restaurants:	8.48
Location:	9.40	Families:	6.00

Royal Marine Hotel

Marine Road, Dun Laoghaire, Dublin, Ireland
T: +353 1 230 0030 **F:** +353 1 230 0029
www.HotelClub.com

Recent visitors to Dublin will know that membership of the EU has been kind to the Irish capital. Billions of Euros thrown at the city has turned it into one of the chicest (and most expensive) in the region. This transformation from provincial backwater to world-class tourist destination made the hotel industry sit up and take stock. At least, that's what the Royal Marine did when it closed in 2004 for a 50-million Euro refurbishment. A Victorian landmark of the city (it has been a hotel since 1828) it is now bang up-to-date with all those modern necessities - plasma LCD TVs, Broadband Internet Access, power showers and Jacuzzi baths - demanded by international jet-setters. They will be following in some illustrious footsteps - Frank Sinatra and Danny Kaye can be counted amongst the Marine's historic guests, and it's safe to assume that the celebrity count will continue. But star spotting is not what you'll come here for. Or if you do you'll soon be sidetracked; first by the warm welcome from the Royal Marine's legendary staff, and then by the spacious guestrooms themselves, which are tastefully decorated, in natural tones and light woods. Big bay windows afford tremendous views across the Dun Laoghaire harbour and if this tempts you to wander further there are great coastal walks to Sandycove and Monkstown. Those of a more hedonistic bent, however, will be more than satisfied by the shopping on George Street, or by wandering over to the nearby Guinness Storehouse.

Rates from: 🐚🐚🐚🐚
Star rating: ★★★★
Overall rating: 🐚🐚🐚🐚🐚

Ambience :	10.0	Cleanliness:	10.0
Value:	10.0	Facilities:	10.0
Staff:	10.0	Restaurants:	10.0
Location:	8.00	Families:	10.0

Radisson SAS St Helen's Hotel

Stillorgan Road, Dublin 4, Ireland
T: +353 1 218 6000 **F:** +353 1 218 6010
www.HotelClub.com

Disappointingly, the hotel's 151 bedrooms are situated in a latter day extension but feather soft beds in both standard rooms and suites ensure heavenly sleep. The holy grail of St Helen's is the spectacle of immaculate terraced gardens. A pilgrimage to this princely home is a tonic for the soul.

Dating back to 1750, the serene Radisson St Helens is a real retreat. The Christian Brothers were former residents in this fine building and set the tone in days gone by. Today it's the tinkling tones of a grand piano emanating from the Ballroom lounge that dictate the mood. Glide up grand entrance steps to an ornate marble reception area before immersing in an afternoon of Victoriana in The Orangerie which dominates the south east wing. At night nibble on fresh Italian antipasti in Tallavera Restaurant which lies secreted in the cellars.

Rates from: 💰💰💰💰
Star rating: ★★★★★
Overall rating: 👐👐👐👐

Ambience :	9.03	Cleanliness:	9.49
Value:	8.24	Facilities:	8.58
Staff:	9.06	Restaurants:	9.03
Location:	8.73	Families:	8.62

The Shelbourne Dublin

27 St Stephen's Green, Dublin 2 , Ireland
T: +353 1 663 4500 **F:** +353 1 661 6006
www.HotelClub.com/hotels/The_Shelbourne_Hotel_Dublin

Hungry mongers head to the Saddle Bar for thoroughbred fodder. Enjoy lip-smacking bivalves at the Oyster Bar or fill up on delectable *petit fours* ensconced within overstuffed sofas at the Lord Mayor's Lounge. Whatever you do, get on your glad rags, glitz it up and get mingling at this elegant but ritzy Irish institution.

All that glitters is gold in the glamorous Shelbourne. The £90 million renovation of this magnificent Irish jewel was worth every shining penny. This history-steeped hotel played a leading role in the theatre of contemporary Irish history, when the Irish Constitution was signed within its curtilage. Feel like a crown royal in any of its 265 regal rooms, all of which are plush with deluxe furnishings. Budget willing, opt for a view (overlooking pretty St Stephen's Green). Huddle over a deal in the diminutive Horseshoe Bar or enjoy stylish refreshments with Dublin's beautiful people at No. 27 Bar.

Rates from: 💰💰💰💰💰
Star rating: ★★★★★
Overall rating: 👐👐👐👐

Ambience :	9.21	Cleanliness:	9.45
Value:	8.12	Facilities:	7.83
Staff:	8.93	Restaurants:	9.03
Location:	9.76	Families:	8.31

Temple Bar Hotel

Fleet Street, Temple Bar, Dublin 2, Ireland
T: +353 1 677 3333 **F:** +353 1 677 3088
www.HotelClub.com

Although traditionally a popular stomping ground for veil-toting hen party celebrants, the unassuming Temple Bar Hotel has grabbed the stag by the horns and is now attempting to amplify its class of clientele, embracing families and business people alike. Staff are eager to underscore the hotel's central location and virtually clamber towards guests with recommendations for The Fair City - with tips that stretch beyond a stout-fuelled stay. After a hard day's pavement pounding, meet fellow guests in the hotel's snug Rendezvous Bar. Far from conservative, The Terrace restaurant, serves up hearty, get-your-day-started full Irish breakfasts in the hotel's conservatory. A table d'hôte menu tenders a tasty variety of options. The hotel's straightforward 129 rooms are functional but surprisingly spacious, with the flexibility to fit family groups. The wheels of commerce need not stop for guests lodging in the hotel's executive suites. With Wi-Fi and full coffee making facilities, business travellers can rest assured of staying on top of things. Rooms are laid out on a grid, so (as with all hotels in this busy Dublin area), guests with aspirations of sound sleep are advised to book interior facing bedrooms overlooking the conservatory. Next door, perennially pulsating Buskers Bar has been revamped with low lighting and artful additions and Boomerangs nightclub has a clientele that just keeps on coming back. Further plans are afoot to develop an outdoor, terraced beer garden. Clearly the Temple Bar Hotel has its finger on the socialising scene in Dublin. Does one hear clucks of approval?

Rates from: 🏠🏠🏠
Star rating: ★ ★ ★
Overall rating: 🎫🎫🎫🎫

Ambience :	8.00	Cleanliness:	8.13
Value:	7.73	Facilities:	7.12
Staff:	8.07	Restaurants:	7.67
Location:	9.47	Families:	8.00

Trinity Capital Hotel

Pearse Street, Dublin 2, Ireland
T: +353 1 6481 000 **F:** +353 1 6481 010
www.HotelClub.com/hotels/Trinity_Capital_Hotel_Dublin

From the people who brought Dublin its blingiest bars, the Trinity Capital Hotel has been designed to bring out the child within. Housed in what was once a Georgian residence, nothing is subtle in these decadently dressed lodgings. The proprietors have splashed its traditionally shaped rooms with sassy attitude, bringing them to life with vibrant colour schemes. Glittering oily-purple mosaics clash wonderfully with pink and purple walls in a fusion of North African souk sensuality and wild *Alice in Wonderland* furniture wares. The 158 rooms range from the standard to the sublime, but its "bazaar" elements work surprisingly well. The oval mini-suite, replete with Jacuzzi, is sure to leave pampered guests purring with pleasure. Alas, the exotically named Café Cairo serves up solely European cuisine, but this more normal nosh is still top notch. Hunt down a nook or cranny in the Café, or sit outside on the terrace and watch Dublin drift by. Reportedly, there are plans to further extend the hotel into the adjacent once booming (now defunct) Fireworks nightclub. The heating levels in the hotel are continuously set at a passionate high, perhaps taking the theme of the North African experience too far. But just remember, it's a jungle of a city, so to snare a lion's share of sleep, be sure to book a room away far from the fire station next door. The hotel's theme is out of this world and when the sun has set, this hotel twinkles, ensuring its guests sparkle back.

Rates from: 🛏🛏🛏🛏🛏
Star rating: ★ ★ ★
Overall rating: 👍👍👍👍

Ambience :	8.87	Cleanliness:	9.27
Value:	8.60	Facilities:	7.90
Staff:	9.13	Restaurants:	8.50
Location:	9.40	Families:	9.56

Westbury Hotel

Grafton Street, Dublin 2, Ireland
T: +353 1 679 1122 **F**: +353 1 679 7078
www.HotelClub.com/hotels/Westbury_Hotel_Dublin

Situated just off the much-touted retail wonderland of Grafton Street, The Westbury Hotel is the distinguished gentleman of Dublin hotels, and much admired for it. Displaying a JR Ewing elegance, its mirrored foyer drips with crystal chandeliers and a sweeping marble staircase invites guests to venture further into its swanky heart. The Terrace Lounge affords a pleasing view of Grafton Street. It's there that pots of steaming tea and delicate *petit fours* teetering on tiered silver trays are wolfed by weary shoppers from far and wide; the Westbury Afternoon Tea is a Dublin institution. If you prefer your tea "Long Island and iced", alight on olive green couches and nibble on colour-coordinated complimentary snacks before ordering evening cocktails in the Orient-oriented Mandarin Bar. Wooden panels line the corridors to the Sandbank Bistro, which serves comfortingly simple victuals while the Russell Room pampers with altogether more serious sustenance. Of the 205 rooms, the recently refurbished, cosy Classic rooms attempt a modern twist with Irish furnishings. The Westbury's luxurious lodgings culminate in the Presidential Suite where celebs like Britney Spears snooze under duck down duvets, soothe their shopped-out bodies in a private sauna or work off guilty pleasures in a mini gym. Allow yourself a deserved wallow in Dublin luxury in the Westbury. Staff reserve old-world manners for all guests, no matter what their Hello! status, and are superbly attentive and polite. A word of warning - leave the "Who Shot JR?" T-shirts and baseball caps at home, as the tuxedoed doorman may not approve.

Rates from: 💰💰💰
Star rating: ★★★★★
Overall rating: 📷📷📷📷

Ambience :	9.26	Cleanliness:	9.45
Value:	7.80	Facilities:	8.29
Staff:	9.17	Restaurants:	8.96
Location:	9.82	Families:	8.41

The Westin Dublin

College Green, Westmoreland Street, Dublin 2, Ireland
T: +353 1 645 1000 **F:** +353 1 645 1234
www.HotelClub.com/hotels/Westin_Hotel_Dublin

The exceedingly good Westin reassures a well-heeled clientele, rich with references to its former life as a bank. By all accounts, The Teller and Shilling Rooms are plush and elegant, with fabulous fixed assets including chandeliers and glistening gold ceilings. Moneyed leather and polished marble are the chosen materials in cappuccino cream tones. Place your standing order at the Mint Bar or the Atrium; cocktails are commendable, but watch your bottom line. The bank's former treasury, the Mint Bar, is renowned in Dublin for its Friday night salsa. Arched ceilings and low lighting make for a cavern reminiscent of Beatlemania. Make believe you're sitting outdoors amongst palm trees, mid-November in the Atrium, a faux-French glass-covered courtyard. Of the 163 stylish rooms, the hotel's traditional guest rooms overlook this central oasis, while deluxe external counterparts peer over altogether more original Dublin architecture. The split-level College Penthouse has a balconied view over Trinity College and a studiously sumptuous interior. Market trackers tap away into the late hours in the Westin Guest Office where modern office facilities supplement restful bedroom environs. Hop into the Westin's Heavenly Bed, a specially designed cloud-soft bed perfect for angelic sleep. The Exchange restaurant puts on a sterling performance with its contemporary menu. But let's get down to brass tax, er, tacks; the Sunday Jazz Brunch sessions at the Westin are a great source of sax in city. An affable staff adds to each experience at this elegant hotel; guests can bank on added interest during a stay at the Westin.

Rates from: 🛏🛏🛏🛏🛏
Star rating: ★★★★★
Overall rating: 🐾🐾🐾🐾

Ambience :	9.00	Cleanliness:	9.45
Value:	8.26	Facilities:	8.28
Staff:	9.00	Restaurants:	8.78
Location:	9.64	Families:	8.25

Castle Durrow

Castle Durrow, Durrow, Co. Laois, Ireland
T: +353 57 873 6555 **F**: +353 57 873 6559
www.HotelClub.com

The land-owning class that was to become known as the Anglo-Irish aristocracy wanted their dwellings to be as different from the traditional farmhouse-type buildings of their predecessors as possible. Castle Durrow, built in 1715 for Colonel William Flower (later Lord Ashbrook), is regarded as one of the finest and best-preserved examples of this "new" country-house style.

Restaurateurs Peter and Shelly Stokes, who turned it into a luxury

hotel in 1998, have managed to incorporate all the modern trappings of today's hospitality industry into this lovingly restored historic setting without impinging one iota on its original 18th-century elegance. From the marbled reception area, filled with the aroma of fresh-cut flowers, to the high-ceilinged bedrooms - 24 of them, each different - Castle Durrow exudes grace, sophistication and tranquillity.

The Restaurant (candle-lit in the evening) serves local produce, with herbs and vegetables from the hotel's own kitchen garden, and gourmets rave about the freshly caught fish from the three local rivers and the wild venison. (A tip - try a sliver of Lavistown cheese from Kilkenny.) During the day, there is a splendid view over the formal gardens, where you may see an elegiac game of boules or croquet being conducted.

More energetic activities can be arranged with a few days' notice and there is an all-weather tennis court. But a game of snooker in the billiards room while the wife/girlfriend is being attended to in the Powder Box Beauty Salon usually suffices. Popular for weddings, these celebrations are held in a separate wing, so no need to worry about any extraneous noises.

Rates from: 🐚🐚
Star rating: ★ ★ ★ ★
Overall rating: 🐚🐚🐚🐚 ½

Ambience :	9.54	Cleanliness:	9.31
Value:	8.77	Facilities:	8.35
Staff:	9.69	Restaurants:	9.08
Location:	8.92	Families:	9.33

Marriott Johnstown House Hotel & Spa

Enfield, Co Meath, Ireland
T: +353 46 954 0000 **F:** +353 46 954 0029
www.HotelClub.com/hotels/Marriott_Johnstown_House_Enfield_Hotel

Although it is centred around a magnificent Georgian manor house, this 126-room Marriott property set in nearly 50 hectares of parkland is a thoroughly modern hotel and until recently it served mainly as an excellent journey-breaker for holidaymakers travelling to and from Dublin (about an hour away), being situated just off the motorway.

All that changed with the unveiling of a spa that is rated by cognescenti as among the best in the business and now attracts dedicated body worshippers in droves. From facials to foot-baths, manicures to massage, this has the lot (including its own restaurant). And there is a 20-metre pool plus a kiddies' pool, a hot tub, Jacuzzi and whirlpool.

The property's rooms are spacious and equipped with almost everything you could possibly need, luxurious bedding being a USP (and under-floor heating in the bathrooms). It specialises in corporate and conference business and there

is a dedicated corporate activity centre actually on site.

There are three restaurants - the Pavilion (elegant casual), the Atrium Brasserie (coffe-shop) and the Coach House Bar (traditional Irish). While waiting for dinner, note the ceiling in the drawing-room - it's by the Francini brothers, renowned for their plasterwork to the gentry.

Although it's a bit isolated for non-drivers (650 free parking spaces, by the way), there are plenty of attractions within easy car (or taxi) access - fishing,

riding, tennis and golf (the hotel has its own simulator); while ankle-biters can be transported to a cinema/bowling alley or a marvellous maze with a pets' corner.

Rates from: 🛏🛏
Star rating: ★★★★
Overall rating: 👍👍👍👍

Ambience :	8.79	Cleanliness:	9.21
Value:	8.64	Facilities:	8.60
Staff:	9.21	Restaurants:	8.50
Location:	8.07	Families:	8.27

Monart Destination Spa

Monart, The Still, Enniscorthy, Co Wexford, Ireland
T: +353 53 923 8999 F: +353 53 923 0944
www.HotelClub.com

If the mere mention of "family friendly" makes you shiver, the Monart's adults-only policy should warm the cockles of your heart. And quite a few other parts of your body as well, as this is arguably one of the swishest spas in the whole of Ireland.

Rather than being something of an afterthought tacked onto an existing hotel, the spa is at the centre of Monart's operations, its *raison d'etre* and trump card.

It's equally adaptable for corporate groups trying out a novel method of brainstorming (though this is not something that actually appears on the treatment menu), or couples simply wanting to kick back and let somebody else do the back rubs rather than simply take it in turns.

While you can pop by for the day, this would entail missing out on staying in one of the 68 luxurious guestrooms. Two suites are in the 18th century Monart House, while the rest are in a separate block with a balcony or terrace, 300-thread-count Egyptian cotton sheets and goose down duvets.

A huge array of options awaits in the spa, from the salt grotto to the outdoor Swedish log sauna with - get this - an ice bucket shower, plus a mud chamber and a 55-square-metre natural spring water hydrotherapy pool. Spa-ing has never been so luxurious or for that matter - so inspirational.

Two restaurants - a fine-diner and a spa café - keeps the culinary side of things modern and healthy (with the occasional sidetrack to wickedness).

An hour or so's drive from Dublin, the Monart is somewhere you simply can't pass by.

Rates from: 💰💰💰💰💰
Star rating: ★★★★★
Overall rating: 🌸🌸🌸🌸

Ambience :	9.29	Cleanliness:	9.86
Value:	9.07	Facilities:	7.73
Staff:	9.43	Restaurants:	9.43
Location:	8.71	Families:	4.60

Falls Hotel Spa Resort

Ennistymon, Co. Clare, Ireland
T: +353 65 707 1004 **F:** +353 65 707 1367
www.HotelClub.com/hotels/Falls_Hotel_Ennistymon

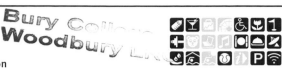

Dylan Thomas, in his cups (inevitably), once said: "Somebody's boring me, I think it's me". It was a great line, from one of the 20th century's greatest poets.

And here, beside the tumbling waters of the River Inagh - as opposed to Under Milk Wood - the man is commemorated in the Dylan Thomas bar, as his wife, Caitlin, lived in the Manor House here once upon a time.

No trace of boredom in the bar or indeed anywhere else in this splendid resort: year-round it's a hive of activity, hosting weddings, conferences and straightforward families and couples looking to enjoy themselves on holiday.

The nine duplex apartments are the obvious choice for parents with youngsters in tow; sleeping as many as seven, they include a kitchen with washer/dryer and access to the Aqua Fitness Club. Smaller parties will be happily accommodated in the resort's 140 regular bedrooms.

One of the Falls' prime attractions is its River Spa, rightly taking its cue from the adjacent waterway. Some might comment that a Turkish soap scrub (for example) being dispensed in such a westerly part of Ireland is just one sign of the country's increasing sophistication. Others would simply remark it's pure bliss, ditto the trio of bathing ceremonies (wasted on just one person).

Two other very good reasons to come here are the restaurants. An Teach Mor is located in the original Georgian part of the resort, open every weekend but only on summer weekdays; Cascades provides not simply top notch food but views of the river as well.

Rates from: 🐚
Star rating: ★★★
Overall rating: 🐚🐚🐚 ½

Ambience :	9.46	Cleanliness:	9.31
Value:	9.08	Facilities:	8.50
Staff:	9.23	Restaurants:	9.23
Location:	9.67	Families:	9.44

Connemara Coast Hotel

Furbo, Galway, Ireland
T: +353 91 592 108 **F:** +353 91 592 065
www.HotelClub.com/hotels/Connemara_Coast_Hotel_Galway

The yellow low-rise Connemara Coast Hotel has taken some of the features of a tropical resort and adapted them to the Irish climate, resulting in a very warm atmosphere - both literally and figuratively. Large rugs heat up the cool white marble lobby floors, and turf-burning fires and a sun-trap balcony do the trick in the Presidential suite. Décor in all 115 rooms, where brown, beige and white are the predominant colours, is classic. Start or finish the day in the Canadian hot tub facing the Galway Bay. Gaelic is spoken fluently in this region so for an initial lesson head to the Sin Sceal Eile (So Long) pub where traditional music is played on selected evenings. It might be that all too quickly it's time to reluctantly bring your newfound linguistic skills into play.

Rates from: 🐻🐻
Star rating: ★★★★
Overall rating: 🐾🐾🐾

Ambience :	8.60	Cleanliness:	9.10
Value:	8.15	Facilities:	8.21
Staff:	8.75	Restaurants:	8.50
Location:	9.00	Families:	8.74

The Ardilaun

Taylors Hill, Galway, Ireland
T: +353 91 521 433 **F:** +353 91 521 546
www.HotelClub.com/hotels/Ardilaun_Hotel_Galway

The Ardilaun house hotel and gate lodge - built by Lady Gregory's family in the 1840s, subsequently owned by Patrick Boland of the toothsome biscuit family, and run since 1962 with dedication to tradition, hospitality and personal attention to detail by the Ryan family - sits amongst long-established flower beds and trees. In fact the garden is eye candy from every window in the hotel. Deep-pile carpets, rich wood furnishings and mirrors; sitting-room tables surrounded by low-backed, high-backed and sink-in-comfy chairs in a huge reception lounge as well as in the Blazers Bar; and enough white linen accessories to sail a ship, confirm the classic luxury. With sneak views of Galway Bay, recent extensions bring the number of ensuite bedrooms to 125 whilst the Leisure Centre boasts an 18-metre Grecian-style swimming pool.

Rates from: 🐻🐻🐻
Star rating: ★★★★
Overall rating: 🐾🐾🐾🐾 ½

Ambience :	9.12	Cleanliness:	9.53
Value:	8.88	Facilities:	8.85
Staff:	9.24	Restaurants:	9.12
Location:	9.00	Families:	8.71

Days Hotel Galway

Dublin Road, Galway City East, Ireland
T: +353 91 381 200 **F:** +353 91 753 187
www.HotelClub.com/hotels/Days_Hotel_Galway

warm service, the Days Hotel offers its recently renovated Leisure Centre and Friendly Fellows Children's Club. It's a modern, bright and contemporary hotel that's best summed up by the free and easy atmosphere in Bar Solo, which moves into top gear with live music most weekends. Slainte!

While you're waltzing down the long tiled reception hall to book into one of the 311 en-suite bedrooms - or 60 self-catering apartments with separate living rooms - you can peep through oblong wood-lined gaps in the wall to the chocolate brown and earthy-

hued décor of Rueben's Restaurant. Wide corridors and lots of empty spaces in the public areas leading to the bedrooms and six conference rooms create a feeling of elegance and peace. Speaking of peace, and in line with their renowned reputation for

Rates from: 🛏🛏🛏🛏🛏
Star rating: ★★★
Overall rating: 🐾🐾🐾🐾 ½

Ambience :	8.60	Cleanliness:	9.53
Value:	9.47	Facilities:	9.24
Staff:	9.27	Restaurants:	8.73
Location:	8.33	Families:	9.40

The g hotel

Wellpark, Co. Galway, Ireland
T: +353 91 865 200 **F:** +353 91 865 203
www.HotelClub.com/hotels/The_G_Hotel

shuffling from sensational treatments at the ESPA to shell-cushioned beds and Connemara marble-tiled bathrooms. Many of the 101 en-suite bedrooms, designed as marine havens of sensual oyster coloured peace, look out over Lough Atalia as it meets Galway Bay. A really stunning property!

Tucked surprisingly into an edge-of-town business centre the g hotel flashes quirky, chic and outright flamboyant allusions of Hollywood grandeur by renowned Galway-born designer Philip Treacy. In a stately mood of serious glamour, take your tea in the silvery Grand Salon. Later, spend a

dizzy hour in the zany Pink Salon with its bull's eye carpet before relaxing in soothing comfort in the Blue Lounge. Mirrors and thousands of Swarovski crystals encased in tables and the bar counter are subtly lit to inspire sophisticated evenings. Privacy is ensured for sleepy-eyed slipper-

Rates from: 🛏🛏🛏🛏🛏
Star rating: n/a
Overall rating: 🐾🐾🐾🐾

Ambience :	9.31	Cleanliness:	9.82
Value:	7.58	Facilities:	8.91
Staff:	9.07	Restaurants:	9.19
Location:	8.30	Families:	6.83

Huntsman Inn

164 College Road, Galway, Ireland
T: +353 91 562 849 **F:** +353 91 561 985
www.HotelClub.com

The Huntsman Inn is downright classy. It's sleek and elegant with a naughty blood red carpet leading to the rooms. The thick pile teases your mind - you'd swear that carpet winks at you as you walk through pools of warm light passing heavy and stylish walnut doors. The walnut touch continues in the floors and furniture of the rooms where a shower and basin stand fit for royalty. Upholstery in velvety charcoal grey set against coffee and cream heavy drape curtains with a

camel-coloured carpet and throw on the bed works in the contemporary setting like you'd never believe.

In the dozen rooms (which comprise three suites with a bath, double bed and sofa-beds for families; one en suite twin room; and eight en suite double rooms) guests can enjoy breakfast almost until lunchtime in one of the three lounge and bar areas downstairs. Featuring organic porridge with local honey, brown sugar and

pouring cream, freshly baked croissants and scones, not to mention The Full Irish, breakfast is without any shred of a doubt one of the highlights of the day. Temptation beckons and it's likely you'll need that 15-minute walk along the banks of Lough Atalia, past the docks and into the centre of Galway.

Overlooking the Lough, an eight-seater conference room is presentation-friendly and Wi-Fi is available in all rooms including the lounge/bar area.

As a final fillip, owners Stephen and Breda Francis take delight in completely refurbishing the Inn every few years keeping it personal yet cutting-edge.

Rates from: 🐚🐚
Star rating: ★★★
Overall rating: 🐚🐚🐚🐚

Ambience :	8.21	Cleanliness:	9.00
Value:	9.50	Facilities:	7.92
Staff:	8.93	Restaurants:	8.08
Location:	9.93	Families:	8.36

Jurys Inn Galway
Quay Street, Galway, Ireland
T: +353 91 566 444 **F:** +353 91 568 415
www.HotelClub.com/hotels/Jurys_Inn_Galway

done with the view and have enjoyed the craic in the bar there's no need to worry about drink driving laws as you step out the front door, turn left and weave into the shops until it's time to collapse into the nearest pub... to enjoy more craic and the live, often traditional, music that's always to be found nearby.

Add two sides water, one side shopping, a beer garden, parking on the premises, shake and enjoy. Around half the 130 ensuite bedrooms look out over the River Corrib as it swishes past ancient buildings; the other half look out to where the river meets the sea at the Claddagh. And whichever part you're looking at you'll have a fine view of Europe's largest flock of Mute Swans. When you're

Rates from: 🐚🐚
Star rating: ★★★
Overall rating: 🐚🐚🐚

Ambience :	8.21	Cleanliness:	9.00
Value:	9.50	Facilities:	7.92
Staff:	8.93	Restaurants:	8.08
Location:	9.93	Families:	8.36

Park House Hotel
Foster Street, Eyre Square, Galway, Ireland
T:+353 91 564 924 **F:** +353 91 569 219
www.HotelClub.com/hotels/Park_House_Hotel_Galway

only lacking the slippers and bathrobe, why move? Sink into one of the deep-cushioned couches surrounded by antiques and collectors' items sitting rich and assured next to you, knowing they make you feel good... and stay there. Your car would already have been valet-parked in one of the 48 bays anyway.

It's temptingly irrelevant that the Park House Hotel is so central to the city of Galway... once you're in there you don't really want to venture out. Why would you? With staff willing to pamper to your needs; an excellent 130-cover restaurant with plush private booths; two equally inviting bars; seven Junior Suites with exclusive 24-hour room service plus all the extra bits including mini bar; 26 Deluxe Suites with almost the same treats; and 51 Superior Suites

Rates from: 🐚🐚
Star rating: ★★★★
Overall rating: 🐚🐚🐚 ½

Ambience :	9.12	Cleanliness:	9.66
Value:	8.79	Facilities:	7.89
Staff:	9.55	Restaurants:	9.41
Location:	9.79	Families:	8.85

Radisson SAS Hotel & Spa, Galway

Lough Atalia Road, Galway, Ireland
T: +353 91 538 300   **F:** +353 91 538 380
www.HotelClub.com/hotels/Radisson_SAS_Hotel_Galway

Sumptuous. *Sum...ptu...ous.* Close your eyes, slowly roll your tongue around the sounds of the word and draw out all the sensuality. That's Level Five and the executive guest rooms where you can revel in an *affaire passionnée* with Galway's Radisson SAS Hotel and Spa. Discreet access leads to the hedonistic swimming pool and softly-lit gym for a gentle or punishing work-out to prepare your body for the delights of what lies a floor below in the chocolatey Spirit One Spa... the Hamman Turkish Bath, Rock Sauna, Aroma Grotto or a laze on the sand in the Beach Room for a full day while the rain pounds down outside.

General Manager Tom Flanagan, a Galway man born and bred, leads his team with solid hotel experience from years spent in Copenhagen, Beijing, Bahrain and Hamburg. The can't-not-do philosophy starts at the top and really does filter down with tremendous impact to guests through Front Office Manager

Micheal Stapleton; the exuberant Hans Prins, the executive chef who has worked in five-star hotels in Germany and Dubai and brought new flavours and menus to the Marinas Restaurant; Barcelona-

born Ferran Bufau, Operations Manager *extraordinaire* who has been with the hotel since its birth in 2001; and the vivacious Karen Jones, Director of Sales and Marketing.

"Live passionately, Live well" advises the classy white welcome card embossed with the hotel logo, continuing German Interior designer Henrik Frischgesel's passion for art to complement the sassy and light contemporary décor. Original paintings by Galway-based and renowned Irish artists hang in happy company with quirky sculptures, their diversity handled with ease in the soaring light and airy lobby, that's not at all dwarfed by the big palm trees and pots of tall leafy bamboo.

Two penthouse suites together with the 16 executive guest rooms on Level Five, 243 standard en-suite rooms and 21 one- and two-bedroom apartments tally up to a grand 282 spacious rooms on offer. And the apartments really are quite something. Thick pile carpets, a mini-business corner, stylish and comfortable décor including plenty of mirrors, and so much more than a kitchenette with all the mod-cons

well-hidden but available. You want more? Well, twice-weekly servicing is included as is breakfast every morning... and the Marinas restaurant has the facility for a separate children's dining area where, in times of high people-traffic, offspring are fed and entertained.

And what would a Radisson SAS Hotel be without fully-equipped conference and business facilities? Galway's hotel has 13 meeting rooms peacefully tucked beside the huge three-part Ballroom; and for the lone business guest a small room off the reception area offers computers and a printer.

City centre location, wide views

over Lough Atalia and Galway Bay, with Galway's social butterflies spicing up the night beside the weekend cocktail pianist in the Veranda Bar may be great but it's really all about service, consistency, service, great rooms, service, well-planned facilities and ... well, service!

Rates from: 🐚🐚🐚
Star rating: ★ ★ ★ ★
Overall rating: 🐚🐚🐚🐚

Ambience :	8.79	Cleanliness:	9.38
Value:	8.29	Facilities:	8.87
Staff:	8.76	Restaurants:	8.77
Location:	9.52	Families:	8.79

Kenmare Bay Hotel & Resort

Sneem Road, Kenmare, Co. Kerry, Ireland
T: +353 64 41300 **F:** +353 64 41749
www.HotelClub.com/hotels/Kenmare_Bay_Hotel

When you have views as magnificent as those in Kenmore Bay you want big windows. So, welcome to the Kenmare Bay Hotel & Resort, a bright, 128-room hotel that's just a three-minute stroll from quaint Kenmore Bay town centre. An extensive refurbishment in 2006 put the hotel firmly in the category of those establishments that call themselves "boutique", though the ambience here is decidedly contemporary and blissfully casual. The exterior may look a little club-house, but once inside cool lines, and sleek fittings will quickly dazzle you. White is the predominant colour in the lobby lending it an air of cleanliness that could almost be considered clinical, were it not for the obvious warmth of the staff. Then you'll notice how happy the other guests appear to be. Perhaps they have just returned from splashing about in the Health Club's 20-metre swimming pool. Or perhaps they've been taking a stroll through the extensive grounds where homebred peacocks amble. One of these beasts has given the hotel restaurant, where locally sourced beef and lamb are served, its name; Jasper may have passed on to pastures new, but his descendants continue to prove a favourite eccentricity.

Perhaps, though, the real reason for the universal smiles is the surrounding scenery; the magical mountains that shadow the Killarney National Park, the rugged beauty of the Ring of Beara, and the justly famous coastline of the Iveragh peninsula, capped off by Kerry's first Heritage Town, Kenmare Bay itself.

Rates from: 𝔅 𝔅 𝔅
Star rating: ★ ★ ★
Overall rating: **Editors' Pick**

Ambience :	n/a	Cleanliness:	n/a
Value:	n/a	Facilities:	n/a
Staff:	n/a	Restaurants:	n/a
Location:	n/a	Families:	n/a

Park Hotel Kenmare

Kenmare, Co. Kerry, Ireland
T: +353 64 41200 **F:** +353 64 41402
www.HotelClub.com

Jolly nice though in-room plasma screens and DVD players may be, there's more of a thrill sitting down in a pukka movie theatre to watch a favourite flick. If you agree with this, then park yourself in this hotel's 12-seater private cinema (The Reel Room) and call "roll 'em".

There's lots more entertainment here of a non-celluloid variety. An 18-hole golf course sits right next door straggling along the shores of Kenmare Bay, and there are five more within easy driving distance.

And there are fewer better ways to conclude a day on the links than slipping into the infinity Jacuzzi bubbling away beside the woods at the Park's spa; while Sanskrit is the usual terminology of choice for such havens, this one's called Samas, a Gaelic word for indulgence of the senses.

On which subject, the hotel's restaurant more than fits the bill, leaning towards local seafood but also with Kerry lamb, beef, pork and duck, dishes that go even

better with the views over the terraced gardens to the mountains across the bay. And whiskey aficionados will more than appreciate the bar's Irish and Scottish single malts.

The hotel, built towards the end of Queen Victoria's reign, comprises just 46 spacious bedrooms, decorated with antiques and objets d'art, and luxuriating in Floris Toiletries, De Witte Lietare towelling and Rivolta Carmignani linen.

Happy to report, there are no meeting or banqueting facilities here - this is a hotel pure and simple, and somewhere to relax well away from the business side of life.

Rates from: 🐚🐚🐚
Star rating: ★★★★★
Overall rating: 🐚🐚🐚🐚

Ambience :	9.52	Cleanliness:	9.65
Value:	8.13	Facilities:	8.14
Staff:	8.89	Restaurants:	9.13
Location:	9.57	Families:	7.90

Sheen Falls Lodge

Kenmare, Co. Kerry, Ireland
T: +353 64 41600 **F**: +353 64 41386
www.HotelClub.com

They don't make 'em like they used to... highly admirable though modern computer-aided auto design may be, there's nothing quite like buzzing through the countryside in a vintage car. The vehicle of choice at this particular establishment is a 1936 Buick Roadmaster (superlative nomenclature!) which - complete with a champagne picnic hamper - makes for a memorable day's touring around the Ring of Kerry.

From classic car to classic (privately owned) hotel. Dating from the 1600s, Sheen Falls (once the home of the Marquis of Lansdowne) provides 66 rooms and rather more in the way of villas which can sleep up to eight, if you are making a party of it. And this is certainly somewhere to enjoy in company - deer and wildlife roam freely on the estate, there are stupendous views of the McGuillicuddy Reeks mountain range, and the sound of cascading waterfalls is never far away.

Like all good country houses, Sheen Falls has a billiard room; the library - a rare beast among hotels nowadays - contains 1,500 volumes; and there's a delightful garden planted in the 19th century in anticipation of a visit by Queen Victoria. Excellent angling is available on a variety of lakes and rivers, in particular the Sheen which is back in action after a year's closure to allow the stock to be replenished.

Excellent dining awaits in both La Cascade and the more informal Oscar's Bistro, and - rounding this whole marvellous property off - there's also a health and fitness spa for those who prefer to get their exercise indoors.

Rates from: 🛏🛏🛏🛏
Star rating: ★ ★ ★ ★ ★
Overall rating: 🐧🐧🐧🐧 ½

Ambience :	9.48	Cleanliness:	9.87
Value:	7.70	Facilities:	8.72
Staff:	9.13	Restaurants:	9.13
Location:	9.26	Families:	8.53

Kilkenny Ormonde Hotel

Ormonde Street, Kilkenny, Ireland
T: +353 56 772 3900 **F:** +353 56 772 3977
www.HotelClub.com/hotels/Kilkenny_Ormonde_Hotel

A tad rarely for an Irish hotel, the Kilkenny Ormonde is not in a castle. But it is overshadowed by one - physically rather than metaphorically, one should hasten to add.

Slap in the centre of town, the Ormonde's array of 118 rooms varies from regular deluxe to a quintet of junior suites to a presidential suite, which is centred around a spacious bedroom and Molton Brown'd bathroom with a sitting room, kitchenette and balcony.

Not that you'd want to dally to long wherever you're putting up for the night. The hotel has a host of places to eat and party;

Fredricks is fine dining, and a two-storey high wall of glass imparts a fine fresh ambience to the Ormonde Lounge; you could invite 500 of your closest friends for a gala dinner in the Kings Ballroom, or tuck in rather less formally at Earls Bistro. Round things off by kicking up your heels in The Venue, which is the venue for bands tributing the likes of U2 and The Wolftones.

Directly across from the hotel stands the Ormonde Leisure Club, championing a 21-metre deck level pool, Jacuzzi, steam room and sauna as well as a zinging fitness centre and aerobics studio. A smaller pool

caters to children, and there's also a crèche for those who have yet to gain their water wings.

This is a modern, friendly and very adaptable property, equally suited to families and executives, and helped enormously by its location at the very heart of Kilkenny.

Rates from: 🛏🛏🛏🛏🛏
Star rating: ★★★★
Overall rating: 👍👍👍👍

Ambience :	8.52	Cleanliness:	9.19
Value:	8.39	Facilities:	8.65
Staff:	8.94	Restaurants:	8.66
Location:	9.65	Families:	8.74

Aghadoe Heights Hotel

Lakes of Killarney, Co. Kerry, Ireland
T: +353 64 31766 **F:** +353 64 31345
www.HotelClub.com/hotels/Aghadoe_Heights_Hotel_Killarney

A state-of-the-art spa, lots of nearby golf, a stunning rural backdrop and you can't go wrong in the hospitality industry in Ireland these days, even if your hotel has no historic associations or olde worlde charm. This newish 74-room property on a hill overlooking the lakes of Killarney and the Kerry mountains is a favourite with footballers' WAGs and you can see why.

The Penthouse Suite is as opulent as they come - silk-lined walls, two kitchens (one for the butler), its own cinema screen, a dining table that seats 20, a bar with draught beer on tap, a hot tub on the terrace and no fewer than six loos. What pampered Premiership pet wouldn't be happy with that, especially if she'd just come from the Aveda Spa, where all kinds of exotic treatments are available, including a Precious Stone Cabinet, "empowered" by a giant amythest crystal?

A makeover is just what the well-known Frederick's Restaurant has undergone, being transformed into the Lake Room, divided by attractive panels into a series of private dining areas. And in the middle, a glass-walled wine "cellar" for you to pick your own poison. A pianist plays in the evenings. Lighter meals, and drinks, can be taken in the Heights Bar and Lounge.

Apart from the pool and the gym, a sauna and a solarium, there is not a great deal to do apart from exploring the lovely grounds or fishing the lake, but hey, who needs distractions when stretched out a heated lounger gazing at one of the world's great views?

Rates from: 💰💰💰
Star rating: ★★★★★
Overall rating: 🐾🐾🐾🐾 ½

Ambience :	9.20	Cleanliness:	9.80
Value:	8.60	Facilities:	9.10
Staff:	9.40	Restaurants:	9.40
Location:	10.0	Families:	8.75

The Brehon

Muckrass Rd, Killarney, Co. Kerry, Ireland
T: +353 64 30700 **F:** +353 64 30701
www.HotelClub.com/hotels/Brehon_Hotel_Killarney

For a thrilling taste of the exotic East, come to ... Killarney. The Brehon, a relatively new hotel (opened 2004) in the rolling green countryside of Ireland's Deep South, boasts Europe's first Angsana Spa, launched in Phuket, Thailand in 1999 and now one of the world's most sought-after body-and-soul restorers, with outlets in Australia, India and Indonesia.

Its tropical scents and the tender touch of its Thai masseuses is a major lure for this 125-room property, which has built up a solid fan base on the back of its luxurious rooms, its unbeatable views - watch the deer nibbling the grass in Killarney National Park

from your bedroom window - and its haute-cuisine restaurant (very popular with the locals).

All hotels everywhere lay claim to great service, but this place really does seem to have found the magic formula. It's the little touches that stick in the memory - such as leaving a book of Irish bedtime stories alongside the chocolates on your pillow when the bed is turned down for the night, or finding your room cleaned and tidied by the time you come back from breakfast.

Another innovation that marks the Brehon out from the crowd is the series of special-interest breaks it organises every Spring and

Autumn. These range from bridge, photography and pottery to gardening, cooking and just plain pampering. There's a pool and a steamroom and a sauna, of course, and invigorating country rambles (you can hire bikes if you prefer). But oh, that spa.

Rates from: 🐚🐚🐚
Star rating: ★★★★
Overall rating: 🐚🐚🐚🐚 ½

Ambience :	9.14	Cleanliness:	9.64
Value:	8.45	Facilities:	9.09
Staff:	8.90	Restaurants:	8.98
Location:	8.86	Families:	8.64

Gleneagle Hotel & Apartments, Killarney

Muckross Road, Killarney, Co. Kerry, Ireland
T: +353 64 36000 **F:** +353 64 32646
www.HotelClub.com

The Gleneagle Hotel & Apartments is synonymous with entertainment in Killarney. The ballroom, which can hold 600, is said to be the biggest entertainment venue outside Dublin. Many a cabaret show is held here during the summer months. In O'D's, the 50- year-old hotel's night club, guests can twist and shake to live rock'n roll every Friday and Saturday. If moving your feet to the rhythm of the wild outdoors is more entertaining, try the hotel's 18-hole Pitch and Putt course, or any of the 20 golf courses around Killarney for that matter. Afterwards, take those tired feet to one of the 250 bedrooms, many of which have stunning views overlooking the surrounding parkland. Just 300 metres away are the hotel's two-bedroom self-catering apartments looking cosy in hues of brown, yellow and red, and a tremendous home away from home.

Rates from: 🐨
Star rating: ★★★
Overall rating: 🐨🐨🐨🐨

Ambience :	9.13	Cleanliness:	9.47
Value:	9.27	Facilities:	9.59
Staff:	9.29	Restaurants:	9.00
Location:	9.27	Families:	9.43

Kathleen's Country House

Madam's Height, Killarney County Kerry, Ireland
T: +353 64 32810 **F:** +353 64 32340
www.HotelClub.com

With a name like Kathleen O'Regan-Sheppard, the owner of this simply lovely hotel could only be Irish. The same goes for the ultra personal brand of hospitality that's dispensed non-stop, with an enthusiasm that's as boundless as it's welcoming. The 17 charming bedrooms are augmented by a quintet of sitting rooms which grant the true flavour of staying in a truly friendly hotel. Breakfast, comprising eminently local produce, is served in the dining room overlooking the gardens, and makes a great start to the day. Drinking water is drawn from the hotel's own spring, and original art works and inspirational verses adorn the walls. Half a dozen golf courses and numerous spas are all within hailing distance, but the temptation to sit tight and lap up Kathleen's is very strong. An invigorating antidote to bland hotels fettered to corporate ideals, this one is a winner, largely thanks to its marvellous proprietor.

Rates from: 🐨🐨
Star rating: ★★★★
Overall rating: **Editors' Pick**

Ambience :	n/a	Cleanliness:	n/a
Value:	n/a	Facilities:	n/a
Staff:	n/a	Restaurants:	n/a
Location:	n/a	Families:	n/a

The Killarney Park Hotel

Town Centre, Killarney, Co. Kerry, Ireland
T: +353 64 35555 **F:** +353 64 35266
www.HotelClub.com/hotels/Killarney_Park_Hotel

Garden Bar and Park Restaurant offer casual and fine dining respectively and The Ross Room caters for private dining. This 75-room hotel believes in anticipating guests' needs - and the spa's eight treatment rooms, relaxation room, hydrotherapy suite and caldarium simply reinforce the fact.

The 1990s saw the arrival of international hotel chains and the construction of numerous golf and entertainment venues in Killarney, but this tourist Mecca remains known for its warmth and hospitality. It's not so surprising then that The Killarney Park, located in the town centre, maintains the charm and warm appeal of a luxury country hotel. The concierge smiles genuinely and the log fires burn brightly in the lobby and the elegant Residents Lounge, where a traditional Afternoon Tea can be enjoyed. The

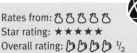

Rates from: 🛏🛏🛏🛏
Star rating: ★★★★★
Overall rating: 🐻🐻🐻🐻 ½

Ambience :	9.59	Cleanliness:	9.68
Value:	8.71	Facilities:	8.86
Staff:	8.88	Restaurants:	9.21
Location:	9.41	Families:	8.88

The Malton

Town Centre, Killarney, Co. Kerry, Ireland
T: +353 64 38000 **F:** +353 64 31642
www.HotelClub.com/hotels/Great_Southern_Hotel_Killarney

dresses to pass without rustling against each other! Food plays a starring role at the Malton. Munch on some home-made bread in the sunny gilded Garden room, or receive the same warm welcome maitre d'Hotel John Fitzgerald has been giving to guests at the à la carte restaurant Peppers for the past 40 years.

Few guests can resist peeping into an empty hotel room, and such curiosity is especially pardonable at the Malton, as each of the 172 rooms sports something different - classy wallpaper, silky curtains or smooth leather headboards. Such modern stylish additions sit well with this very Victorian structure, which dates all the way back to 1854, when the hotel was known as the Great Southern Hotel Killarney. The original staircase was designed to allow two ladies in hooped

Rates from: 🛏🛏🛏🛏
Star rating: ★★★★
Overall rating: 🐻🐻🐻🐻

Ambience :	10.0	Cleanliness:	10.0
Value:	9.00	Facilities:	10.0
Staff:	9.63	Restaurants:	10.0
Location:	9.00	Families:	9.63

Muckross Park Hotel & Cloisters Spa

Lakes of Killarney, Killarney, Co. Kerry, Ireland
T: +353 64 23400 **F:** +53 64 31965
www.HotelClub.com

As George Bernard Shaw opined: "There is no love sincerer than the love of food". And so it came to pass, most notably at the restaurant named for GBS which occupies pride of place at Muckross Park. Mind you, it faces quite a lot of internal competition, as owners Bill Cullen and Jackie Levin have spent the past decade and a half piling on the pleasure at the hotel which originally opened as The Herbert Arms in 1795. More recent innovations include conference and events facilities, 68 spruced-up guestrooms (including two sumptuous historic suites), a rip-roaring pub and of course, the Gothic-inspired spa. As the old saying goes, you have to move with the times, however Muckross would appear to be setting the pace. All in all, this is a very smart property.

Rates from: 🛏🛏🛏🛏🛏
Star rating: ★ ★ ★ ★ ★
Overall rating: 👍👍👍👍 ½

Ambience :	9.14	Cleanliness:	9.64
Value:	8.50	Facilities:	9.42
Staff:	9.43	Restaurants:	8.86
Location:	9.50	Families:	9.11

The Heritage Golf & Spa Resort

Killenard, Co. Laois, Ireland
T: +353 57 864 5500 **F:** +353 57 864 2350
www.HotelClub.com

To work it all off, there's a fitness centre, dance studio and large indoor pool, plus a spa that specialises in Pevonia Botanica skincare and offers 70 types of treatment in some 20 rooms. But what about the golf? How about a Seve Ballesteros-designed course that encompasses five lakes and a stream, 7,000 trees and no inclines?

Forget the blarney and the begorra, this staggering resort, built in 2005, is all about the new Irish economic powerhouse and the aspirations of its nouveau riche. A sprawling hotel in the grand style, with spacious rooms and suites that put the emphasis on unobtrusive luxury, is the centrepiece of complex that also includes self-catering apartments and a second-home village that threatens to dwarf quaint old Killenard. Eating and drinking well is one of the main attractions - no fewer than three top-of-the-line restaurants and five bar/lounges to tempt the tastebuds.

Rates from: 🛏🛏🛏🛏🛏
Star rating: ★ ★ ★ ★ ★
Overall rating: 👍👍👍👍 ½

Ambience :	8.78	Cleanliness:	9.70
Value:	8.65	Facilities:	9.51
Staff:	9.09	Restaurants:	9.22
Location:	8.41	Families:	8.68

Cabra Castle Hotel

Kingscourt, Co. Cavan, Ireland
T: +353 42 966 7030 **F:** +353 42 966 7039
www.HotelClub.com/hotels/Cabra_Castle_Hotel_Kingscourt

It looks like a castle. And it's been a castle since 1760. But the Cabra Castle Hotel has got all the trappings of modern times, right down to those little essentials like a helipad.

With a plethora of rooms to choose from, selecting the right place to stay from among the 80 on offer isn't as easy as it sounds. There is the splendour of an oversized suite or quaint attic room in the Lords Chamber. Retreat to a room in the old outhouses of Cabra Castle and have access to the walled garden. And then for the perfect private retreat there is the four bedroom gate lodge. Wherever you lay your head, comfort and excellent service are assured.

From the castle grounds head out to explore the nearby Wishing Well or Cromwell's Bridge and return to the castle for a meal whose ingredients are either home grown or sourced elsewhere in the country. Of course, it's well nigh imperative to start the day with a Full Irish Breakfast - bacon, egg, sausage, tomato and white or black or both sorts of pudding.

And you don't have to be a dyed-in-the-wool romantic to guess that this is as fine a spot as any to celebrate your nuptials. Add to the splendid backdrop the sterling local services of McCrum Carriage Hire, the Celtic Thunder band, photographers Seamus Farrelly or Finbarr O'Donoghue, and Rocket Pyrotechnics (who round off the day with fireworks) and your long years of married bliss are off to a tremendous start.

Rates from: 🪙🪙🪙
Star rating: ★★★★
Overall rating: 🗝🗝🗝🗝

Ambience :	10.0	Cleanliness:	10.0
Value:	8.00	Facilities:	8.50
Staff:	10.0	Restaurants:	8.00
Location:	8.00	Families:	10.0

Kinnitty Castle

Kinnitty, Co. Offaly, Ireland
T: +353 57 913 7318 **F:** +353 57 913 7824
www.HotelClub.com

mysteries and "pistols at dawn" recreations, forsooth!

But equestrian holidays are Kinnitty's speciality, offering everything from pony-trekking to fox-hunting. After a hard day in the saddle, you can enjoy a restorative drink in the wood-panelled, book-lined Library Bar, or repair straight to the gourmet Sli Dala restaurant, the Monks Kitchen (buffet served on platters and goblets) or the Dungeon Bar (live folk music).

There is a spa at the castle's lodge (Jacuzzi, sauna, steam room, high-pressure showers, plus a variety of skincare and body treatments). Between the castle itself and the estate's venerable Moneyguyneen Guesthouse, 37 rooms range from standard (though no two are alike) to four-poster Baronial. But you must be prepared to enter into the time-machine spirit - none has TV.

It could be argued that the rise of luxury countryside hotels has saved many an historic building from going to ruin - and they don't come much more historic than Kinnitty Castle, which dates back to the Druids and whose timeline marks most of the major wars, incursions and rebellions that have shaped Ireland. The present neo-Gothic incarnation only arose in 1929, but its owners, the Ryan family, play the "olde worlde" card for all its worth.

The ambience is aided by suits of armour and animal trophies, creaking corridors and candles, peat fires and medieval banquets, with huntin', shootin' and fishin' in the 4,000-plus hectares of grounds in the foothills of the Slieve Bloom Mountains. Corporate "bonding" is catered for with hot-air ballooning, paint-balling, quad-biking and orienteering, as well as archery, falconry, treasure hunts, murder

Rates from: 🍶🍶🍶	
Star rating: n/a	
Overall rating: 🐚🐚🐚🐚 ½	
Ambience : 9.82	Cleanliness: 9.47
Value: 8.29	Facilities: 8.51
Staff: 9.44	Restaurants: 9.18
Location: 9.00	Families: 8.30

Absolute Hotel

Sir Harry's Mall, Limerick, Ireland
T: +353 61 463600 **F:** +353 61 463601
www.HotelClub.com

Long for lovely days in Limerick if you're staying at the Absolute Hotel. It's a chic 99-room establishment that is the epitome of modern-day Ireland.

If a roof garden with 360-degree panoramic views of the city weren't enough, there are floor-to-ceiling windows that flood the lobby with light, several outdoor terraces and a splendid riverside restaurant that sits on a bend of the Abbey River and offers thoroughly sumptuous al fresco dining.

But if those lovely days prove elusive, fear not; it also boasts a spa offering volcanic mud wraps, cocktails in the elegant Cocktail Bar and a range of rooms that capitalise on bespoke design touches. There are even "Rain Dance" Power Showers in every guestroom, proving that the Absolute is also fond of a little joke.

Rates from:
Star rating: ★★★★
Overall rating: **Editors' Pick**

Ambience :	n/a	Cleanliness:	n/a
Value:	n/a	Facilities:	n/a
Staff:	n/a	Restaurants:	n/a
Location:	n/a	Families:	n/a

The George Boutique Hotel

O'Connell Street, Limerick, Ireland
T: +353 61 460400 **F:** +353 61 460410
www.HotelClub.com

If The George is anything to go by then the historic city of Limerick means serious business as it squares up to the challenges of the 21st century.

There has certainly been little in the way of modesty, with little held back in the furnishing of the 125 guestrooms and suites at this contemporary boutique hotel.

Stylish artwork, chic fabrics, 350-thread count luxurious Egyptian linens, rainforest power showers and 26-inch flat screen TVs are all requisite in a hotel of this class, but a choice of expensive teas and coffees and a nightcap liqueur in every room is a nice and novel touch.

The dark walnut panelling and flickering candles create a sumptuous atmosphere and for those with plenty of cash to splash out on the Presidential Suite, the views from the seventh floor are simply sensational.

Rates from:
Star rating: ★★★★
Overall rating:

Ambience :	8.00	Cleanliness:	9.20
Value:	8.20	Facilities:	7.25
Staff:	7.80	Restaurants:	7.40
Location:	8.60	Families:	6.50

Clarion Hotel Limerick

Steamboat Quay, Limerick, Ireland
T: +353 61 444 100 **F:** +353 61 444101
www.HotelClub.com/hotels/Clarion_Hotel_Limerick

Whether you see it as ship-shaped, cigar-shaped or just a stunning piece of contemporary architecture, Ireland's tallest hotel has probably inspired a limerick or two in the town after which this comic-verse form is named. If nothing else it has certainly become an instant landmark.

Some 70 metres and 17 storeys high, it offers 158 rooms, including suites and a penthouse, all done out in warm colour schemes and attractive maple-wood furniture, and boasting such touches as steam-free mirrors and seaweed-extract toiletries in the bathrooms, Egyptian-cotton duvets and high-performance hairdryers (2,000 watts).

The property's USP is the fabulous views it affords of the River Shannon, on a bank of which it resides. Both the Sinergie Restaurant and the Kudos Bar (exotic Thai and Malay food) overlook it. And given its central business-district location, there are plenty more F&B options nearby (try Dolan's pub, which has traditional Irish music seven nights a week).

Individual TVs fronting the equipment in the gym take the boredom out of exercise, and you can gaze at the riverine goings-on while swimming in the (smallish) pool - both part of the SanoVitae Health and Fitness Centre, which also boasts the obligatory sauna, steamroom and Jacuzzi.

Only 15 minutes' drive from Shannon airport, it could take you just as long again to reach the hotel via the frustrating one-way traffic system unless you receive clear instructions in advance. And another small tip - make sure the blinds in your bedroom close properly if you want a sound night's sleep because the hotel is powerfully illuminated after dark.

Rates from: 🛏🛏
Star rating: ★★★★
Overall rating: 👍👍👍👍

Ambience :	8.77	Cleanliness:	9.27
Value:	8.23	Facilities:	8.64
Staff:	8.45	Restaurants:	8.85
Location:	8.77	Families:	8.54

Radisson SAS Hotel & Spa, Limerick

Ennis Road, Limerick, Ireland
T: +353 61 456 200 **F:** +353 61 327 418
www.HotelClub.com/hotels/Radisson_SAS_Limerick

This 154-room, low-rise property, once known as the Limerick Inn and looking out onto the Woodcock Mountains, affords the best of both worlds: it is set in its own grounds (worth a stroll at any time of day) on the outskirts of the city (Ireland's third largest) thus having the feel of a country house hotel. Yet it's only a taxi ride away from the attractions downtown.

Both its public spaces and its bedrooms are refreshingly spacious. The latter, as well as suites and family rooms, include Business Class accommodation, with which you receive a complimentary buffet breakfast, bathrobe and slippers, free movies and a daily newspaper. And there also is a Ladies Level, serviced only by female staff and featuring such feminine extras as satin-padded hangers, lavender-scented cushions, hot chocolate and glossy magazines.

The distaff side will also enjoy the nine treatment rooms (Elemis beauty products), hair salon, al fresco Canadian hot tub and Leisure Club at the spa, which also encompasses a pool, sauna, stream room and gym. And there are outdoor tennis courts for the more energetically inclined.

Dining, whether it be the Full-Irish buffet breakfast, lunch or dinner, is in the 120-seat, split-level Porters Restaurant, off which there is a bar where you can eat, drink, watch sports events on plasma TV screens or listen to live music at weekends. Plus the Lobby Bar for more tranquil whistle-whetting.

Excellent conference and business facilities and free parking round out the allure of this hotel that has one foot in the country, one in the city.

Rates from: 🏠🏠
Star rating: ★★★★
Overall rating: 🏠🏠🏠🏠

Ambience :	8.87	Cleanliness:	9.33
Value:	8.20	Facilities:	8.59
Staff:	9.31	Restaurants:	8.40
Location:	7.27	Families:	9.18

The BrookLodge Hotel & Wells Spa

Macreddin Village, Co. Wicklow, Ireland
T: +353 402 36444 **F:** +353 402 36580
www.HotelClub.com/hotels/Brooklodge_Hotel_Maccredin

About an hour's drive out of Dublin, you'll come across the quaint old village of Macreddin... built (on the shell of the original, deserted one) just a few years ago and turned into a self-contained country resort, with its own pub, chapel, bakery, micro-brewery and shops selling free-range food. Brainchild of the Doyle brothers, it offers a de-stress experience for city slickers, with the accent on fresh air and exercise, healthy eating and body toning (the requisite golf course opens in 2008).

Accommodation (66 rooms) is country-house style, with some overlooking the village green and some in a separate building (which has conference facilities) by the brook. Apart from Acton's Pub and the Orchard Café, the big dining attraction is The Strawberry Tree, Ireland's only certified organic restaurant. A feature of this is the Big Table, where dishes are presented to groups of eight to 40 diners to dip into communally.

The Wells Spa is another major enticement, as you can tell from its inclusion in the property's name, offering Finnish and mud baths, hot tubs, a floatation room, beauty and skin treatments galore, a gym and an indoor-outdoor pool, with heated loungers. All the usual rugged open-air activities can be arranged, but BrookLodge specialises in two - equestrianism and off-road driving.

The former encompasses show-jumping and dressage in a purpose-built arena, as well as just hacking, while a fleet of Land Rovers caters for the 4x4 crowd. Imagine the look on the face of a born-and-bred Macreddin villager paying a return visit.

Rates from: 🛏🛏🛏
Star rating: ★ ★ ★ ★
Overall rating: 🛏🛏🛏🛏 ½

Ambience :	9.23	Cleanliness:	9.54
Value:	8.62	Facilities:	8.71
Staff:	9.37	Restaurants:	9.66
Location:	8.77	Families:	8.72

Killashee House Hotel and Villa Spa

Killashee, Naas, Co. Kildare, Ireland
T: +353 45 879277 **F**: +353 45 879266
www.HotelClub.com

If you've had a good win at the races - three of Ireland's best-known courses, The Curragh, Punchestown and Naas, are all just a 15-minute drive away - then this may be the place to spend it. Not for a raucous celebration, mind, but for a sedate taste of upper-class living.

Although dating back to the fifth-century days of missionary St. Auxillius (from whom the name Killashee somewhat mysteriously derives), the present building was designed as a hunting lodge for descendants of the earls of Drogheda by Thomas Turner in 1861, and it was run as a boys' boarding school by an order of nuns between the wars.

Today, the imposing greystone manor, with its striking bell tower beckoning from the end of a majestic driveway, oozes elegance. Its 141 rooms and suites, some with four-poster beds, all look out over manicured gardens to the Wicklow Mountains (visibility permitting). While the plasterwork

in the scarlet-and-gold Turner's Restaurant (Irish with a Mediterranean twist) is superb, the aesthetic impact heightened by a house harpist.

Traditional Irish music enlivens the Nun's Kitchen Bar ("creative" Irish cuisine) and two lounges, the Gallery and the Residents', are resplendent with antiques, chandeliers and sink-into sofas.

As if all this were not enough, the 18-room Villa Spa is world-class (try the spectacular Moroccan Suite) and there is a 25-metre pool, a gym, Jacuzzi,

steamroom and even a tylarium.

All sorts of strenuous activities can be arranged, but with all this sybaritic luxury at your disposal, why bother?

Rates from: 🏠 🏠 🏠
Star rating: ★ ★ ★ ★
Overall rating: 🏠 🏠 🏠 🏠

Ambience :	9.17	Cleanliness:	9.54
Value:	8.63	Facilities:	8.36
Staff:	8.92	Restaurants:	8.83
Location:	8.75	Families:	8.50

Osprey Hotel & Spa

Devoy Quarter, Naas, Co. Kildare, Ireland
T: +353 45 881 111 F: +353 45 881 112
www.HotelClub.com

The Irish are always in search of a good "craic" (which for the uninitiated essentially means having a high old time) and the Osprey is predicated on providing exactly that.

A self-contained complex on the edge of town, it caters for conferences, corporate parties and stag and hen get-togethers, so if you're the retiring, Greta Garbo type, it may not be for you.

Fun-lovers, however, will adore the huge nightclub, with five DJs and lots of live entertainment, and the state-of-the-art spa to "recover" in. The former is dubbed "Time", the latter "Life", presumably without reference to the legendary American publisher of those magazine titles.

Accommodation is probably best described as funky - up-to-the-minute amenities and colourful décor in rooms that lead off a somewhat confusing layout of corridors due to the hotel's unusual shape (great for getting tipsily lost in around 4am).

The 80-seater Mash restaurant

(fusion cuisine) overlooks a fountain, and food is also served in the Statler Bar and Waldorf Lounge.

The spa is full of innovative features, such as Salt and Snow Grottos, a low-temperature steam room with crystal lighting, and a low-humidity sauna that allows longer lingering. Plus flotation tanks, solarium, mud baths - and pool and gym, of course.

There are no fewer than nine bars spread over four floors in the Time nightclub, one of which is dedicated to music from the 80s so that the 30-somethings shouldn't feel left out. As the Dubliners who flock here at weekends say, it's a great craic.

Rates from: 🛏🛏🛏
Star rating: ★★★★
Overall rating: 👍👍👍👍

Ambience :	8.00	Cleanliness:	9.00
Value:	8.00	Facilities:	8.00
Staff:	8.00	Restaurants:	9.00
Location:	7.00	Families:	6.00

Dromoland Castle Hotel

Newmarket-on-Fergus, Co. Clare, Ireland
T: +353 61 368 144 **F:** +353 61 363 355
www.HotelClub.com/hotels/Dromoland_Castle_Newmarket_on_Fergus

There's probably an EU directive forbidding the utterance of that well-worn saw "an Englishman's house is his castle" on grounds of racism, sexism, elitism, or all three. Mind you, Ireland has plenty of

similarly politically risqué sayings - "many an Irish property was increased by the lace of a daughter's petticoat" springs to mind. And so, by a commodius vicus of recirculation, we come to

Dromoland Castle and environs.

Tracing its roots back to the 16th century - though the present structure was built in the 19th - Dromoland ("Hill of Litigation") could well have been ordered up by Hollywood's central casting. The ancestral resting spot of the O'Briens, descendants of Brian Boru, High King of Ireland, its statuesque neo-Gothic battlements and towers could easily have been wafted out of a tale by Somerville and Ross. Small wonder it was snapped up for hotel conversion by the wealthy American philanthropist Bernard McDonough when the 16th Baron Inchiquin, Donough O'Brien, ran into a little financial difficulty in the 1960s. The current owners have invested substantially to sustain the legend,

similarly baronial. The Earl of Thomond is a thoroughly inspiring name for a restaurant, and both menus and wine list fall into line throughout the day; dinners are especially evocative, with music from the resident harpist giving executive chef David McCann's creations an extra lilt. The Fig Tree provides lighter fare, and afternoon tea in the drawing room is an immovable date in many residents' diaries.

Like many properties of its size, Dromoland has evolved from pure hotel into a wider ranging "estate". A golf course - par-72, 18 holes, and rated one of the best in Europe - is the prime example of this, followed closely by a brand new spa which opened within the castle in the summer of 2007. Fans of neither of these recreations might seek solace in more traditional country pursuits such as fishing on the lake, archery, or clay pigeon shooting, while horse riding is available at a nearby stables.

while the staff, many of whom have spent much of their working lives here, are endlessly, Irishly, cordial.

If there's a degree of theatricality about Dromoland - oak panelling, open fires, winding corridors and rooms constructed on luxurious scales - it's altogether welcome and its staging is almost always entirely authentic; those so inclined could live out every aristocratic fantasy they've every entertained here. Whether it's a stateroom, suite or merely an ordinary guestroom - all blend ancient and modern in the right places, and impart that all-essential "knight for a night" feeling.

Dining, in fact all aspects of eating and drinking here, are

Naturally, such an agglomeration of facilities attracts corporate visitors in fairly substantial numbers (especially given Dromoland's proximity to Shannon Airport), who tend to cluster in the Brian Boru Hall. Those with time and inclination to sidestep the official programme could do a lot worse than pop outside to revel in the 166 hectares that surround this powerfully inspirational hotel, somewhere that gives everyone the chance to become landed gentry, however briefly.

Rates from: 💰💰💰💰
Star rating: ★ ★ ★ ★ ★
Overall rating: 🐾🐾🐾🐾

Ambience :	9.58	Cleanliness:	9.52
Value:	8.00	Facilities:	8.68
Staff:	9.31	Restaurants:	9.31
Location:	8.92	Families:	8.66

Marriott Druids Glen Hotel & Country Club

Newtownmountkennedy, Wicklow, Ireland
T: +353 1 287 0800 **F:** +353 1 287 0848
www.HotelClub.com

Some restaurants in the more touristy parts of Spain fix a droll plaque to their doors proclaiming that "Hemingway never ate here". James Joyce certainly never stayed at this hotel, yet the reception area, the ballroom and a corridor are all named after him. On the other hand, the Druids Glen Golf Club in Seattle was almost certainly named after the one in County Wicklow, which is known as the "Augusta of Europe" and has staged four Irish Opens.

The Marriott forms part of the 160-hectare Druids Club Golf Resort and will naturally make its strongest appeal to those whose passion is whacking little white

balls into far-off holes. But being a Marriott, it is a thoroughly dependable, up-market property, just 40 kilometres south of Dublin, and has plenty to offer non-golfers, including their children.

Its 145 rooms are as state-of-the-art as you would expect and come with the multinational chain's "bedding package", which "addresses clean and fresh bedding concerns, including a bed skirt and bed scarf, feather and foam pillows, sheeted duvet cover and comforter and softer fitted bottom and flat top sheets". You also get free tea or coffee and a daily newspaper, and the bathrooms have walk-in showers with a separate tub.

There are seven treatment rooms in the Elemis Spa, a business centre and extensive corporate and wedding facilities. Flynn's Restaurant specialises in beef, seasonal game and freshwater fish, and there's a Brasserie for more casual dining. James Joyce would have loved it.

Rates from: 🏯🏯🏯
Star rating: ★★★★★
Overall rating: 🦢🦢🦢🦢

Ambience :	9.06	Cleanliness:	9.48
Value:	8.55	Facilities:	8.98
Staff:	9.20	Restaurants:	8.90
Location:	8.74	Families:	8.55

Portlaoise Heritage Hotel

Town Centre, Portlaoise, Co Laois, Ireland
T: +353 57 86 78 588 **F:** +353 57 86 78 577
www.HotelClub.com/hotels/Heritage_Hotel_Portlaoise

Teleported into the Irish midlands, the Heritage Hotel (the name notwithstanding) is all that's bright and best about the new generation of the country's accommodation.

Only a short stroll from the town centre, the place pretty obviously says Conference loud and clear, and attendees will be more than well fed, bedded and entertained. The dedicated conference wing can cater for up to 500, though some doubling up might be required at night as there's only 110 guest rooms. These include both regular rooms and suites, blending classic design with modern elegance and decorated with rich warm colours.

Of the restaurants, Fitzmaurice signs its signature with a flourish, while the Spago Italian bistro imports a touch of Mediterranean colour - not to mention taste. Both Molly's and the Charter Bar can cater to those who've decided to skip food to concentrate on the essentials, however Kelly's Foundry Grillhouse is probably the most charismatic eatery on the premises. It stands of the site of a former ironworks, and patrons are invited to cook their steaks on a volcanic stove.

No self-respecting 21st-century Irish new-build comes without fitness facilities, and the Heritage is no exception.

As well as a 22-metre swimming pool, a sauna and a Jacuzzi, there's a top notch gym, plus a spa with the onomatopoeic handle, Ealu, with a wide range of inspiring treatments.

Finally, bowls fanatics hankering for a game can assuage their lust at the sister Heritage hotel in Killenard, whose 14 rinks are just 20 minutes' drive away.

Rates from: 🛏🛏🛏
Star rating: ★★★★
Overall rating: 🐦🐦🐦🐦

Ambience :	8.43	Cleanliness:	9.50
Value:	7.69	Facilities:	8.65
Staff:	8.62	Restaurants:	8.08
Location:	8.86	Families:	7.89

Kelly's Resort Hotel & Spa

Rosslare, Co. Wexford, Ireland
T: +353 53 913 2114 **F:** +353 53 913 2222
www.HotelClub.com

Kelly's is not so much a family hotel as a thorough-going dynasty. If guests don't know when they arrive that William J Kelly opened his tearooms here in the 1890s, it's not too long before they're let in on the Sunny South East's worst-kept secret. Kellys are still running Kelly's, and the resort is thriving.

From dispensing cakes and cuppas, Kelly's has grown over the years, but has never lost the family touch which keeps guests coming

back for more, attended, as time wears on, perhaps by first their own children and then their grandchildren. The eight kilometres of sandy beach is as lovely as it was a century ago, but Kelly's itself, which now hosts 118 rooms, has definitely moved with the times.

Most guests will be staying in a standard room, which are homely, comfortable, and invigorated by views of Rosslare Strand and the Irish Sea. A recently-built clutch of

16 hovers above the spa, accessed by a splendid sightseeing glass lift. However there's also a pair of junior suites, while on the top floor William Crozier and Tony O'Malley - named after the artists and featuring much of their work - are a perfect blend of luxury and contemporary.

Possibly the most revolutionary addition to Kelly's of late is SeaSpa, separate from the main building and a cool £6 million's

worth of treatment rooms (one's Thai), ice fountains, pebble walks, and seawater vitality pools plus loads of space to chill on heated loungers, if that's not a contradiction in terms. Consultants E'Spa sorted out the treatment menu, and there's also a private garden for relaxation.

There's plenty to keep all ages occupied at Kelly's, from a crazy golf course to a dedicated card room, plus four tennis courts - two indoor and two out. And within

striking distance of the resort there's such traditional Irish rural activities such as fishing and golf. But few would want to miss out on breakfast, lunch and dinner, unarguable highlights of any stay here. The L-shaped Beaches is the focal point of the resort's food, however La Marine Bistro and Bar flourishes under the creative inspiration of head chef Eugene Callaghan - his crab and shrimp lasagne with rocket and parmesan salad is a gem.

Perhaps not too remarkably, long service is very much part of the scene at Kelly's; Tom and Josie Bishop have each been with the resort for 40 (that's not a typo) years, and quite a few others have worked here for three decades or more. Their, and the other staff's, loyalty and dedication are all too apparent in everyday operations. This is very much a happy ship.

Finally, there is very little chance of Kelly's being swallowed up by a chain. The current Mr and Mrs Kelly have six daughters - Laura, Clara, Eva, Anna, Faye and Grace - so there should be few problems handing over the reins to the next generation. As William J Kelly surely once thought to himself, there's nothing like investing in the future!

Rates from: 🝳🝳🝳
Star rating: ★★★★
Overall rating: 🝳🝳🝳🝳 ½

Ambience :	9.27	Cleanliness:	9.42
Value:	8.79	Facilities:	8.40
Staff:	9.32	Restaurants:	9.61
Location:	9.27	Families:	9.75

Galway Bay Hotel Conference & Leisure Centre

The Promenade, Salthill, Galway, Ireland
T: +353 91 520 520 **F:** +353 91 520 530
www.HotelClub.com/hotels/Galway_Bay_Hotel

A casual observer could be forgiven for thinking this hotel has a long, grand history watching generations of visitors walk the prom with Galway Bay lapping at their feet. But it's just ten years old, yet a stately sense of timelessness in architecture, décor and service brings guests back time and again.

This hotel doesn't hide behind a huge gym, swimming pool and spa. Those facilities are good but weekly book chats with Galway's Des Kenny in the library; history sessions with a local history professor in the Leather Lounge, and day tours to the Burren and Connemara take higher priority. For youngsters, the Penguin Kids Activity Camp fulfils "if the kids are happy then the parents are happy". In fact whatever your age or need it's likely to have been thought of and catered for with 'It's a pleasure!' in response.

Food is important and executive chef Robert Bell has been wooing diners in the traditional luxury of the Lobster Pot restaurant since the hotel doors first opened.

Thanks to banqueting rooms which can accommodate 1,000 people, the romance of great photo opportunities on the wide sea-facing balcony, canopied beds in the bridal suites, a business centre and event co-ordinators to smooth out the stresses, weddings and conferences are huge.

In the 153 rooms, big comfy beds take precedence over big bathrooms but eat-off-the-floor clean tiles, and goodies on the bathroom shelves, provide fair compensation. You can choose from suites, superior suites, sea-view, family, ground-floor and bog-standard rooms, with two rooms fully equipped for people with disabilities.

Rates from: 🛏 🛏
Star rating: ★ ★ ★ ★
Overall rating: 🛏 🛏 🛏 🛏

Ambience :	8.95	Cleanliness:	9.40
Value:	8.50	Facilities:	8.58
Staff:	8.98	Restaurants:	8.80
Location:	9.52	Families:	9.20

Clarion Hotel Sligo

Clarion Road, Sligo, Ireland
T: +353 171 911 9000 **F:** +353 171 911 9001
www.HotelClub.com/hotels/Clarion_Hotel_Sligo

Fittingly, the owner of this imposing 1848 Gothic-style granite building that was a hospital before it became a hotel, runs a charitable organisation (Patron The Duchess of York) called The Daisychain Foundation, which offers free holidays at all its properties for Ireland's disabled. You can get a taste of the pleasures that await them by staying at the Clarion in Sligo.

As you might imagine, it is very child-friendly, which may or may not appeal to you. The kids have their own mysteriously named Minnalouse Club, with a cinema and playroom, their own splash pool and access to a selection of children's movies (there are DVD players in all rooms).

Its 167 rooms and suites are spacious and well equipped with all the accoutrements today's traveller requires. You have a choice of Italian or Asian food respectively in the two main restaurants - the Sinergie and the Kudos (which is a lively bar in the evenings), and the Savour lounge does lunches.

A highlight of the hotel is the SanoVitae Health Centre and Spa. This has a gym with over 60 pieces of equipment (each with its own flat-panel TV for allaying the tedium of exercise), an aerobics studio, some 268 lockers complete with hairdryers and shower gel, sauna, steamroom, Jacuzzi and 20-metre heated indoor pool.

The spa has eight individual rooms and a couple of hydrotherapy baths and offers plenty of beauty treatments, massages and wraps.

A hotel with a heart, then, on Ireland's wild Atlantic coast, watched over by the towering Benbulben Mountain.

Rates from: 🛏🛏
Star rating: ★★★★
Overall rating: 🐾🐾🐾🐾

Ambience :	8.87	Cleanliness:	9.40
Value:	8.70	Facilities:	8.86
Staff:	8.97	Restaurants:	9.04
Location:	8.59	Families:	9.12

Radisson SAS Hotel & Spa, Silgo
Ballincar, Rosses Point, Sligo, Ireland
T: +353 71 91 40008 **F:** +353 71 91 40005
www.HotelClub.com

With a song in your heart by Westlife and a WB Yeats poem on your lips, where else could you be but in Sligo, birthplace of both? And where better to stay than what was once the much-loved Ballincar House Hotel, now a super-duper new Radisson?

With 132 rooms, including junior suites and business class, all done

out in warm scarlet hues and most with views of Sligo Bay and Benbulben Mountain, it offers all the amenities of a first-class modern hotel behind a somewhat underwhelming façade.

Simple but classy - as indeed is the Classiebawn Restaurant, with its sweeping ceiling and sub-divided dining areas. There's food too in the Benwiskin Bar, which comes alive in the evenings, especially Saturday night, which is live-music night. And the Memory Harbour Lounge is always buzzing.

The Solas Spa and Wellness Centre utilises the E'spa product range in its seven treatment rooms, and features a Razul chamber, inspired by the exotic rituals of the Middle Eastern harem, plus a Balenotherapy bath and a dry flotation tank, and Jane Iredale makeup.

A major attraction, apart from the sandy beaches and rugged scenery, is the County Sligo Golf Club at Rosses Point, just down the coast road. In 2007, the hotel sponsored the West of Ireland Championship there and it is regarded as one of Ireland's premier links courses.

So what are you waiting for? Dig out those old Westlife boy-band classics and a copy of Yeats's collected verse and come see what inspired them.

Rates from: 💰 💰 💰
Star rating: ★ ★ ★ ★
Overall rating: 🏩 🏩 🏩 🏩

Ambience :	8.78	Cleanliness:	9.33
Value:	8.52	Facilities:	9.00
Staff:	8.60	Restaurants:	8.46
Location:	8.52	Families:	8.83

Parknasilla Hotel

Sneem, Co. Kerry, Ireland
T: +353 64 45122 **F:** +353 64 45323
www.HotelClub.com

"This place does not belong to any world that you and I have ever worked or lived in - it is part of our dream world," said George Bernhard Shaw after visiting the Parknasilla Hotel. And while visiting, it is a dream world guests need never leave as a range of activities is available right on the sprawling estate. Meander down to the ruins of Derryquin castle, view the grounds from horse back, go clay pigeon shooting, try your hand at archery or indulge in croquet or petanque. Reluctant to leave the countryside behind? Gaze at Kenmore Bay from the wide bay window in Pygmalion Restaurant or feast your eyes upon the ocean from Doolittle Bar or more tempting yet, the balcony of the Princess Grace suite (one of 95 rooms and suites).

Rates from: 🏵🏵🏵🏵🏵
Star rating: ★ ★ ★ ★
Overall rating: 🏵🏵🏵🏵 ½

Ambience :	9.57	Cleanliness:	9.32
Value:	8.50	Facilities:	8.39
Staff:	9.41	Restaurants:	8.78
Location:	9.86	Families:	9.39

Tullamore Court Hotel

Tullamore, Co. Offaly, Ireland
T: +353 507 93 46666 **F:** +353 507 93 46677
www.HotelClub.com

Much of the architecture in the heritage town of Tullamore dates back to the 1750s but the Tullamore Court Hotel is an example of the contemporary style that is starting to make a frequent appearance in the entertainment capital of central Ireland. Recent renovation has introduced 33 new executive rooms and suites, bringing the total to 105. Recognising that much of the town's growth was due to the milling industry's expansion, Tullamore Court's fine dining restaurant is called Windmill and diners may find expansion of a different kind - in particular around the waistline - might occur here. For more casual dining head to Furlong Bar and sip an Irish Mist, a liqueur that originated in Tullamore. And if you need an excuse to get away from the hotel, many of the larger shops in town offer ten per cent discount to Tullamore Court guests.

Rates from: 🏵🏵🏵🏵🏵
Star rating: ★ ★ ★ ★
Overall rating: 🏵🏵🏵🏵

Ambience :	8.00	Cleanliness:	9.40
Value:	8.20	Facilities:	8.02
Staff:	8.25	Restaurants:	8.60
Location:	8.60	Families:	8.93

The Mount Wolseley Hotel Spa & Country Club

Tullow, Country Carlow, Ireland
T: +353 59 918 0100 **F:** +353 59 915 2123
www.HotelClub.com /hotels/Mount_Wolseley_Country_Resort

Heaps of history attaches to this 1995 golf resort on an 80-hectare estate on the banks of the River Slaney in County Carlow. It was given to a captain at the Battle of the Boyne in 1725 who lent King Billy his horse when the royal steed stumbled. The gallant captain's best-known descendant was Frederick York Wolseley, who used his fortune from a mechanical sheep-shearing business in Australia to launch the eponymous motor car.

Though horse-riding, fishing, archery and clay-pigeon shooting can all be arranged, it is the golf on a course designed by Christy O'Connor Jr, with water hazards on 11 holes, that is the main attraction. Indeed, with non-players barred from strolling the fairways, a minor point raised by some guests is that there is grass, grass everywhere with nary a blade to walk upon.

But the splendid views and elegant charms of the old house are worth the stay and if you don't

play golf, you can always drive into nearby Tullow, where there are some 15 pubs all within a dog-end's throw of one another. Back at the hotel, you can dine at Frederick's Restaurant, named after himself, relax at the bar or in the graceful drawing rooms, work out in the gym, tone up in the Spa, or play tennis.

The property's 40 rooms are comfortable and well-equipped, with separate bath and shower areas and an outside loo (no, not outside the hotel, outside the bathroom). USPs: a thrill-a-minute ice-skating rink at Christmas and a heli-pad for those truly in a hurry.

Rates from: 💰💰💰
Star rating: ★★★★
Overall rating: 🌀🌀🌀🌀

Ambience :	9.10	Cleanliness:	9.10
Value:	8.57	Facilities:	8.80
Staff:	9.00	Restaurants:	8.90
Location:	8.10	Families:	9.21

Faithlegg House Hotel & Golf Club

Faithlegg, Co. Waterford, Ireland
T: +353 51 382 000 **F:** +353 51 382 010
www.HotelClub.com/hotels/Faithlegg_House_Hotel_Waterford

If Irish country house living is what you're looking for, Faithlegg House has 14 master rooms with four-poster beds and forthrightly panoramic views. There are also 68 new rooms which were added as a discreet extension in 1999, while in the grounds of this magnificent 18th-century house stand 51 self-catering houses called Faithlegg Mews, whose off-season rates for four people would make a budget traveller blush. But even if you're staying in The Mews, you can still avail yourself of the tennis courts, swimming pool, and leisure centre with its funky three-square-metre Jacuzzi; and you still get to drink cocktails in the piano lounge after a long day playing golf on the 18-hole championship golf course. Sounds too good to be true? Book early, it's very often full, and with very good reason.

Rates from: ☝☝☝☝
Star rating: ★ ★ ★ ★
Overall rating: 👣👣👣👣

Ambience :	8.76	Cleanliness:	9.38
Value:	8.29	Facilities:	8.72
Staff:	9.00	Restaurants:	8.86
Location:	8.90	Families:	8.13

Tower Hotel, Waterford

The Mall, Waterford, Ireland
T: +353 51 862 300 **F:** +353 51 870 129
www.HotelClub.com/hotels/Tower_Hotel_Waterford

Few city hotels are as well situated as the Tower Hotel Waterford. It stands at one end of the main thoroughfare, overlooking the quay and the marina. This means that the Adelphi Riverside Bar overlooks the River Suir, and if you ask at the desk, they will try to get you a room that overlooks the river. No extra charge. But be warned, they hand out these rooms on a first-come, first-served basis, so they might not be available. You just have to be lucky.

The Tower Hotel has a goodly stack of conferencing facilities and a dedicated business centre. It also has a gym and a pool, so it's by no means all work and no play. Reginald's Tower, one of the oldest such structures in the country, stands opposite the hotel, giving it both its name and a nice historical note.

Rates from: ☝☝☝
Star rating: ★ ★ ★
Overall rating: 👣👣👣👣

Ambience :	8.56	Cleanliness:	9.22
Value:	8.67	Facilities:	7.90
Staff:	8.89	Restaurants:	8.67
Location:	9.67	Families:	8.85

Waterford Castle

The Island, Waterford, Ireland
T: +353 51 878 203   **F:** +353 51 879 316
www.HotelClub.com/hotels/Dooleys_Hotel_Waterford

Arriving at the Waterford Castle is a fabulous experience in itself. On the River Suir at the edge of the city, a small car ferry chugs across to The Isle of the Castle. A short drive through some of the 125 hectares of parkland leads to the castle entrance, beyond which lies a hotel Reception like no other. The ornate 16th-century plaster ceiling and the Elizabethan oak panelling on the walls are entirely original. As you check into one of only 19 bedrooms, you will be informed that dinner is served in the Munster Room (no connection with that 1960's US sitcom) and there is a dress code - long trousers, jacket and tie. Quite right. Who could possibly eat dinner without a tie?

All the rooms are individually designed and all have fantastic views of the river and parkland, while some look over the golf course. Waterford Castle wouldn't be a top class Irish hostelry if it didn't have its own 18-hole golf course. In fact, it's Ireland's only island golf course. But there's still space to wander around the rest of the island on your own. Plans for a full-on spa are in the works; meantime beauty treatments are dispensed in guestrooms. For more rural diversion, there's clay pigeon shooting at hand, and a

stables nearby for equestrian stuff.

Most mornings you'll see guests taking photos of the castle before they leave. It's understandable. Waterford Castle Hotel looks the way a castle should: staying there makes you feel like you own the place.

Rates from: 🏰🏰🏰
Star rating: ★★★★★
Overall rating: 🏰🏰🏰🏰 ½

Ambience :	9.62	Cleanliness:	9.62
Value:	9.00	Facilities:	8.11
Staff:	9.54	Restaurants:	9.15
Location:	9.77	Families:	9.50

Carlton Atlantic Coast Hotel

Westport, Co. Mayo, Ireland
T: +353 98 29000 **F:** +383 98 29111
www.HotelClub.com/hotels/The_Carlton_Atlantic_Coast_Hotel_Westport

Three centuries ago Westport was a thriving sea port. Today, it still thrives, albeit because of importing tourists rather than exporting grain. Transformed from an 18th-century mill into an 85-room hotel, The Carlton embraces nature in many ways; through the golf, fishing, boating, walking, mountain climbing and sea angling all a stone's throw away; with the fresh fish available daily in the roof top Blue Wave restaurant and the Harbourmaster Bar; or via the views of Croagh Patrick and the shores of Clew Bay, which look especially amazing both from the balcony and the roll-top bath in the Clew Bay suite. At least one couple of former guests agrees. A successful proposal one year ensured the return of Mr and Mrs a few months later. You really can't ask for a better recommendation.

Rates from: 🐚🐚🐚
Star rating: ★★★★
Overall rating: 🐾🐾🐾🐾

Ambience :	8.95	Cleanliness:	9.30
Value:	8.85	Facilities:	7.86
Staff:	9.06	Restaurants:	9.60
Location:	9.10	Families:	8.60

The Castlecourt Hotel

Castlebar Street, Westport, Co. Mayo, Ireland
T: +353 98 55088 **F:** +353 98 28622
www.HotelClub.com

This is definitely Ireland and not Italy, but the Castlecourt's 20-metre indoor pool - from whose balmy depths guests can gaze at Romanesque statues and warm yellow walls - has a decidedly Mediterranean feel to it. But the warmth imbued here is all utterly Irish and managers Joe and Ann Corcoran pride themselves on the welcoming atmosphere - whatever the age of their guests. The Golden Years Programme, organised by the 149-room hotel's own "Golden Girl", provides seanachai (story-telling) sessions, bingo, quizzes, cookery demos and Beauty by Rose. Kids can enjoy a plethora of delights such as beach parties, pyjama breakfasts, discos and (presumably non-alcoholic) cocktail nights. As the name suggests, business is not forgotten here and together with the adjoining Westport Plaza hotel, the Castlecourt has the largest conference resort in Connaught, seating 750 theatre-style.

Rates from: 🐚🐚
Star rating: ★★★
Overall rating: 🐾🐾🐾🐾

Ambience :	8.93	Cleanliness:	9.48
Value:	8.79	Facilities:	8.52
Staff:	9.32	Restaurants:	8.48
Location:	9.28	Families:	9.46

Hotel Westport

Newport Road, Westport, Co. Mayo, Ireland
T: +353 98 25122 **F:** +353 98 26739
www.HotelClub.com/hotels/Hotel_Westport

It's not every hotel where patrons can check in on a Friday night and be asked to investigate the mysterious death of another guest, spend Saturday trying to figure out whodunit, and have it all explained that evening; after which a 70s and 80s disco is on the agenda. It's all part of "The Incredibal Murdur Mistry Weekend" available at the 129-bedroom Hotel Westport. After all that excitement, head to the Ocean Spirit Spa and enjoy a Cleopatra bath with essential oils and salts or a Hamam traditional Turkish massage on a heated stone table. Even the conference facilities are just that bit out of the ordinary. The Cara conference suite has doors wide enough to accommodate large vehicles and the Mayo suite comes complete with dance floor and private bar.

Rates from: 🐚 🐚 🐚
Star rating: ★ ★ ★ ★
Overall rating: 🐚 🐚 🐚 🐚 ½

Ambience :	8.80	Cleanliness:	9.47
Value:	9.20	Facilities:	8.64
Staff:	9.25	Restaurants:	9.11
Location:	9.50	Families:	9.40

Knockranny House Hotel & Spa

Westport, Co. Mayo, Ireland
T: +353 98 28600 **F:** ++353 98 28611
www.HotelClub.com

Having a fine dining restaurant on the premises is nothing unusual for a luxury hotel, but the Knockranny's La Fougère prides itself on ensuring the food goes beyond just looking good. One of the reasons the food tastes superb is because the herbs are grown in the garden, the bread is home-baked and the chicken is smoked on site. More homely touches, such as open log fires and antique furniture, greet guests upon entering the 97 rooms. The décor is kept light in the standard rooms. The presidential suite, which just opened last autumn, is decked out with shades of green and burgundy and hosts a few additional perks, such as a four-poster bed. For more pampering, head to the mud chambers or dry floatation tanks at Spa Salveo.

Rates from: 🐚 🐚 🐚
Star rating: ★ ★ ★ ★
Overall rating: 🐚 🐚 🐚 🐚 ½

Ambience :	9.33	Cleanliness:	9.57
Value:	8.73	Facilities:	8.73
Staff:	9.54	Restaurants:	9.52
Location:	9.10	Families:	9.05

Ferrycarrig Hotel

Wexford, Ireland
T: +353 53 912 0999 **F:** +353 53 912 0982
www.HotelClub.com/hotels/Ferrycarrig_Hotel_Wexford

When John F Kennedy's great-grandfather fled Wexford in 1848 to escape the great potato famine, he can have had no idea of what an affluent little town it would turn out to be a century and a half later (or how well his great-grandson - who visited the place in 1963 - would do, come to that). And he could certainly never have envisaged a luxurious modern hotel like the Ferrycarrig.

Each of its 102 comfortable, contemporary rooms has a view over the tranquil waters of the River Slaney estuary - many from their own balconies - and despite its popularity as a wedding-banquet venue, and the fact that it is child-friendly, the loudest noise you're liable to hear in the morning is that of the vast variety of local bird-life. If you want to make really sure of a good night's sleep, you can book a room on the adults-only floor.

Dining at the formal Reeds Restaurant (fresh local produce a speciality) is a far cry from what poor old Patrick Kennedy had to put up with. The wine list, organised by grape variety, is especially informative. While the Dry Dock Bar, with its spectacular riverside deck, is a more laid back affair (ask for the Texas Steak Sandwich and sticky-toffee pudding).

Gym equipment at the Active Club is the same as that used by athletes at the Olympic Village in Athens, and you also have a pool, Jacuzzi, sauna and beauty salon. But for most people, it's the peace and quiet that puts this place in a class of its own.

Rates from: 👜👜👜👜👜
Star rating: n/a
Overall rating: 👜👜👜👜

Ambience :	7.00	Cleanliness:	9.00
Value:	9.00	Facilities:	9.00
Staff:	9.00	Restaurants:	9.00
Location:	10.0	Families:	10.0

Talbot Hotel

On the Quay, Wexford, Ireland
T: +353 53 9122566 **F:** +353 53 9123377
www.HotelClub.com/hotels/Talbot_Hotel_Wexford

That the history of this iconic 1960s Wexford hotel actually stretches back more than 100 years is evidenced by some of its architectural features - a bar built where an old bonded warehouse once stood and a health centre that used to be a grain mill, for instance. But with its central location (close to both the station and the sea), it has long been a focal point for local people.

Its 107 rooms and suites (including eight for families and four for the disabled) are all airconditioned, with double-glazed windows, and despite showing some signs of their age, offer most of the expected modern amenities, though room-service is limited. A feature of the property is the array of original oil-paintings on display throughout.

The Quay Leisure Centre in the building's basement has a pool, Jacuzzi, sauna and steam room, as well as a hi-tech gym and a spa where you can receive massage and other relaxing therapies or make yourself look even lovelier in the Essence Beauty Suite. It is well patronised by Wexfordians.

Gourmet dining is in the intimate Oysters Lane Restaurant, where fresh local ingredients form the basis for some adventurous Cordon Bleu cooking. You can also eat in the Ballast Bank Bar & Grill (try the carvery lunch), which features live music every night and, again, attracts a lot of non-residents. It also stays open well into the night.

The Talbot has a kids' club and is child-friendly. Indeed, it is friendly all-round, which probably accounts more than anything for its enduring appeal.

Rates from: 🐾🐾
Star rating: ★★★★
Overall rating: 🐾🐾🐾🐾 ½

Ambience :	9.10	Cleanliness:	9.45
Value:	9.25	Facilities:	9.24
Staff:	9.35	Restaurants:	9.60
Location:	9.55	Families:	9.64

Whites of Wexford

Abbey Street, Wexford, Ireland
T: +353 53 912 2311 **F:** +353 53 914 5000
www.HotelClub.com

Histories don't come much more colourful that that of this venerable establishment, which started life as a lodging house called The King's Arms in 1715. When it was run by the original

John White, commercial travellers used to carve their own roasts in the restaurant - and write their reports upstairs in the "commercial room" (an early manifestation of the business centre).

It is still a centre-piece of Wexford life, especially during the Opera Festival in June. Completely transformed during a two-year re-development terminating in 2006, the hotel now has 157 rooms, standard ones done out in crimson and white, superiors and suites on the top (fifth) floor coming with harbour views as well as robes and slippers and free mineral water and daily newspaper.

As well as a luxurious Leisure Club, boasting a gym using the Fitlinxx computerised training system and individual TVs, a 20-metre pool with reduced levels of chlorine, and a spa containing nine treatment rooms, scented showers, an ice fountain and a hydropool, plus a beauty salon, it also offers Ireland's and the UK's first cryotherapy clinic for treating muscle strain and arthritis.

You can dine by candlelight in The Terrace Restaurant (French cuisine with fresh local ingredients) or sit outside in the courtyard on fine summer evenings, and food is also served in the Library Bar, which has live music every Friday and Saturday. La Speranza Café Bar looks onto Wexford's main drag and a disco called Exile On Main Street is just round the corner. It's pretty likely that old John White wouldn't recognise the place.

Rates from: 🕯🕯🕯
Star rating: ★★★★
Overall rating: 🕯🕯🕯🕯 ½

Ambience :	9.10	Cleanliness:	9.35
Value:	9.15	Facilities:	9.26
Staff:	9.60	Restaurants:	9.42
Location:	9.45	Families:	8.89

Isle of Man

The British Isles abound with delicious anomalies, and one of the most toothsome is the semi independent Isle of Man, which can justly claim credit for the world's oldest parliament, the tailless Manx Cat, and The Bee Gees.

Its other major lures include fairly relaxed tax regulations, and a brace of spectacular motorcycle races - the Tourist Trophy, or TT, and the Grand Prix - each summer, when accommodation can be expected to be at a premium.

Home to some 80,000 souls, the island is otherwise pretty much off the main tourist track, to the undoubted delight of scenic railway and horse-drawn tram buffs who flock here in considerable number.

While the island is hardly a time capsule, it is reminiscent of Britain of yesteryear; those visitors not drawn here on business may well have time to discover a charm and distinction not always readily apparent on the mainland.

HOTEL	PAGE
I **Douglas**	
The Sefton	227

The Sefton

Harris Promenade, Douglas, IM1 2RW, Isle of Man
T: +44 1624 645501 **F**: +44 1624 676004
www.HotelClub.com/hotels/Sefton_Hotel_Douglas

If there's a pleasant echo of Victorian days at The Sefton, it takes second place to the modern atrium water garden, the highly imaginative, eco-friendly, predominant feature of this 95-room property. So picking an atrium room is a natural choice, though some guests may prefer accommodation whose windows open onto the Irish Sea.

Expect solid comfort (plus Wi-Fi access) rather than any avant garde moves in the interior design stakes. Days here start in the congenial breakfast room; a spa and library beckon if it's too chilly to venture to the promenade. Manx produce enlivens meals at the Gallery restaurant, while quaint tribute is paid to one of the island's most celebrated immigrants in the hotel bar, named for Sir Norman Wisdom. Younger readers may need reminding Sir Norman was a popular actor and comedian in the 1950s and 60s and is reputedly the most popular foreign entertainer in Albania.

Rates from: 🛏 🛏 🛏
Star rating: ★ ★ ★ ★
Overall rating: 🏵 🏵 🏵 🏵

Ambience :	9.17	Cleanliness:	9.50
Value:	8.00	Facilities:	9.60
Staff:	9.40	Restaurants:	9.20
Location:	9.50	Families:	9.50

Northern Ireland

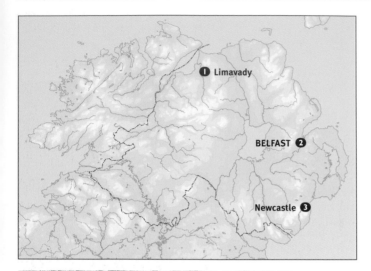

"There's never been a better time to visit Northern Ireland," trumpet various people paid to do so, or who stand to make a bit of money out of increased arrivals figures.

"Shush!" hiss the region's long-time aficionados, who have previously revelled in Northern Ireland's multifarious but little-visited attractions, and look askance at the prospect of more folks muscling in on their fun.

And fun there most certainly is, and scads of it.

The Troops Out campaign is a thing of the past, and Belfast is back in the headlines for all the right reasons, doing the urban regeneration thing with a certain amount of gusto, while the rest of the province provides both natural beauty and man-made attractions in ample measure. To cite just a few examples, the Titanic was built here, CS "Narnia" Lewis was born here (so there's a well defined heritage trail), the legendary Finn McCool - or more prosaic volcanic activity - produced the spectacular Giant's Causeway on the north coast of Antrim, there's angling for anglers, golfing for golfers, and a strongly emergent arts and culture scene.

However the most enjoyable facet of the new Northern Ireland is the palpable confidence and energy that's evident everywhere, from that omniscient, irrepressible conversationalist propping up the bar to the hotel's most junior porter. Gone are The Troubles, and now's the time to get going as part of Europe, imitating the Celtic Tiger to the south.

Executives passing though the capital will find plenty of hotels to choose from, while visitors with a less hectic schedule, and perhaps with families in tow, may be tempted by the gentler rhythms of places to stay in the countryside.

That eminent hotelier Dr Billy Hastings features large in subsequent pages, and deservedly so as his achievements for Northern Ireland's accommodation industry merit high praise, and act as a beacon for the future.

Anyone looking for a refreshingly unusual holiday spot in the British Isles would do well to delve deeper here, while those flitting in and out on business could easily be forgiven for extending their trip "for pressing personal reasons".

After all, as just about anyone who is anyone around these parts would happily admit "there's never been a better time to visit Northern Ireland".

Hastings Culloden Estate & Spa

Bangor Road, Holywood, Belfast, BT18 0EX, Northern Ireland
T: +44 28 9042 1066 **F:** +44 28 9042 6777
www.HotelClub.com/hotels/Culloden_Hotel_Belfast

World-famous in Northern Ireland, Dr Billy Hastings has been running hotels in the province since 1968, surfing the exigencies of The Troubles and building up a stable of properties that could impart a thing or three to certain rather better known international chains. Supremely good service in hotels to match could be the good doctor's watchword, and it's very much on display at this particular Hastings hotel, the Culloden Estate and Spa.

As might be expected, the hotel comes with a rousing history attached. A Gothic mansion raised in the late 19th century on a site chosen especially for its (relatively) clement climate, it later became a Bishop's Palace, then passed to a succession of gentry before taking on its present incarnation.

While its surrounding five hectares of garden and woodland lend the air of a country estate, the 79-room Culloden is only eight kilometres from Belfast city centre, drawing folk of all different stripes. The Stuart Suite can hold up to 600, the Highland Business Centre caters to smaller gatherings, while the Cultra Inn is popular with both stags and hens; keeping with the theme, the Culloden also makes for rather a nice wedding venue. And where better for Mr and Mrs Newly-Spliced to repair when the nuptial celebrations are over than the Palace Suite, apex of the

Culloden's accommodation and previously host to U2's Bono, travel guru Alan Whicker and former prime minister John Major, though not all at the same time?

Further down the line, there's a selection of slightly more modest suites, 38 double rooms and 25 twins, all very pleasantly upholstered and many with inspiring views of the gardens and down to Belfast Lough.

One of the prime reasons for coming to the Culloden is not necessarily to check in, but to check out what chef Paul McKnight has been up to. The Mitre is his main stage, but private dining performances are also enacted in the Drawing Room, with very fresh and very Irish produce taking key roles.

Perhaps the Culloden's pièce-de-resistance is its spa, importing treatments from around the world - Thai, Swedish, Indian - and dispensing them in surrounds that suggest pure luxury. There's also a regular fitness centre, an indoor pool that's exceptionally welcoming especially when its supposed to be summer outside, and an aromatic eucalyptus steam room, all granting extra amperage to the term pampering. Day-long programmes suggest extended stays, while a menu aimed specifically at men should reassure chaps who find the

whole concept a little too girlie.

Guests putting up here for a while will find plenty in the way of recreation beyond the bounds of the Culloden, be it the neighbouring transport museum, the Royal

Belfast Golf Course (Culloden's concierge fixes the best tee times) or the magnificent gardens of the National Trust's neo-Classical Mount Stewart House.

With the British Army's withdrawal in the summer of 2007, Northern Ireland has entered a new era. The Culloden, like all the Hastings hostelries, fared very well in the past. Nothing should stop them now!

Rates from: 🐚🐚🐚🐚🐚
Star rating: ★★★★★
Overall rating: 🎷🎷🎷🎷 ½

Ambience :	9.39	Cleanliness:	9.64
Value:	8.45	Facilities:	9.42
Staff:	9.19	Restaurants:	9.30
Location:	9.15	Families:	8.59

Hastings Europa Hotel

Great Victoria Street, Belfast, BT2 7AP, Northern Ireland
T: +44 28 9027 1066 **F:** +44 28 9032 7800
www.HotelClub.com/hotels/Europa_Hotel_Belfast

The posse of journalists based in the Europa during what Northern Ireland people coyly refer to as The Troubles usually didn't have far to go to find the site of the latest bomb.

The reason was simple: they were at it, for the 240-room property was blasted 33 times in 30 years, making it the world's most bombed hotel.

These days, the only conflagration you'll find is the open fire in the wood and marble lobby, with pilots and politicians checking in and live jazz or classical strings floating from the perennially lively public bar.

If you're a resident, you can potter up the stairs to the first-floor piano bar, passing as you do photographs of the great and the good who have stayed at the hotel, from Rod Stewart to Archbishop Desmond Tutu, although not sharing the same room, tragically.

That would have been a story even greater than the 1997 overnight of President Bill Clinton, who impressed the staff so much they named a suite after him.

Check into it, feel suitably presidential as you look out over magnificent views of the city, then make your way down to eat at the Piano Restaurant, where languid bronze nudes grace the tables and the food is a notch and a half above your average hotel nosh.

And then wander across the road to The Crown Bar, the Victorian pub beloved of John Betjeman and movie makers alike, for one last pint of Guinness before bed.

Just one, mind. You wouldn't want to miss breakfast, after all.

Rates from: 🛏🛏🛏🛏
Star rating: ★★★★
Overall rating: 👏👏👏👏

Ambience :	8.63	Cleanliness:	9.06
Value:	8.31	Facilities:	7.91
Staff:	9.00	Restaurants:	8.63
Location:	9.63	Families:	8.38

Hilton Belfast Hotel

4 Lanyon Place, Belfast, BT1 3LP, Northern Ireland
T: +44 28 9027 7000 **F:** ++44 28 9027 7277
www.HotelClub.com/hotels/Hilton_Hotel_Belfast

Pass the compulsory friendly nod from Charlie the top-hatted doorman, and you enter a world of light and air, with pale walls, bonsai trees silently striving to outdo each other in understated elegance, and chaise longues in vibrant reds and shades of blue.

When the 195-room Hilton opened as Belfast's first city centre five-star hotel in 1998, its designers set out to create an interior that was timeless, and proof that they've succeeded is the fact that it would still make any Japanese-Scandinavian sumptuous minimalist nod their discreet approval, pop into the gym to work up a subtle glow, then go off for a dry Martini in the Cables Bar, a contemporary take on the traditional Irish snug, with squishy leather sofas in front of a painfully stylish gas fire.

The riverside Sonoma Restaurant echoes the lobby's theme of colour and light, with a perfect view across the River Lagan of Samson and Goliath, the twin cranes of Harland and Wolff, once the world's biggest shipyard and birthplace of the Titanic.

That was old Belfast, but here you will find yourself rubbing shoulders with the pre-theatre crowd heading for a show at the adjacent Waterfront, the iconic concert hall which more than anything else marked the birth of the new city.

You'll see it even more when you make your way up to one of the light, airy and spacious bedrooms for panoramic views of the hammer and buzz of a city freeing itself with vigour from a troubled past.

Rates from: 🐚🐚
Star rating: n/a
Overall rating: 🐚🐚🐚🐚

Ambience :	8.24	Cleanliness:	8.94
Value:	7.94	Facilities:	7.82
Staff:	8.82	Restaurants:	8.60
Location:	9.35	Families:	8.71

Jurys Inn Belfast

Fisherwick Place, Great Victoria Street, Belfast, BT2 7AP, Northern Ireland
T: +44 28 9053 3500 **F:** +44 28 9053 3511
www.HotelClub.com/hotels/Jurys_Inn_Belfast

If you look out of the window of your room at Jurys to see an antiquated London Routemaster bus, don't change your medication just yet. It's just offering city tours, next door to the one offering trips up the dramatic north coast; and the one offering an express service to Dublin. If you're beginning to suspect that Jurys is the perfect budget base for exploring Belfast and beyond, you wouldn't be far wrong. Add in the extremely reasonable rates for 190 functional but comfortable rooms in which you can fit three adults (or two adults and two children), an Inntro bar with an entirely tasty and inexpensive daily special,

broadband in every room, and a location which is next door to the Grand Opera House and only five minutes' walk from City Hall, and you've got a bargain in any language. It's all very much above par for what is after all a humble three-star, and the staff are friendly even by local standards. And that's saying something.

Rates from: ☾ ☾ ☾
Star rating: ★★★
Overall rating: 🦋🦋🦋🦋

Ambience :	8.24	Cleanliness:	8.94
Value:	7.94	Facilities:	7.82
Staff:	8.82	Restaurants:	8.60
Location:	9.35	Families:	8.71

Malmaison Belfast

34-38 Victoria Street, Belfast, BT1 3GH, Northern Ireland
T: +44 28 9022 0200 **F:** +44 28 9022 0220
www.HotelClub.com/hotels/Malmaison_Belfast

French cooking using seasonal local produce such as Finnebrogue venison, washed down with the 240-strong list of sommelier Stefan Sanchez. Upstairs, the 64 rooms are lighter than expected, including two penthouses you could happily live in, and all with music systems ready to play a CD from the hotel library. Cohen, naturally.

Enter a world of black wood and stygian velours, the only relief the dully glinting brass of an ancient plate camera and several Granny Smiths in shadowy pigeonholes. The apples, that is, not the relatives. This pair of listed 150-

year-old former grain warehouses may sound like Leonard Cohen's living room, but it is strangely cosy, creating an atmosphere of intrigue in which you are surprised to see men with their wives. Downstairs, the brasserie boasts excellent

Rates from: ☾ ☾ ☾
Star rating: ★★★★
Overall rating: 🦋🦋🦋🦋

Ambience :	9.00	Cleanliness:	9.50
Value:	7.79	Facilities:	7.05
Staff:	8.93	Restaurants:	9.00
Location:	9.00	Families:	8.00

The Merchant Hotel

35-39 Waring St., Belfast, BT1 2DY, Northern Ireland
T: +44 28 9023 4888 **F:** +44 28 9024 7775
www.HotelClub.com

Their gaze could equally be directed at the staff uniforms, blue and black striped shirts echoed in the orange, red and brown striped carpet of the 26 rooms upstairs which will have Gustavian minimalists feeling quite faint.

But then, this is not a hotel for the faint-hearted, whether you're ordering cocktails or booking the hotel Bentley Arnage to collect you and yours from the airport.

The good news is that the Great Room, the main restaurant, lives up to its name, with faultless food served by matching and perpetually friendly staff.

Upstairs, the bedrooms are a sumptuous riot of lush patterns and colours, with five suites named after local writers.

The CS Lewis, naturally, has a large wardrobe, and check-out is at noon, so you can have a "lion" in the morning.

One of the finest Victorian buildings in the city, the Merchant was once the headquarters of that venerable institution, the Ulster Bank.

Today, the discreet rustle of money still fills its marble halls, but the customers are spending rather than withdrawing: particularly the local businessmen who celebrated a deal by ordering the world's most expensive cocktail, a Trader Vic's

Mai Tai for £750 based on a 17-year-old Wray and Nephew rum worth £26,000 a bottle.

In the opulent lobby, ladies who lunch, watched by myriad gilded cherubim and seraphim, celebrate a hard morning's shopping with afternoon tea and Champagne, while the Old Masters on the walls look on with a Victorian frown at such extravagance.

Rates from: 🏨🏨🏨🏨
Star rating: ★★★★★
Overall rating: 🏨🏨🏨🏨

Ambience :	9.40	Cleanliness:	9.53
Value:	7.47	Facilities:	7.64
Staff:	9.13	Restaurants:	9.08
Location:	9.53	Families:	7.83

Stormont Hotel

Upper Newtownards Road, Belfast, BT4 3LP, Northern Ireland
T: +44 28 9065 1066 **F:** +44 28 9048 0240
www.HotelClub.com/hotels/Stormont_Hotel_Belfast

Once upon a time, children, the Stormont was the Cinderella of Belfast hotels, looking across the road with a pout at the great and the good making their way up the mile-long drive to the other Stormont: the great white monolith of the Northern Ireland Parliament.

Then along came a fairy godmother in the shape of affable local magnate Billy Hastings, who got it to the ball at last with a comprehensive makeover.

Today, the stark white exterior of the 110-room Stormont may never make style bunnies hop for joy, but inside, all is pale wood and primary fabrics, counterpointed by the open fire, an ironic nod to the traditional Ulster cottage welcome, which is a hallmark of Hastings hotels across Northern Ireland.

The staff are a wonderful combination of eager and relaxed: the former because they know they're still one star short of nearby sister hotel the Culloden, and the latter because they're 15 minutes away from the hurly burly of the city.

That means you will need your own car or a rental, but with free parking, who cares?

For dining, the La Scala Bistro and more formal Shiraz Restaurant, are both above average, and to work up an appetite, there's the hotel's own fitness suite, the complimentary, superbly equipped David Lloyd tennis centre just minutes away, or just a bracing walk a mile up the landscaped hill to the province's seat of power where you can declare your manifesto to the wind.

Rates from: 🐚 🐚 🐚
Star rating: ★ ★ ★ ★
Overall rating: 🐚 🐚 🐚 🐚

Ambience :	8.78	Cleanliness:	8.94
Value:	8.72	Facilities:	8.91
Staff:	8.89	Restaurants:	8.73
Location:	8.83	Families:	8.17

Radisson SAS Roe Park Resort

Limavady, Co Londonderry, BT49 9LB, Northern Ireland
T: +44 28 777 22222 **F:** +44 28 777 22313
www.HotelClub.com/hotels/Radisson_SAS_Roe_Park_Resort_Limavady

The moment you pass the happy couple enjoying a moment of passion on the lush fairway, you know you're somewhere romantic.

But enough about the rabbits: humans too come back here time and again, to take a deep breath, roll their shoulders and look forward to a couple of days getting to know each other again and doing as little or as much as they want in a resort which has location in triplicate.

That little could be pampering in the spa, lounging in the hot tub, or sitting in front of the fire in The Coach House and watching the waiter approach with the legendary Big One starter, your thoughts a fine balance of anticipation and fear as to where you're going to put your main course.

And the much? Well, it could be shaving away at your handicap on the glorious 18-hole parkland course, or jumping in the car and heading off on one of the great drives of the world, the rugged Antrim north coast, taking in the Giant's Causeway, views which don't stop until they get to America, and Bushmills, the world's oldest distillery, where they started making whiskey in 1608 and have been getting better ever since.

The only caution, and it is a small one, is that the place's romantic setting makes it a big favourite for wedding receptions, so if you fancy an early night after all that passion on the fairway, book an upstairs room from the 118 on offer.

Rates from: 🏠🏠🏠
Star rating: ★★★★
Overall rating: 🐾🐾🐾🐾

Ambience :	8.95	Cleanliness:	9.05
Value:	8.33	Facilities:	8.77
Staff:	9.00	Restaurants:	8.95
Location:	8.48	Families:	9.06

Hasting Slieve Dornard Resort & Spa

Downs Road, Newcastle, Co. Down, BT33 0AH, Northern Ireland
T: +44 28 4372 1066 **F:** +44 28 4372 4830
www.HotelClub.com/hotels/Slieve_Donard_Hotel_Newcastle

Canadian Pacific Railways had the Banff Springs Hotel, and the Belfast and County Down Railway had the Slieve Donard. The distances involved may have been different, but the principle was the same: to create a luxury at the end of the line impossible to resist for well-heeled travellers.

In the case of the Slieve Donard, when it was finished in 1898 for a whopping £44,000, complete with its own bakery, vegetable gardens, pigs, laundry and generator to provide electricity for the railway station, it was probably the most magnificent hotel in Ireland.

Not surprisingly, it attracted guests to match: from King Leopold and Charlie Chaplin to songwriter Percy French, whose line "where the mountains of Mourne sweep down to the sea" still serves well enough as directions to get there.

They came, of course, for golf,

sallying forth with their trusty mashie niblicks to thrash their way around Royal County Down, then as now one of the world's great links course.

Others came to stride into the mountains in plus-fours and stout boots, or to breath in the sea air and take the waters, in the form of douche, spray, needle and Turkish baths, before making their way up the grand staircase past flunkeys polishing the brass carpet rods twice a day, to take their ease in rooms with Chippendale furniture, Persian carpets and coal fires.

In 1972, it was bought by Billy Hastings, the Dalai Lama of Northern Ireland hotels, and for years slumbered on as the grand dame of his group, stolid but dull.

Today, a £15 million makeover has changed all that: the once homely interior is now a hymn to good taste, the once unremarkable food is something to write home about and the new spa is the equal of anywhere in the known universe.

Not that all of this has stopped the affable Billy from retaining the Hastings trademark; the open fire in the grand lobby. And it's a real one, none of your gas nonsense.

Upstairs, the 178 bedrooms are a happy marriage of history and hip, with sofas the size of baby elephants (although more comfortable) from which you can watch the flatscreen TV if you ever tire of the view.

Not that you will, particularly if you make your way down to the spa, to luxuriate in that wonderful feeling of being utterly cared for with a massage or a facial, before padding across the wooden floor to a sauna with a glass wall giving you an elemental and utterly satisfying view of sea and sky, mountain and forest.

Spend an hour at peace there, or in the adjacent hot pool, watching the sun fall to kiss the ocean, before sighing with contentment and thinking to

yourself that it's maybe time for a spot of dinner.

And with it that most satisfying of adult feelings, of dressing and making your way down a grand staircase to cocktails and a meal that you feel quietly confident will exceed your expectations. What more could you want of a grand hotel?

Rates from: 🝔🝔🝔🝔🝔
Star rating: ★★★★
Overall rating: 🝔🝔🝔🝔

Ambience :	8.85	Cleanliness:	9.23
Value:	8.04	Facilities:	9.20
Staff:	8.63	Restaurants:	8.73
Location:	9.59	Families:	8.38

Scotland

creation of the Scottish Executive, or Government, which keeps Westminster at slightly more than arm's length. The world's largest wave energy project may be under way in Orkney, and the Och The Noo souvenir shop off Edinburgh's Royal Mile might be run by a family of Sikhs, but traditional Scotland at its bonniest - interpret the adjective how you will - lies waiting.

A sovereign state until 1707, Scotland has maintained a healthy independence - twice rising in rebellion in the 18th century - although of late rivalry with England has been concentrated on sporting fixtures and media banter. Europe's largest oil reserves lie off the coast, and their profits are the key to the swagger of Aberdeen and the northeast. Elsewhere, post-industrial Scotland encompasses everything from high finance to low call centres.

It's hard to conceive of a more attractive capital than Edinburgh, dominated by the castle (the site of a riveting night-time military tattoo

Glorious as budget airlines may be, and while vestiges of romance may still cling to the railways ("pulling up Beattock, a steady climb, the gradient's against her, but she's on time"), the quintessential entry to Scotland is motoring up the A68 and over Carter Bar. Like as not, there'll be a piper at the border to offer a hearty welcome, and whatever

your views on bagpipe music, it's cheering to discover that he's not been stationed there by the tourist board. And that there's a pile of CDs up for sale just goes to show that the Scots' reputation for canniness remains as strong as ever it was.

Just about everything that lies to the north is thriving in a similar vein. Recent years have seen the

each summer), which looks down on the central thoroughfare of Princes Street and its adjacent gardens. A maze of intriguing alleyways burrows through the older parts of the city, while to the south the Braid Hills and the Pentlands grant a reminder of the broad green acres which make up the greater part of this country. Edinburgh has inspired numerous writers, from Robert Louis Stevenson to Muriel Spark, and more recently Irvine Welsh and Alexander McCall Smith, whose Scotland Street series was initially serialised in The Scotsman newspaper. Few visitors depart The Festival City without a similar feeling of artistic stimulation.

Scotland's second city, Glasgow, prospered in the 19th century, and more recent economic woes have been set aside as it surfs a cultural renaissance. A thriving history is recorded in a rash of museums from the Victoriana of the Kelvingrove and The Burrell Collection (gifted to the city by the wealthy and philanthropic Sir William), to the latest art and design in GOMA and The Lighthouse. High property prices and the Bohemian café society found in The West End are two sure signs of regeneration in a city which has more green space

per capita than any other European metropolis. Further north, Dundee has bypassed memories of the Three Js (jam, journalism and jute) which were once its economic mainstays with its own brand of redevelopment, not least Sensation, one of the country's most entrancing and intelligent museums.

Away from the cities, the highlands and islands provide numerous opportunities for outdoor pursuits, be it fishing, deer stalking or simply climbing Ben Nevis, which at 1,344 metres is the highest peak in the British Isles. A bridge has linked the Isle of Skye to the mainland since 1995, but other islands retain their remote beauty, and the roads in the north must be some of the least trafficked in Britain.

For a sampler of Scottish accommodation, a brisk walk between The Balmoral and Tigerlily in Edinburgh is not only to journey from the sublime to the fabulous,

but to bridge the twin poles between not exactly ancient and ultra modern. In between, sterling bastions of hospitality await on outlying islands such as Colonsay, Skye and Jura, and even if you adopt the Kingsley Amis stance on golf ("a game I hope fervently to go

to my grave without ever having had to play") you'll be aware of Gleneagles and St Andrews.

Given Scotland's latitude and longitude, the weather makes its presence felt most of the year, to the extent of almost hoping that part of what Al Gore says about

global warming might come true. Like Scottish Boy Scouts, and Girl Guides for that matter, learn to be well and truly prepared.

And if it's inclement without, some rather neat spas (The Scotsman hotel's Cowshed is particularly notable) beckon inside, while local chefs have put haggis (sonsie-faced or otherwise) and black pudding on the back burner to experiment and dazzle in a Scotland's brave new culinary world.

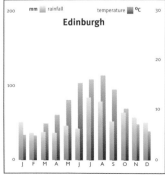

The Gleneagles Hotel

Auchterarder, Perthshire, PH3 1NF, Scotland
T: +44 1764 662 231 **F:** +44 1764 662 134
www.HotelClub.com

If it doesn't sound too much like heresy, you don't have to like golf (or be attending a G8 Summit) to enjoy Gleneagles. Built in the more gracious 1920s by the Caledonian Railway Company (before trains had been overtaken by planes and automobiles), it has metamorphosed into a comprehensive resort that defines "up market" and brooks few rivals.

It would be disadvantageous to attempt to cover more than a few aspects of Gleneagles, whose original advertising slogan described it as the Eighth Wonder of the World. Set among some 340 hectares an hour's drive from Edinburgh or Glasgow, its natural beauty is perhaps its greatest asset. Three championship golf courses - King's, Queen's (both of which actually predate the hotel) and what used to be known as Monarch's, but which now goes under the prosaic moniker of PGA Centenary - provide a sizeable number of visitors with the reason for coming here. It's interesting to remark that while the original greens were hacked out of the wilderness with pick and shovel, students at the golf academy nowadays are filmed with a digital camera and given the resulting CD-Rom to take home.

It's a parallel tale with the accommodation, which is spread between 232 guestrooms,

combining modern technology with the grandeur of an age-old country estate. Cream of the crop are the ten "spirit" suites - named not for anything New Agey but in tribute to Gleneagles current owner, drinks colossus Diageo.

On which subject, there's 120 single malt whiskies just aching to be tippled here, as well as more than 250 different wines, more than adequate accompaniment for chef Andrew Fairlie's double Michelin-starred, Gallically-accented menus.

And striking a contrast with some particularly toothsome Scottish produce - salmon, Dundee cake, Highland grouse - is the newly opened Deseo, which styles itself as a Mediterranean food market.

If all this sounds very much adult-oriented, it's worth noting that Gleneagles is the thinking child's playground, where an especially indulgent (and flush) godparent might provide a series of highly original birthday presents in the form of gift vouchers; six-year-olds may try their hand at off-road driving, and ten-year-olds may take their places on the archery and rifle ranges, while boys and girls two years their senior can pilot all-terrain vehicles and attend gundog training sessions. Organised birthday parties include chariot racing among a list of diversions (which rather put clowns and conjurers in the shade) and falconry, golf and horse riding are open to all. These activities, with the possible exception of the Ben Hur stuff, are also available for over-18s.

Never somewhere to let the grass grow under its feet, Gleneagles will open a brand new destination spa in January 2008, to be managed by ESPA, with a score of treatment rooms, a vitality pool and a veritable host of heat treatments. And looking a little further into the future, anyone looking to fill up their 2014 diary should note that the Ryder Cup is scheduled to be played here then.

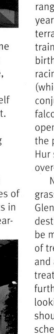

Rates from: 🛏🛏🛏🛏🛏
Star rating: ★ ★ ★ ★ ★
Overall rating: 🐾🐾🐾🐾 ½

Ambience :	9.54	Cleanliness:	9.48
Value:	7.97	Facilities:	9.29
Staff:	9.36	Restaurants:	9.51
Location:	9.21	Families:	8.69

Hilton Coylumbridge

Aviemore, PH22 1QN, Scotland
T: +44 1479 810 661 **F:** +44 1479 811 309
www.HotelClub.com/hotels/Hilton_Coylumbridge_Hotel_Aviemore

"If my kids are happy, I'm happy," is a parental truism - and if you want to put it to the test, try this 88-room Hilton in the Cairngorms, one of Scotland's leading ski resorts. It is low-rise and nothing much to look at (or to look out onto, come to that), with so-so rooms, unspectacular décor and average f&b outlets, but what lifts it into a class of its own is its appeal to the younger members of the family. They will gravitate to the Fun House, with its mini-golf and bowling, air hockey, soft-play areas and tree house, and the outdoor adventure park, with a dry ski slope and climbing wall. Dad can watch over them while munching a burger or hot dog in the 1950s-themed American Diner, then challenge the son and heir to a game of pool. Or he and "mom" can retire to the Woodshed Bar, an all-day-dining log cabin that screens major sports events.

The indoor swimming-pool complex, with sauna, solarium and Jacuzzi, is another family favourite. And there is often live entertainment in the evenings, with a disco for that precocious daughter. The restaurants - Grant Room and Caffe Cino - and Foyer Lounge & Bar all have roaring log fires.

Boasting extensive conference and business facilities, the property also targets groups of "bonding" business executives: "team-building" activities include rafting and skiing, clay-pigeon shooting, horse-riding and quad-biking in the 26-hectare grounds.

But then, what are off-duty business types but little kids at heart, anyway?

Rates from: 🐚🐚🐚
Star rating: ★★★★
Overall rating: 👐👐👐👐

Ambience :	8.93	Cleanliness:	9.00
Value:	8.60	Facilities:	7.47
Staff:	9.15	Restaurants:	8.20
Location:	9.27	Families:	9.33

Crieff Hydro

Crieff, Perthshire, PH7 3LQ, Scotland
T: +44 1764 651 670 **F:** +44 1764 656 315
www.HotelClub.com

For nearly a century and a half, this Victorian spa hotel has been a landmark for the Highlands-bordering town of Crieff, but in recent years it has morphed into a much more modern rural resort, with a very un-Victorian attitude to those whom our forebears believed should be "seen but not heard".

There is a Big Country club for two-to-12-year-olds and teenagers are catered for as well as their more energetic parents with horse-riding, quad-biking (mini vehicles for the kids), mountain-biking, rope courses, badminton, tennis, golf and archery in the 365-hectare wooded grounds.

The 213 rooms and suites come in two categories - traditional and contemporary, or you have the option of self-catering in the property's stand-alone cottages, lodges and chalets (a ten-unit "village" has recently been added to the mix). You can even bring the family dog.

There is a pool in the Victorian Spa, which also features a sauna and steamroom, while you can tone your muscles in the gym or enhance your appearance at the Hair, Health and Beauty Salon.

The Meikle Restaurant affords the opportunity to dress for dinner, The Brasserie is more informal and the Winter Garden coffee shop even more so - as is The Hub, a newly opened light-snackery with big-screen TV for sports events.

For all its concessions to the demands of today's holidaymakers, the Hydro manages to retain a whiff of its Victorian origins, with traditional ceilidhs round the fireside, tumbler of local malt in hand, and free sledges for guests when winter snows lay thick upon the ground.

Rates from: 🛏🛏🛏🛏
Star rating: ★ ★ ★ ★
Overall rating: 🐾🐾🐾🐾

Ambience :	8.00	Cleanliness:	8.00
Value:	7.50	Facilities:	8.50
Staff:	7.50	Restaurants:	9.00
Location:	7.50	Families:	7.50

Apex City Quay Hotel & Spa

1 West Victoria Dock Road, Dundee DD1 3JP, Scotland
T: +44 1316 665 124 **F:** +44 1316 665 128
www.HotelClub.com/hotels/Apex_City_Quay_Hotel_Spa_Dundee

This staid old Scottish city is in the throes of re-inventing itself, and at the heart of this makeover, on the Victoria dockside where trendy boutiques and restaurants are springing up almost overnight, is the Apex City Quay.

Its 152 rooms range from standard to Master Suite and have all the contemporary accoutrements you would expect, from wide-screen TVs and mood lighting to power showers and oversized desks. It is also, somewhat surprisingly for such an "adult" hotel, very child-friendly - two kids under 16 can stay for free if sharing a room with mum and dad, while those under ten eat for nothing as well.

The Alchemy Restaurant magics French fare out of Scottish ingredients, while the Metro Brasserie & Bar is the sort of place you'd expect to feature a Sunday jazz brunch (which it does). Then there's the Japanese-influenced Yu Spa, with wooden hot tubs, Elemis treatment rooms, ozone pool, solarium, steamroom and sauna, as well as a "techno-gym".

Contemporary Scottish artwork fills the walls and when you've had your fill of that, you're about as close as you can get to most of the sightseeing splendours of Dundee, such as Captain Scott's Arctic-exploration vessel and a wooden warship, *HM Frigate Unicorn*, as well as the Verdant working jute mill (once one of Dundee's major industries), the late Queen Mum's childhood home, Glamis Castle, and Scone Palace, home of Scotland's kings. If you want to enquire about any of these attractions, local phone-calls are free!

Rates from: 🏯🏯🏯
Star rating: ★★★★
Overall rating: 😊😊😊😊

Ambience :	8.25	Cleanliness:	9.38
Value:	8.81	Facilities:	8.55
Staff:	8.50	Restaurants:	8.13
Location:	8.56	Families:	7.70

Hilton Dunkeld House Hotel

Dunkeld, Perthshire, PH8 0HX, Scotland
T: +44 1350 727 771 **F:** +44 1350 728 924
www.HotelClub.com/hotels/Hilton_Dunkeld_House_Hotel

The chain may have mixed feelings about one of its properties breaking the corporate mould, but many visitors to Dunkeld House come away with the comment: "It doesn't feel like a Hilton." What it does feel like is a Scottish country-house hotel, which is what the seventh Duke of Atholl's former summer home has been turned into.

Lots of leather and log fires (albeit mock in many cases), rich furnishings and wood panelling, and some quirky touches (the bed in the Bothy Room is made out of a boat). Ask for a Club Room with a river view. It is wheelchair-friendly and very environmentally

conscious. One can't imagine many guests rushing to get away, but if you are in a hurry you can request an express check-out.

Set in 113 park-like hectares on the banks of the Tay, its outdoor activities are a prime attraction - everything from tennis, putting, volleyball, croquet and petanques to archery, clay-pigeon shooting, quad-biking, 4X4 driving and, of course, angling (salmon and trout). The LivingWell health club has a pool, sauna and gym, while Natural Beauty offers massage, facials, aromatherapy and hair care.

Fare in the Garden Restaurant and Garden Bar is locally sourced

where possible (a bottle of whisky is available at breakfast for pouring over your porridge!) And guests are greeted on arrival with a wee dram - of whisky or sherry. There is an 18-hole golf course just a short drive away, but a walk through the grounds is pleasant enough exercise for most.

Rates from: 🌳🌳🌳
Star rating: ★★★★
Overall rating: 👋👋👋👋

Ambience :	8.76	Cleanliness:	8.88
Value:	8.35	Facilities:	8.55
Staff:	8.76	Restaurants:	8.88
Location:	9.12	Families:	8.75

The Balmoral

1 Princes Street, Edinburgh, EH2 2EQ, Scotland
T: +44 1315 562 414 **F:** +44 1315 578 740
www.HotelClub.com/hotels/Balmoral_Hotel_Edinburgh

After the Castle, The Balmoral hotel clock is one of the best-known landmarks in Edinburgh. It is always set three minutes fast to ensure travellers make it to their train in the neighbouring Waverley Station on time - except on New Year's Eve, when it is a focal point for Hogmanay revellers. Inside the hotel itself, things also run like clockwork. The service is so super-efficient, guests may find themselves with more time on their hands than they bargained for. The hotel's airy Palm Court is a good place to spend it - sample some fizz from the Bollinger Bar, the only one of its type in the United Kingdom, or destroy your diet with an afternoon tea. The décor has a timeless quality, embracing the past and reflecting the Scottish landscape with the use of earthy colours such as subtle lilacs, greens and blues. The 188 bedrooms - including 20 suites - are refreshingly unfussy, with a mixture of contemporary styling and a scattering of antiques. Thanks to the age of the building, which opened in 1902, the ceilings are high throughout giving the already spacious rooms a feeling of added grandeur. Many feature views of the Castle, the city's Old

Town or the hills beyond. Perhaps surprisingly for a hotel with so much history and tradition, it is also at the cutting edge when it comes to new ideas. It isn't just adults that get five-star service, babies, kids and teens also get a taste of the highlife. The hotel's Five-star Babies programme provides toys, bottle warmers and sterilisers, while older kids get luxury bathtime treatment, including bubble bath and ducks. A teddy turndown service will see them tucked up tight with a Balmoral bear and customised kids' robes and slippers are also provided. Teenagers won't feel left out, either, with PlayStation 2s, non-alcoholic mocktails and books and DVDs all available. Hogwarts fans will also be interested to learn that JK Rowling put the finishing touches to *Harry Potter And The Deathly Hallows* in the hotel - and signed an antique bust in the room where she stayed to mark the event. Guests who can bear to tear themselves away from their rooms can enjoy informal dining in Hadrian's brasserie or opt for the more decadent surroundings of the Number One restaurant, with its red lacquer walls, artwork from the Institute of Art in London and, most importantly for food buffs, a Michelin star. The Balmoral Bar underwent an extensive redesign in autumn 2007 and now has a chic, contemporary feel, drawing on the heather hues of the Scottish landscape for its colour scheme. Those who have over-indulged can salve their consciences by heading to the gym and award-winning spa in the basement. That said, even the 15-metre pool has an air of hedonism, thanks to a candle-lit relaxation area beside it. The spa area also

features a candle-lit Relaxation Suite, to get guests in the mood for the range of skin care and massage packages on offer. In short, this old lady of Princes Street - like her clock - keeps on moving with the times, but always seems to be just a little bit ahead of the competition. If you can't hack the rates, at least drop in for a glimpse.

Rates from: 𖤐𖤐𖤐𖤐𖤐
Star rating: ★★★★★
Overall rating: 𓃰𓃰𓃰𓃰

Ambience :	9.02	Cleanliness:	9.42
Value:	7.69	Facilities:	8.54
Staff:	8.74	Restaurants:	8.86
Location:	9.70	Families:	8.36

The Bonham

35 Drumsheugh Gardens, Edinburgh, EH3 7RN, Scotland
T: +44 1312 26 6 050 **F:** +44 1312 266 080
www.HotelClub.com/hotels/Bonham_Hotel_Edinburgh

Previously a university hall of residence, and even more previously a private clinic, this hushed and plush boutique hotel can now teach a thing or two about style. Two wooden-fronted telephone booths stand sentinel by the entrance offering a quirky nod to its former undergraduate residents. The fine wood finishings have been retained throughout the hotel – which comprises three 19th-century townhouses connected by a warren of corridors and staircases, splashed with colour thanks to canvases from up-and-coming artists.

All of the 48 rooms – each individually designed by Janey Armstrong – has a cosy but classy feel, and although some feel a little tired a refit is planned by mid 2008. Many rooms offer views to die for out towards the Firth of Forth and one even features a glass roof above the bath so guests can watch for shooting stars. Other welcome surprises include an Edwardian copper bath and an arresting spiral sofa bench in Reception. The overall vibe is of dash and verve, combining with a general feeling of calm and comfort.

Fine dining in the Restaurant at the Bonham, run by Frenchman Michel Bouyer, gives Scots tradition a European twist. As a single example, the Sunday three-course Boozy Snoozy lunch – £75 for a table of four including two bottles of wine – deserves a double prize for both nomenclature and culinary wizardry. As a final note, motorists wearied of being stung for the privilege of stabling their vehicle while they sleep will rejoice at The Bonham's free parking facility.

Rates from: 🛏🛏🛏🛏
Star rating: ★★★★
Overall rating: 🐾🐾🐾🐾

Ambience :	8.94	Cleanliness:	9.50
Value:	8.88	Facilities:	6.96
Staff:	8.56	Restaurants:	9.07
Location:	9.38	Families:	7.44

Caledonian Hilton Edinburgh

Princes Street, Edinburgh, EH1 2AB, Scotland
T: +44 1312 228 888 **F**: +44 1312 228 889
www.HotelClub.com/hotels/Hilton_Caledonian_Hotel_Edinburgh

prefer to get sweaty in private, may prefer to opt for the yoga mat provided in all bedrooms. Fine dining can be had in the elegant Pompadour Restaurant, with its beautiful bird murals, or in the brasserie-style Chisholm's Restaurant, while whisky lovers can take their pick of more than 140 in The Caley Bar.

The rose-coloured brick of this 251-bedroom hotel provides a warm welcome, echoed by the attentive staff. Opened in 1903 as a station hotel it ushered in an era of luxury that endures to this day. Although much of the architecture is Victorian, there is a host of art deco fittings and these period touches have been carried into the rooms. Many have views out over Princes Street Gardens and Edinburgh Castle and all come with plenty of little extras as standard, including PlayStations and bathrobes. Use of the LivingWell health club is free for guests, although those who

Rates from: 🛏🛏🛏🛏
Star rating: ★ ★ ★ ★ ★
Overall rating: 🐾🐾🐾🐾

Ambience :	9.00	Cleanliness:	9.28
Value:	8.03	Facilities:	8.11
Staff:	8.92	Restaurants:	8.76
Location:	9.36	Families:	8.12

Dalhousie Castle Luxury Castle Hotel and Spa

Bonnyrigg, Edinburgh, EH19 3JB, Scotland
T: +44 1875 820 153 **F**: +44 1875 821 936
www.HotelClub.com/hotels/Dalhousie_Castle_Hotel_Edinburgh

enjoy traditional Scottish fare. Those who prefer their food with a view can opt for The Orangery, a bright, conservatory-style space that looks out onto the South Esk river, which runs through the hotel grounds. Anyone looking for something more indulgent can opt for a spot of pampering in the Aqua Sulis spa.

No 13th-century castle would be complete without a ghost and the resident spook at the 37-room Dalhousie is the Grey Lady, a mistress of one of the Castle's lairds in the 16th century, who was locked up in a turret until she wasted away. There's no danger of starving to death in the dungeons these days, however, since they have been converted into the Dungeon Restaurant. Cosy, welcoming - and complete with suits of armour - this is an intimate space in which to

Rates from: 🛏🛏🛏🛏
Star rating: ★ ★ ★ ★
Overall rating: 🐾🐾🐾🐾 ½

Ambience :	9.77	Cleanliness:	9.85
Value:	8.92	Facilities:	8.42
Staff:	9.46	Restaurants:	9.38
Location:	9.31	Families:	9.30

The George Hotel

19-21 George Street, Edinburgh, EH2 2PB, Scotland
T: +44 1312 251 251 **F:** +44 1312 265 644
www.HotelClub.com/hotels/George_Intercontinental_Hotel_Edinburgh

It may be more than 200 years old but this elegant 197-room hotel in the city's upmarket George Street still has a few new tricks up its sleeve - including plans to build an additional 50 bedrooms by the end of 2008. The rest of the Grade II listed building has recently undergone a £12 million refurbishment. This makeover has brought a breath of fresh air to the original architecture, rather than blowing your mind with modernity, and the understated décor brings out the best in the hotel's traditional trappings. Rooms in the Forth Wing have a chic, contemporary feel, with a lily motif used on cushions, artwork and even on the backs of the desk chairs.

The more traditional Adam Wing, meanwhile, has had a subtler spruce-up, with the rooms featuring Scottish thistles as their badge of honour. The rooms come in all shapes and sizes and the suites are particularly generous, with high ceilings giving an added feeling of space. Those at the back of the hotel look out towards the River Forth, while bedrooms at the front gaze onto George Street - which with its bank-balance busting designer shops makes for a tempting stroll.

Equally tempting is the Tempus Restaurant Bar. Here dark wood hints at the palette of the past while the artwork and the cuisine - indulgent breakfasts and an evening menu that places the emphasis on locally sourced produce such as Buccleuch beef and Loch Fyne salmon - are fiercely up to date.

Rates from: 🛏🛏🛏🛏🛏
Star rating: ★★★★
Overall rating: 📷📷📷📷

Ambience :	8.75	Cleanliness:	9.20
Value:	8.15	Facilities:	8.15
Staff:	8.89	Restaurants:	8.80
Location:	9.75	Families:	8.50

The Glasshouse

2 Greenside Place, Edinburgh, EH1 3AA, Scotland
T: +44 1315 258 200 **F:** +44 1315 258 205
www.HotelClub.com/hotels/Glasshouse_Hotel_Edinburgh_The

The appeal of this boutique hotel, just five minutes' walk from Princes Street, is as much about the outside as the inside. Its 150-year-old façade was once part of Lady Glenorch Church which, thanks to the numerous windows, gives the thoroughly modern interior a light, bright and airy ambience. This feeling of space extends to the 65 bedrooms, all of which feature private terraces - reached via windows stretching from floor to ceiling windows - either looking out on to the city and the Forth Estuary in the distance, or opening on to the hotel's most surprising and seductive secret - its roof-top garden. This lovely oasis offers unrivalled views of Calton Hill and, if the weather obliges, a quiet spot to catch some sun. The Snug lounge provides a cosy alternative if the weather turns wet, with a crucible of fire giving the place a homely atmosphere. This is aided by an honesty bar - guests take what they like and 'fess up to it on a sheet so that they can pay at the end of their stay. All the rooms are spacious and include nice touches, such as complimentary business cards and shoe shine. The suites are each named after a different malt whisky and, as an added boozy bonus, feature a free decanter of the relevant tipple inside, while the deluxe suite also boasts a private Jacuzzi and sauna. Although the hotel doesn't serve evening meals, round-the-clock room service is available, including a competitively priced tapas menu, and breakfast is served in The Observatory, which also features floor-to-ceiling views out onto Calton Hill.

Rates from: 🛏🛏🛏
Star rating: ★★★★★
Overall rating: 👏👏👏👏

Ambience :	8.88	Cleanliness:	9.54
Value:	8.00	Facilities:	7.67
Staff:	9.04	Restaurants:	7.77
Location:	9.04	Families:	7.67

Macdonald Roxburghe Hotel, Edinburgh

38 Charlotte Square, Edinburgh, EH2 4HQ, Scotland
T: +44 8701 942 108 **F:** +44 1312 405 555
www.HotelClub.com

They say you can't please all the people all the time – but when it comes to a choice of styles, this 197-room hotel makes an accomplished stab at it.

Partly situated in a Georgian townhouse in the west end of Edinburgh - less than a minute from Princes Street and the uber-fashionable George Street - many of the rooms and suites feature the furnishings of the period, including original artwork.

Those who like their tradition tempered by modern design will not be disappointed either, since several of the rooms in the older part of the hotel have been given a contemporary flourish thanks to stylish wallpapers and textured fabrics. Guests who think history is for has-beens, meanwhile, can choose to sleep soundly in one of the rooms in the hotel's new portion - built in 1999. Connecting the old and the new is a bright and breezy conservatory and courtyard area, perfect for sampling afternoon tea. Many of the rooms in the newer part of the hotel look out towards Edinburgh Castle, while guests staying at the front of the Georgian section can gaze out onto the green oasis of Charlotte Square Gardens.

Families will appreciate the 12-metre indoor swimming pool, while visitors wishing to work off some of the belt-busting buffet breakfast served in the hotel's Melrose Restaurant can do so in the large, fully-equipped gym. Guests who have had enough exercise walking up and down the city's many hills, can indulge in one of the spa treatments on offer or relax in the sauna and steam room.

Rates from: 🏠🏠🏠
Star rating: ★★★★
Overall rating: 👍👍👍👍

Ambience :	8.65	Cleanliness:	9.00
Value:	8.18	Facilities:	8.64
Staff:	8.88	Restaurants:	8.60
Location:	9.41	Families:	8.45

Malmaison Edinburgh

1 Tower Place, Edinburgh, EH6 7DB, Scotland
T: +44 131 468 5000 **F:** +44 1314 685 002
www.HotelClub.com

Of the 11 Malmaisons across the UK, none can claim a better location than this one in the port of Leith. While the hoi polloi tumble over one another in the centre of the city, Malmaison guests find themselves at the heart of the vibrant Shore area - chock-a-block with bars and bistros, with not a tourist trap in sight. The hotel is just a five-minute walk from cinema, shopping and restaurant complex, Ocean Terminal, which is also the berthing place of the *Royal Yacht Britannia*. The hotel's Brasserie - which also offers al fresco dining - features a Home Grown & Local menu, boasting ingredients such as Buccleuch estate steak, while the chic Mal bar manages the clever trick of being airy in the daytime and cool but cosy by night. Overlooking the picturesque Water of Leith and the (slightly more industrial) Firth of Forth, the hotel was once a Seamans' Mission. Today its mission is much more modern, with asymmetrical furniture giving the reception area a whisper of *Alice In Wonderland*. There are nine suites among the 100 rooms, all of which have an individual feel, from roll-top baths to four-poster beds. All come with flatscreen TVs, CD players and free Internet. The gym is small but well-equipped, although the hotel's helpful jogging map may well encourage a spot of cardiovascular sight-seeing. If the Scottish weather is kind, town is around 45-minutes' stroll away, along the Water of Leith Walkway or, if rain stops play there is a regular bus service which will put you on Princes Street within 20 minutes.

Rates from: 🛏🛏🛏
Star rating: n/a
Overall rating: 🛏🛏🛏🛏

Ambience :	9.07	Cleanliness:	9.41
Value:	8.41	Facilities:	7.81
Staff:	9.12	Restaurants:	8.92
Location:	8.26	Families:	7.50

Marriott Dalmahoy Hotel & Country Club

Kirknewton, Edinburgh, EH27 8EB, Scotland
T: +44 1313 331 845 **F:** +44 1313 331 433
www.HotelClub.com/hotels/Marriott_Dalmahoy_Hotel_Country_Club

Gazing out over the surrounding 400 hectares, guests at this 215-room hotel could be forgiven for assuming they are in the heart of the countryside. Yet, despite being home to Scotland's longest golf course, the Dalmahoy (laid out in 1725) is a mere ten or so kilometres from Edinburgh city centre. Guests can play a round on the championship 18-hole East Course or tackle the slightly less intimidating West Course. If all that sounds like a good walk spoiled, there are plenty of other leisure options - from the heated indoor swimming pool to dance studio, gym and outdoor tennis courts. Those who prefer to bunker down inside will not be disappointed, since the house has been sympathetically refurbished and features the manor-house style Douglas Lounge, traditional fine dining in the Pentland Restaurant and cheap and cheerful eats in The Long Weekend Café Bar. The highlight of the bedrooms is the super-comfy beds, which all have down mattress toppers and high-thread Egyptian cotton linen.

Rates from: 💰 💰 💰
Star rating: ★★★★
Overall rating: 💰 💰 💰 💰

Ambience :	9.06	Cleanliness:	9.24
Value:	8.53	Facilities:	8.90
Staff:	8.94	Restaurants:	9.06
Location:	8.29	Families:	9.17

Paramount Carlton Hotel

19 North Bridge, Edinburgh, EH1 1SD, Scotland
T: +44 1314 723 000 **F:** +44 1315 562 691
www.HotelClub.com

With Edinburgh's historic Royal Mile on its doorstep and the New Town's Princes Street just a couple of minutes' walk away, the Carlton offers the best of both the old world and the new. The same is true inside where a recent refurbishment has seen the Bridge Restaurant and Bar given a new lease of life. A sweeping staircase leading up from reception harks back to the glamour of the 1930s and this styling extends throughout the building. There are 189 spacious bedrooms, many of which look out over the Royal Mile or towards the greenery of Arthur's Seat. Several also have quirky shapes, such as those that sit within the hotel's corners, which have turret-style architecture. The hotel's hidden surprise is its enormous Bodysense Health & Leisure Club, which not only features the obligatory gym, but also a swimming pool, dance studio and two squash courts.

Rates from: 💰 💰 💰 💰
Star rating: ★★★★
Overall rating: 💰 💰 💰 💰

Ambience :	8.50	Cleanliness:	9.00
Value:	7.50	Facilities:	7.00
Staff:	9.50	Restaurants:	8.00
Location:	9.50	Families:	7.00

Point Hotel

34 Bread Street, Edinburgh, EH3 9AF, Scotland
T: +44 1312 215 555 **F:** +44 1312 219 929
www.HotelClub.com/hotels/Point_Hotel_Edinburgh

Leonardo Da Vinci said "simplicity is the ultimate sophistication" and it's an adage the interior designers at this 138-bedroom hotel have clearly taken to heart. Clean lines and light, bright walls dominate, from the cool white reception area, offset by a slightly retro acid yellow, through to the bedrooms, where furniture is kept simple and bathrooms small to maximise living space. Currently midway through a four-year refurbishment, all the beds will soon have an art deco look and walnut veneer finish. Many of the bed headboards are used as crafty room dividers, concealing storage space, tea-making facilities and ironing boards. Offering very reasonably priced standard rooms, the hotel also boasts some of the best views on a budget in the city, with many of the windows looking out towards Edinburgh Castle. Mirrors have also been placed strategically to reflect the view into the rooms so you can wake up to a castle view without leaving your bed. Coloured neon lights in the corridors have a retro feel which may not be for everyone, but as the Point Hotel is not part of a group, it has an attractive air of quirky independence. Free Wi-Fi is offered in the hotel's communal areas, including the sleek, ebony-finished Monboddo Bar, which is noted for its cocktails. Each year the hotel sponsors a student from the Edinburgh College of Art, who produces pieces that hang in the reception and Point Restaurant, completing the contemporary vibe. Leonardo would doubtless approve.

Rates from: 🐚🐚
Star rating: ★★★
Overall rating: 🐚🐚🐚🐚

Ambience :	9.21	Cleanliness:	9.00
Value:	8.38	Facilities:	8.06
Staff:	8.71	Restaurants:	9.00
Location:	9.14	Families:	8.43

Prestonfield

Prestonfield House, Priestfield Road, Edinburgh, EH16 5UT, Scotland
T: +44 1312 257 800 **F:** +44 1312 204 392
www.HotelClub.com

Describing the Aladdin's cave of antique furnishings at this 22-room hotel as opulent is akin to saying Edinburgh Castle is a bit old. The decadent display - incorporating everything from 17th-century leather to Chinese lacquer cabinets and converted kettle drums - is as breathtaking as the peacocks that wander the grounds. It may be exuberant, but it is also very welcoming - with staff attentive but relaxed. Guests are treated to a bottle of Champagne on arrival, adding to an air of deliciously wanton wickedness, as pervasive as the scent of lavender wafting up from dishes in the hallways. The indulgence extends to the food, served in the Rhubarb restaurant, with the menu featuring luxuries such as lobster, truffles and caviar. There are no hidden catches either - Internet access, DVDs and an alarming array of other little extras are all included within the room rate.

Rates from: 🛏🛏🛏🛏
Star rating: ★★★★★
Overall rating: 👌👌👌👌

Ambience :	10.0	Cleanliness:	9.88
Value:	7.50	Facilities:	8.02
Staff:	9.63	Restaurants:	9.75
Location:	8.63	Families:	7.00

The Scotsman Hotel

20 North Bridge, Edinburgh, EH1 1YT, Scotland
T: +44 1315 565 565 **F:** +44 1316 523 652
www.HotelClub.com/hotels/Scotsman_Hotel_Edinburgh

This century-old, one-time headquarters of the eponymous daily newspaper has been described by a former employee as "the kind of building a clever child might have designed, and hugely satisfying to work in". Likewise to kick back in. From the 16-metre stainless steel swimming pool and the engagingly witty environs of the Cowshed spa in the basement (where once printing presses rumbled), to the Gothic eyrie of the duplex Penthouse, there is much to surprise and delight here. Hi-techery in the 69 rooms and suites augments rather than invades, and there are welcome traditional recreations like board games (Edinburgh Monopoly) and a box of short stories by Scottish writers. Breakfasts (the whole 8.2296 metres of kedgeree, kippers etc) go with a bang at the North Street Brasserie. And the 43-seat private cinema is pure class.

Rates from: 🛏🛏🛏🛏
Star rating: ★★★★★
Overall rating: 👌👌👌👌

Ambience :	9.31	Cleanliness:	9.38
Value:	8.06	Facilities:	8.71
Staff:	8.78	Restaurants:	8.55
Location:	9.66	Families:	7.11

Sheraton Grand Hotel & Spa

1 Festival Square, Edinburgh, EH3 9SR, Scotland
T: +44 1312 299 131 **F:** +44 1312 299 631
www.HotelClub.com/hotels/Sheraton_Grand_and_Spa_Hotel_Edinburgh

Caledonia stern and wild? Hah! It would be perfectly forgivable if guests never made it to Princes Street or the Castle (both on the doorstep) having checked in to this ultra happy lap of luxury. The 260 rooms and the public facilities are all that might be wished for, but the prime reason for booking here is the spa, memorably named One. It's drawn endless rave-heart reviews, ranging from "possibly the most extraordinary in Britain"

to "not off-putting poncey", both of which are intended as high praise. Both hardware (as in equipment and design), and software (which you might take to mean therapists' touch or the complimentary robes, towels and slippers) are exceptional, as is the treatment menu. Pop into the café for a bite or grab some ESPA products on the way out - this is very much a spa with a hotel attached. That said, the Sheraton's

drinking and dining venues - yang to the spa's yin - deserve a fair measure of praise. They strike a neat balance between the solidly traditional, like the Grill Room, which is equally suitable for a romantic dinner or a business lunch, and Santini, which contrasts fine Italian cuisine with the surrounds of the Scottish capital, while the Exchange Bar is the spot for drams both wee and not so. As an endnote, meeters and eventers will be thrilled to observe the international conference centre directly opposite, but there is probably no greater attraction at this hotel than its spa.

Rates from: 𝕭𝕭𝕭𝕭𝕭
Star rating: ★★★★★
Overall rating: 👍👍👍👍

Ambience :	8.63	Cleanliness:	9.34
Value:	8.29	Facilities:	8.88
Staff:	8.90	Restaurants:	8.81
Location:	8.95	Families:	8.52

Thistle Edinburgh

107 Leith Street, Edinburgh, EH1 3SW, Scotland
T: +44 8703 339 153 **F:** +44 8703 339 253
www.HotelClub.com/hotels/The_Thistle_House

When it comes to location on a budget this modern 143-room hotel is hard to beat. Just three minutes' walk from Waverley Station and Princes Street and adjoining the St James Centre mall, it is a shopaholics' dream and with rates starting from well under £100 a night per person, it won't break the bank. Currently undergoing a gradual refurbishment, the rooms will all be sporting contemporary and comfy chocolate brown and dark red décor by 2009. The Boston Bean Bar serves up light meals while Craig's Restaurant stresses the à la carte option. Those feeling tartan-tastic can indulge in the hotel's Ultimate Scottish Experience evening between April and November. This is an ever-popular evening of traditional – and more importantly good quality – Scottish food, music and dance, featuring free-flowing wine and, of course, the chieftain o' the puddin' race, haggis.

Rates from: 🛏🛏🛏🛏
Star rating: ★★★★
Overall rating: 👣👣👣👣

Ambience :	8.19	Cleanliness:	8.81
Value:	7.88	Facilities:	6.60
Staff:	8.60	Restaurants:	8.13
Location:	9.06	Families:	8.36

Tigerlily

125 George Street, Edinburgh, EH2 4JN, Scotland
T: +44 1312 255 005 **F:** +44 1312 257 046
www.HotelClub.com/hotels/Tigerlily

The heady scent of tigerlilies on the doorstep hints at the opulence within this 33-room boutique. The rather austere Georgian facade belies its vibrant, modern interior which stretches well to the rear. The ground floor features two bars and a restaurant, while the Lulu nightclub - free to guests - gives a boudoir feel to the basement. The furnishings have a tactile appeal, with patterned wallpaper recalling the building's past, while bright, textured cloth and curtains of steel ball bearings are as sharply modern as Keira Knightley's cheekbones. The staff are utterly charming and the decadent air extends to the bedrooms whose bespoke furniture comes with an individual twist - in the loft-style Black Room, for example, even the loo roll is black. While some may find the gadgets a bit bewildering, those who want to sample the technology of tomorrow will be in their element.

Rates from: 🛏🛏🛏🛏
Star rating: ★★★★
Overall rating: 👣👣👣👣 ½

Ambience :	10.0	Cleanliness:	9.75
Value:	8.50	Facilities:	7.75
Staff:	9.25	Restaurants:	9.67
Location:	9.50	Families:	9.10

The Witchery by the Castle

Castlehill, The Royal Mile, Edinburgh, EH1 2NF, Scotland
T: +44 1312 255 613 **F**: +44 1312 204 392
www.HotelClub.com

Those who think Gothic equals gloom are in for a surprise when they visit this small hotel with a big character. Each of the seven suites is an extravaganza of architectural salvage, from altar rails and pews to tapestries, which lend them an air of cosy grandeur. The sumptuous surroundings also harbour hidden secrets. The Old Rectory suite has a chapel-style bathroom, complete with Gothic ceiling, while in The Library suite, the bathroom is squirreled away behind a false wall of books and the television pops up from the blanket box at the foot of the bed. Champagne is provided on arrival and breakfast is served in your room, while lunch and dinner are available in the decadent Witchery restaurant, or bright and breezy Secret Garden restaurant. Edinburgh Castle is just moments away but you may be too busy worshipping the sinful self-indulgence to care.

Rates from: 🛏🛏🛏🛏
Star rating: ★★★★★
Overall rating: 👣👣👣👣

Ambience :	9.94	Cleanliness:	9.59
Value:	8.24	Facilities:	4.30
Staff:	9.41	Restaurants:	9.29
Location:	9.82	Families:	6.50

City Inn Glasgow

Finnieston Quay, Glasgow, G3 8HN, Scotland
T: +44 1412 401 002 **F**: +44 1412 482 754
www.HotelClub.com/hotels/City_Inn_Glasgow

It's not perhaps the most inspiring name ever granted to a hotel, but be it known that the City Inn enjoys a deserved reputation as one of Glasgow's foremost design-led bolt holes. The 164-room inn enjoys dynamic Clydeside views and easy access to Glasgow's adjacent Scottish Exhibition and Conference Centre, the city's business district and the myriad delights of the west end - a bohemian enclave marketed (with some justification) by the council as Glasgow's answer to Greenwich Village. Conceived as an affordable urban hotel, good food as much as good rooms upholds the Inn's reputation through a formula that allies contemporary European culinary finesse to peerless local seasonal produce. Amongst Glaswegians, and a fair few visitors too, al fresco terrace dining overlooking the dramatic river vista is as popular as it is delightful. When the weather cooperates, of course.

Rates from: 🛏🛏🛏
Star rating: ★★★★
Overall rating: 👣👣👣👣

Ambience :	8.67	Cleanliness:	9.64
Value:	8.80	Facilities:	7.61
Staff:	9.20	Restaurants:	8.93
Location:	8.60	Families:	9.00

Glasgow Marriott

500 Argyle Street, Anderston, Glasgow, G3 8RR, Scotland
T: +44 1412 265 577 F: +44 1412 219 202
www.HotelClub.com/hotels/Marriott_Hotel_Glasgow

Set in the city's financial district, the Marriott is marketed as a business hotel but that shouldn't discourage visitors here on hols - as long as they are prepared to use Glasgow's plentiful cheap taxis and public transport.

Nominally, the Marriot is one of the best placed hotels in Glasgow, everything you could want as a work tripper, shopper or sightseer is just a short walk, train, bus or underground ride away. Central Station and Buchanan Street, the gateway to Glasgow's key shopping locations are easily within walking distance. The boutiques and bars of the chic Merchant city are further eastwards and the parks and galleries of the southside and west end are easily accessible a full seven days a week.

However, it may be just as well that the Glasgow Marriott makes most sense as a base to explore the city because its immediate motorway-side location is off-puttingly desolate, particularly after dark. It is certainly not recommended for a romantic midnight stroll.

Visitors using the 300-room hotel as a base to explore Central Scotland can access 180 spaces of on-site parking. The Marriott unsurprisingly boasts all the usual brand staples - wireless Internet, meeting facilities, indoor pool, sauna and gymnasium - making it ideal for both city breaks and work appointments alike.

Regardless of the reason for your visit you are sure to appreciate the work-sized desks, large beds, cotton sheets, down comforters, and additional pillows that, regrettably, are too seldom standard issue in Scotland's hotels.

Rates from: 🐾🐾
Star rating: ★★★★
Overall rating: 🐾🐾🐾🐾

Ambience :	8.61	Cleanliness:	9.59
Value:	8.52	Facilities:	8.98
Staff:	9.00	Restaurants:	8.77
Location:	8.57	Families:	8.92

Hilton Glasgow

1 William Street, Glasgow, G3 8HT, Scotland
T: +44 1412 045 555 **F:** +44 1412 045 004
www.HotelClub.com/hotels/Hilton_Hotel_Glasgow

Glasgow's structured city centre layout ensures that prime real estate really is at a premium when it comes to building large hotels. As such, and unlike most European cities, Glasgow's finest hotels are often peripheral or inaccessible to the city centre on foot. The 331-room Hilton Glasgow is a case in point, abutting the M8 motorway on one side and, on the other, a corporate hinterland that becomes Glasgow's, ahem, red light district after dark.

Still, with its 20 storeys offering breathtaking views along the spectacularly illuminated Clydeside and over Glasgow's prestigious west end, its location need not over irk a clientele that will be primarily non-pedestrian when it comes to getting around.

As you'd expect, this slick, modern hotel rigidly adheres to Hilton's conservatively plush formula. The package of heated pool, exercise facilities, a sauna, concierge service and business centre are Hilton staples the world over. The stylish rooms are generous in size, well appointed and the PlayStations in situ are a thoughtful addition, especially for travellers with youngsters.

With only three lifts servicing this skyscraping tower, the Hilton may frustrate the impatient, but over all, attentive staff, pleasingly familiar design and bucket-loads of slick surface gloss should more than compensate for any sense of inconvenience.

Guests on the executive floors benefit from a semi-private club, Minsky's offers a casual New York style deli buffet, while Camerons represents a fine concession to location, serving up the kind of upscale seasonal Scottish food that has become emblematic of Scotland's newfound cultural confidence.

Rates from: 🛏🛏🛏🛏
Star rating: ★★★★★
Overall rating: 👐👐👐👐

Ambience :	8.40	Cleanliness :	9.10
Value:	8.15	Facilities:	8.91
Staff:	8.81	Restaurants:	8.89
Location:	8.30	Families:	8.57

Hotel Du Vin Glasgow

1 Devonshire Gardens, Glasgow, G12 0UX, Scotland
T: +44 1413 392 001 **F:** +44 1413 371 663
www.HotelClub.com

There is a terrific amount to admire about this northerly outpost of the splendiferous Hotels du Vin, but being welcomed by the kilted and bonneted concierge (who blends solicitude with a twinkling eye and a hearty handshake) on the very pavement of Devonshire Gardens makes for a marvellous beginning.

Artfully woven between what originally were five contiguous town houses (imagine the priciest Monopoly board quintet cheek by jowl) the hotel's staircases, corridors and public rooms are a joy to explore, while each of the 49 guest rooms is a metropolitan haven without peer.

There are ten different categories - from up in the eaves, to duplexes, to suites that open onto the garden - primarily graded by size, yet all are imaginatively furnished with more than a discreet nod to both high-end luxury and excellent taste.

Mention of which leads to the *vin* and *bistro* bits, and it's fair to say that neither kitchen nor cellar has much of a rival anywhere in the city. The oak-panelled dining room presents both classic and modern dishes with a truly Scottish skirl; breakfast, incidentally, is to diet for, while afternoon tea goes down a treat either by a roaring fire in the lounge or (more rarely) in the sunny terraced garden.

Naturally, the Hotel du Vin exercises a certain magnetism on the corporate sector, and there's an array of rooms that convert neatly for presentations, meetings, or simply private dining. And whatever their reason for staying here, all guests will enjoy the Botanical Gardens, which lie a few minutes' walk away.

"My first thought on seeing my enormous suite," wrote one guest, "was that I'd like to live here" - a sentiment which many others since have echoed with varying degrees of vigour.

As a parting note, guests are positively encouraged to make away with the bathroom unguents, thus combining a beautifully subtle sales technique with a really memorable souvenir!

Rates from: 🪙🪙🪙
Star rating: ★★★★★
Overall rating: ✋✋✋✋✋

Ambience :	10.0	Cleanliness:	10.0
Value:	9.33	Facilities:	9.00
Staff:	9.33	Restaurants:	9.00
Location:	10.0	Families:	9.48

Jurys Inn Glasgow

80 Jamaica Street, Glasgow, G1 4QG, Scotland
T: +44 1413 144 800 F: +44 1413 144 888
www.HotelClub.com/hotels/Jurys_Inn_Glasgow

Situated on a busy southern artery that crosses the Clyde, Jurys Inn is one of Glasgow's most popular budget hotels.

Handily placed for both The Sub Club and The Arches, Glasgow's internationally renowned cutting edge dance clubs, Jury's Inn is also a Mecca for weekend clubbers and stag parties drawn to this renowned party city.

The 321-room hotel, within two minutes' walk of the city centre's Golden Z of shopping streets, is ideal for a short stay.

Locally, it enjoys a good reputation for comfortable if utilitarian rooms, cleanliness and friendly staff. It is best described as a good all-rounder catering expertly

to the demands of both weekday business visitors and weekend tourist trade alike.

A sauna, Laundromat, fitness room and pay-per-view TV should correspond to most budget travellers' expectations.

The Clydeside views are generally appealing and the hotel is perfectly situated for both of Glasgow's key railway stations and the underground train network that can be accessed in St Enoch Square, just arround the corner.

Jurys Inn Glasgow boasts conference facilities for up to 100 delegates a popular coffee bar, Il Barista, that is ideal for small scale meetings, a bar (Inntro Bar) offering live sports TV coverage and an

informal restaurant, Innfusion.

The hotel's clubland location and potentially boisterous weekend clientele ensures that it may not be the obvious choice for guests seeking repose.

However, there is no doubt that in terms of all round convenience, Jurys Inn Glasgow offers genuine value for money.

Rates from: 🏵🏵🏵
Star rating: ★ ★ ★
Overall rating: 🏵🏵🏵🏵

Ambience :	7.69	Cleanliness:	9.14
Value:	8.14	Facilities:	7.56
Staff:	8.14	Restaurants:	7.62
Location:	8.86	Families:	8.11

Malmaison Glasgow

278 West George St, Glasgow, G2 4LL, Scotland
T: +44 1415 721 000 **F:** +44 1415 721 002
www.HotelClub.com

Ken McCulloch's seriously swish Malmaison chain now features in many UK cities but it was born here in this converted Episcopal church, just five minutes' walk from bustling Sauchiehall Street.

The 72 rooms vary from the intimate to the subtle but the décor remains pleasingly slick throughout. All the facilities are well appointed and include thoughtful additions such as contemporary artworks and CD players with their own library of music in each room. Generous rations of complimentary designer toiletries ensure that the Malmaison is the hotel of choice for visiting beauty industry PR staff. Indeed, they typically host their press briefings in the hotel's airy atrium-

like bar, accessed from reception by a winding spiral staircase.

The French-style crypt-based Brasserie is notable for its generous portions and a menu that boasts simple staples such as steak frites and roast rack of lamb alongside more uncommon fare such as swordfish. A specially selected wine list completes the offer of stylish, unfussy dining that is central to the Malmaison experience.

The Mal, as it's known locally, also boasts free Internet access, satellite TV and same-day laundry whether you're lodging in one of eight sumptuous mezzanine suites or a modest single room.

Perhaps Malmaison's biggest plus point is the seclusion and

tranquillity offered in many of the rooms' atypically high-ceilinged interiors. Despite the hotel's city centre location returning guests confirm that it is one of the best Glasgow hotels to get a good night's sleep. Consequently, it is popular with insomniacs and audiophiles alike.

Rates from: 🛏🛏🛏
Star rating: n/a
Overall rating: 🐚🐚🐚🐚

Ambience :	8.40	Cleanliness:	8.80
Value:	7.87	Facilities:	7.99
Staff:	8.60	Restaurants:	8.00
Location:	8.33	Families:	7.00

Marks Hotel

110 Bath Street, Glasgow, G2 2EN, Scotland
T: ++44 1413 530 000 **F:** +4 1413 53 0 900
www.HotelClub.com

It's not a million years ago that Glasgow felt somewhat bruised. An early casualty of chronic 1980s unemployment gave it a reputation as the booze capital of Britain. Yet the city's ability to re-invent itself has been astonishing and it's happening again. But Glasgow - "City of Love"? Well it's been inspired by the discovery of some St Valentine's relics in a local church, and now Glasgow has its own love festival on Valentine's Day. Still not convinced? Try

walking into the deliciously opulent Marks Hotel. It used to be the Bewleys, but a £1million makeover by Catherine Henderson Design has given it a strikingly sensual feel. The angular exterior and informal lobby give a handful of clues, with jet-black walls contrasting sharply with bright, orange chairs. No, it's when you're safely inside one of the 103 guestrooms that the secrets unfurl; soft fabrics in vibrant reds; swirling, contemporary Design Guild

wallpaper; graceful bathrooms with Arran aromatic toiletries. How could you not fall in love?

If you need a little help there's an extensive selection of champagnes in the bar, including lively bottles of salmon pink Billecart; and a rather naughty chocolate cake amongst the dinner desserts in the One Ten Grill.

But really all this talk of love is a little spurious. Owner Stuart Wilson renamed the hotel after his baby son and intends it to be for everyone; singles, couples and families. Even Valentine's Day hopefuls. As long as they have a love for the stylish.

Rates from: 🛏🛏
Star rating: ★★★★
Overall rating: **Editors' Pick**

Ambience :	n/a	Cleanliness:	n/a
Value:	n/a	Facilities:	n/a
Staff:	n/a	Restaurants:	n/a
Location:	n/a	Families:	n/a

Radisson SAS Hotel

301 Argyle Street, Glasgow, G2 8DL, Scotland
T: +44 1412 043 333 **F:** +44 1412 043 344
www.HotelClub.com/hotels/Radisson_SAS_Hotel_Glasgow

Since it opened in 2002, the GM+AD designed Radisson has become one of Glasgow's great contemporary landmarks, as well as being savvy Glaswegians' favourite local hotel. Scotland's premier architects gained their spurs with a series of commercial projects that have dragged the tired grid-like city centre right into the 21st Century. This copper-fronted 250-bedroom property, just a caber toss from Central Station, is unequivocally their masterwork. With its quirky curved façade and a style inspired by Arne Jacobsen's 1960 Gothenburg Royal Hotel (also a Radisson), this Glasgow addition bristles with Scandinavian cool, blonde wood detailing, and dramatic lighting. It's a remarkable achievement, given Radisson's commitment to a moderate pricing structure. Unsurprisingly you're just as likely to bump into Justin Timberlake or a touring rap icon in the fitness centre as you are visiting conference delegates.

Rates from: 🏵 🏵 🏵
Star rating: ★★★★★
Overall rating: 🌷 🌷 🌷 🌷

Ambience :	8.61	Cleanliness:	9.22
Value:	8.09	Facilities:	8.76
Staff:	8.87	Restaurants:	8.35
Location:	8.70	Families:	7.75

Dunain Park Hotel

Inverness, IV3 8JN, Scotland
T: +44 1463 230 512 **F:** +44 1643 224 532
www.HotelClub.com

If seclusion is what you are looking for then the eleven-room Dunain has got that estate agent's mantra, 'location, location, location' with three capital 'L's.' To the northeast lies the picturesque city of Inverness, to the south the haunting Loch Ness, and all around are distilleries that conjure up Scotland's most famous export; single malt whisky. You better believe they save the best for themselves, however, and there are over 200 varieties on offer in the well-stocked bar. If that's not enough to persuade you to linger at this traditional country pile then try the classic Scottish cuisine in the restaurant (think turrets of haggis and creamy leek broth) or midsummer midnight walks in the lovely Victorian gardens where roe deer and hares can sometimes be spotted.

Rates from: 🏵 🏵 🏵 🏵 🏵
Star rating: ★★★
Overall rating: **Editors' Pick**

Ambience :	n/a	Cleanliness:	n/a
Value:	n/a	Facilities:	n/a
Staff:	n/a	Restaurants:	n/a
Location:	n/a	Families:	n/a

The Colonsay

Isle of Colonsay, Argyll, PA61 7YP, Scotland
T: +44 1951 200 316 F: +44 1951 200 353
www.HotelClub.com

There is no formal Reception at The Colonsay and the impression is of walking into someone's stylish beach-house. You enter through French doors into uncluttered, spacious interiors painted in the colours of the sea on a beautiful day - turquoise, baby blue and slate-green. Floors are wooden and either pale and waxed or painted slate-grey. Smart modern sofas in neutral beiges or creams are set in front of open fires and the tables are decorated with sprigs of island flowers - rhododendrons perhaps, magnolia, orchids or crocosmia.

The walls are hung throughout with a collection of early sepia photographs of the island and its inhabitants, alongside original works by contemporary artists.

There are also homely touches; in a peaceful airy sitting room shelves are stocked with a good assortment of books and games to play - backgammon, cards and scrabble. Upstairs the nine bedrooms, named after locations on Colonsay, have the same understated charm, with high-quality, super comfortable beds made up with finest Egyptian cotton, and views of the sea and surrounding countryside.

There is a sureness of touch about The Colonsay, a relaxed informal chic; it feels confident in its own skin. This is not surprising when you find out that the owners Jane and Alex Howard have lived on the island for many years so have an implicit understanding of the place. Further professional input has then been added by friends and business partners Hugo Arnold, food writer and adviser to the Conran Group, and Dan Jago, director of wine at Tesco.

As the only hotel on the island

The Colonsay has an important dual role; it is essential to the island residents as well as to tourist incomers. As a result it is not swanky, which the islanders would hate and which would also make it too expensive both for them and for the majority of island visitors. Instead it is simple, elegant and well-run by a young team headed by the charming combination of manager Scott Omar and his wife Becky. Keith Trevena, a promising young Geordie chef, directs in the kitchen and produces a short but varied menu which aims to provide for both conservative and more adventurous options. There will usually be a hearty steak at dinner time, local fish or shellfish and an interesting vegetarian dish such as handmade spaghetti with mascarpone and wild island garlic. Local fisherman Bill Lawson provides the hotel with crab, lobster and langoustine, while islander Andrew Abrahams supplies

oysters and honey. Fish is generally sourced in Oban, though trawlers occasionally call in to the pier and sell their fish directly. Vegetables come where possible from Howard's own kitchen garden at Colonsay House. There is wholesome, often home-made, bar food for those on smaller budgets and a lively, informal atmosphere enhanced by the stream of local regulars who take advantage of entertainments laid on at the hotel - regular quiz nights and a DVD evening for children.

More remote country hotels should take note of the way they do it at The Colonsay.

Rates from: ☁☁		
Star rating: ★★★		
Overall rating: **Editors' Pick**		
Ambience :	n/a	Cleanliness: n/a
Value:	n/a	Facilities: n/a
Staff:	n/a	Restaurants: n/a
Location:	n/a	Families: n/a

Jura Hotel

Craighouse, Jura, Isle of Jura, PA60 7XU, Scotland
T: +44 1496 820 243 **F:** +44 1496 820 249
www.HotelClub.com

It's part of the allure of travel; finding that empty, glorious spot where you can just leave everything behind.

Enter the Jura Hotel. Set in Craighouse, the only village on the 48-kilometre slice of moor and hill that makes up the island of Jura, this is one hotel where the word remote is rightly applied.

Secreted off the western coast of Scotland and surrounded by some of the most treacherous sea currents around the whole of Great Britain, it is easy to see how this rugged isle is famed for being something of a retreat.

One Eric Blair came to Jura in 1946 to pen one of the greatest novels of the 20th century. Better known as George Orwell, Mr Blair headed to what he termed as this "completely un-gettable" island and produced his classic vision of a dystopian future, *1984*. And, he wrote it all at the furthest, bleakest corner of Jura in a cold, windswept house.

Maybe if he'd chosen to stay at the Jura Hotel his book might have turned out differently. Arrive at this hotel on a wet Scottish evening off the Islay ferry and you'll find a warm, convivial welcome, a dram of local whisky and a piece of the local venison, fresh off the hills. The rooms offer simple comforts and spectacular views across to the mainland and the Paps - Jura's distinctive hills.

Then, after a sound night's sleep, start the day with a mammoth cooked breakfast - the perfect fuel to begin the hunt for your own little bit of solitude, on this magnificently remote and starkly beautiful island.

Rates from: ☙
Star rating: ★★
Overall rating: **Editors' Pick**

Ambience :	n/a	Cleanliness:	n/a
Value:	n/a	Facilities:	n/a
Staff:	n/a	Restaurants:	n/a
Location:	n/a	Families:	n/a

Flodigarry Country House Hotel

Flodigarry, Isle of Skye, IV51 9HZ, Scotland
T: +44 1470 552 203 **F:** +44 1470 552 301
www.HotelClub.com

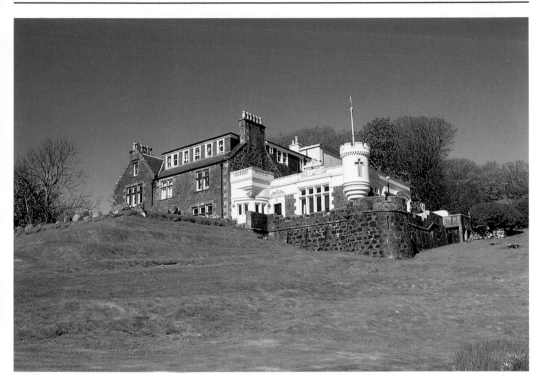

Welcome to Skye's own Jurassic Park. The landscape may be ancient and littered with dinosaur remains, but there is nothing prehistoric about the facilities at the Flodigarry Country House Hotel.

There's an excellent choice of 18 ensuite bedrooms to suit all requirements. There are eleven bedrooms in the main house of the hotel with a further seven bedrooms in Flora MacDonald's cottage next door. Yes, that's *the* Flora MacDonald who came to the rescue of Bonnie Prince Charlie - Flodigarry was her home.

When booking a room you should consider the type of view you're after. Some windows look out onto the other-worldly Quirang, a range of thrusting post-glacial escarpments, or over Staffin Bay to the Torridon hills on the mainland. Whichever aspect you choose there's nothing but natural majesty beyond every window.

After a day's sightseeing, you'll want some healthy Highland food, and lots of it.

At Flodigarry you can try pan-fried wood pigeon on a potato scone with a Drambuie and thyme sauce, or a baked filo parcel of Minch seabass.

Head chef Jeff Johnston extols the virtues of both the local produce he includes in his sumptuous dishes and the hotel itself, maintaining that the emphasis here will continue to be on home-grown and locally-caught Skye produce.

Traditional, friendly Flodigarry has great appeal - it is a perfect haven for people on short-break retreats escaping hectic city life as well as a glorious back-drop for weddings and private functions. And Chef Jeff and his team will more than match the stunning surroundings with their own special ingredients.

Rates from: 💰💰
Star rating: ★★★
Overall rating: 👏👏👏👏

Ambience :	9.00	Cleanliness:	10.0
Value:	9.00	Facilities:	10.0
Staff:	9.00	Restaurants:	7.00
Location:	10.0	Families:	7.00

Ullinish Country Lodge

Struan, Isle of Skye, IV56 8FD, Scotland
T: +44 1470 572 214 **F:** +44 1470 572 341
www.HotelClub.com

As long ago as 1773, visitors were lavishing praise on the Ullinish Country Lodge in north-west Skye. Back then, the great lexicographer Dr Samuel Johnson had this to say about the place: "There was ease in this house and an appearance as if everything went on daily just as we saw it, that was very agreeable. It made one quite free of the idea that our company was a burden." He would be similarly delighted that standards have not slipped in the intervening 200-plus years.

Following a top-to-bottom refurbishment in 2005, the lodge - wild ocean and plunging sea cliffs on one side, the imposing Black Cuillin mountain range on the other, with sea eagles wheeling high above - offers a degree of comfort which might have rendered Dr Johnson gobsmacked, even supposing the term was in his dictionary. With six luxury en-suite and characterfully named bedrooms, complete with king, super king and half-tester beds, Ullinish offers both refinement and isolation. And the highly reasonable rates, albeit increased since the 18th century, won't break the bank either.

As far as cuisine is concerned, the ethos - under the skilful eye of celebrated chef Bruce Morrison - is local and lush, from hand-dived scallops caramelised with cepes, pancetta and capers to turbot poached in red wine with spinach. Cheeses from the West Island Dairy, with a scoop of pear and tamarind chutney, top meals off to perfection.

For entertainment, there's a fair selection of outdoor pursuits, including deer-stalking, and fly fishing in nearby Loch Bracadale. And could anyone seriously turn down a tour of the Talisker distillery?

Rates from: 𝔅 𝔅 𝔅 𝔅
Star rating: ★ ★ ★ ★ ★
Overall rating: **Editors' Pick**

Ambience :	n/a	Cleanliness:	n/a
Value:	n/a	Facilities:	n/a
Staff:	n/a	Restaurants:	n/a
Location:	n/a	Families:	n/a

The Black Bull Lauder

13-15 Market Place, Lauder, Berwickshire, TD2 6SR, Scotland
T: +44 1578 722 208 **F:** +44 1578 722 419
www.HotelClub.com

Sir Harry Lauder (1870 - 1950), The Laird of the Music Hall, gets less press nowadays than when he was the highest-paid entertainer in the world, writing and singing songs like *I Love a Lassie* and cracking jokes about tight-fisted Scots while pulling in a substantial £12,700 per night plus expenses. Similarly, the town that bears his name is rather less well known than it might be, straddling what has long been the broad main road from Edinburgh to England.

The Black Bull's right beside the A68, and started welcoming visitors around 250 years ago when coaches used to stop here for a change of horses. A superior gastro pub rather than a fully fledged hotel, it's charming in its modesty, its size, and above all its seasonal cuisine. The last is the personal fiefdom of Maureen Rennie, who with her husband Tony restored the Bull after it had fallen into disrepair at the turn of the century. It was a brave venture, and one that's paid off handsomely. There's just eight bedrooms, some large enough to accommodate extra beds for children, and all sympathetically tricked out and given the Gilchrist & Soames treatment in the bathrooms.

Secure in the knowledge of being amply quartered and fed, guests can sally forth around the area's manifest attractions. Thirlestane Castle is within bowshot; spectacular equestrian events are held every summer; and the thrill of catching a salmon or rainbow trout is made all the sweeter by knowing Mrs Rennie will happily cook it for dinner.

Surrounded by the undulating Lammermuir Hills, The Black Bull and Lauder make for an excellent Borders base. Note that drink-driving regulations being what they are nowadays, "a wee deoch an doris, afore ye gang awa" is probably inadvisable, whatever Sir Harry used to sing.

Rates from: 🛏🛏
Star rating: ★ ★ ★ ★
Overall rating: **Editors' Pick**

Ambience :	n/a	Cleanliness:	n/a
Value:	n/a	Facilities:	n/a
Staff:	n/a	Restaurants:	n/a
Location:	n/a	Families:	n/a

De Vere Deluxe Cameron House Hotel

Loch Lomond, Dunbartonshire, G83 8QZ, Scotland
T: +44 1389 755 565 **F:** +44 1389 759 522
www.HotelClub.com

You can hardly visit Scotland without taking in the bonnie, bonnie banks of Loch Lomond - so why not stay right on them, as British royalty, Sir Winston Churchill and Samuel Johnson and James Boswell have done before you, albeit when Cameron House was home to the shipbuilding Smollett family (paddle steamers to the world), whose best-known scion was the novelist Tobias.

For a couple of decades now, the stately pile has been a luxury hotel, whose 96 rooms and suites have just undergone a major renovation. Ask for one with a loch view. A new restaurant has opened, Lomond's, to go with the Marina (open kitchen, wood-burning oven, Californian-Mediterranean fare), Great Scots Bar and the Claret Jug, overlooking the new golf course, the Carrick (named after its designer, the legendary Doug of that ilk). Though you might prefer a quick nine holes round the adjoining, devilishly tough, aptly

named, Wee Demon course.

And there is a new spa, too - set some way apart from the hotel (from which you can be shuttled). A laguna-style pool, plunge pool, sauna and gym will tone you up for more demanding pursuits such as tennis, squash, archery, mountain or quad biking. Kids are catered for at the Cammie Club.

But wherever you go in the 40-hectare grounds, you'll feel the brooding presence of Britain's largest lake. And the way to get the best out of this is to book a champagne cruise on it, aboard the hotel's luxury vessel Celtic Warrior or restored Henley launch Belle Epoque.

Rates from: 🏰🏰🏰🏰🏰
Star rating: ★★★★★
Overall rating: 🐾🐾🐾🐾 ½

Ambience :	9.40	Cleanliness:	9.52
Value:	8.92	Facilities:	9.08
Staff:	9.33	Restaurants:	9.26
Location:	9.80	Families:	9.12

Stobo Castle Health Spa
Stobo, Peebles, EH45 8NY, Scotland
T: +44 1721 725 300 **F**: +44 1721 760 294
www.HotelClub.com

It's not quite a castle, as even the mildest belligerents could get in round the back. It's very definitely a spa. But above all, Stobo is a magnificent retreat, beautifully and imposingly located making the most of its historical antecedents and blending in the sort of health treatments, cuisine and comfort that the building's original owners could barely have dreamed of.

Winding up the drive and rattling over the cattle grids guests should feel a sense of anticipation, one that's augmented by the flight of stone steps leading up to Reception and the grand lobby beyond. The first impression is of a country house, and the rustic views from dining and drawing rooms reinforce this, however the back of Stobo opens out into a truly impressive spa, with a galaxy of treatments and some extremely switched-on staff.

Larger parties (and Stobo is a natural host for weddings and similar get-togethers) may opt for the stand-alone lodges at the rear of the hotel, however the main accommodation attraction is the Cashmere Suite, designed with a certain flair by Lizzie Bell, using a wealth of the eponymous wool as well as plenty of silks and lacquer. Large screen TVs and a DVD player provide the tech side of things, while a control panel allows for 20 different light settings.

For exercise beyond the gym and indoor pool, there's a tennis coach and mountain bikes. In need of a minor surprise? Take a stroll round the Japanese water garden at the edge of the property.

Rates from: 🐻🐻
Star rating: n/a
Overall rating: **Editors' Pick**

Ambience :	n/a	Cleanliness:	n/a
Value:	n/a	Facilities:	n/a
Staff:	n/a	Restaurants:	n/a
Location:	n/a	Families:	n/a

Knockinaam Lodge

Portpatrick, Wigtownshire, DG9 9AD, Scotland
T: +44 1776 810 471 **F**: +44 1776 810 435
www.HotelClub.com

So remote and idyllic is the setting of this grey-stone lodge at the end of a single-track country lane, in a sheltered cove by the Irish Sea, that it inevitably suggests an air of mystery and intrigue. Which is undoubtedly why Scottish thriller-writer John Buchan set his classic *The 39 Steps* here - and (perhaps inspired by the book) Sir Winston Churchill and General Eisenhower met here to map out the top-secret D-Day invasion (one wonders where the aides-de-camp stayed since the place only has nine bedrooms).

One of these, named after the wartime PM, still has the 100-year-old enamel bath that he probably smoked a cigar in while soaking before dinner (think Albert Finney in *The Gathering Storm*). The other eight are equally idiosyncratic. There is a restaurant, of course, enhanced by the pleasure of pre- and post-prandial snifters in the wood-panelled Whisky Bar, offering some 120 single malts. Try the local Bladnoch.

Lounging by the log fires in the drawing rooms; taking afternoon tea on the lawn when the weather's fine (which it surprisingly often is - thanks to the protected location and proximity of the Gulf Stream); shell-collecting and rockpool-exploring on the beach - these are the gentle pursuits offered at this historic haven.

Those of a more energetic disposition can make the eight-kilometre clifftop walk to Portpatrick, or go golfing, horse-riding, fishing (the lodge will lend you a rod) or even rough shooting. But the greatest thrill this intimate little hideaway affords is the simple but all too rare pleasure of listening to the silence late at night before nodding off.

Rates from: 😛😛😛😛
Star rating: ★ ★ ★ ★
Overall rating: 😛😛😛😛

Ambience :	10.0	Cleanliness:	9.50
Value:	5.50	Facilities:	5.25
Staff:	10.0	Restaurants:	10.0
Location:	9.00	Families:	10.0

Fairmont St Andrews, Scotland

St Andrews, KY16 8PN, Scotland
T: +44 1334 837 000 **F**: +44 1334 471 115
www.HotelClub.com

When American hotelier Don Panoz learned that 200-plus hectares of land overlooking St. Andrews Bay, empty apart from a few potato patches, was for sale, he must have thought he'd found his field of dreams. At a cost of £50 million, he built a 209-room golf resort, with two courses attached, and it is now one of Scotland's leading conference and leisure centres (though it was taken over by Fairmont in 2006).

In contrast with all those history-dripping castles and baronial mansions that abound in Scotland, this place is pure California with a tartan twist, though the low-rise, E-shaped building is neutral enough to blend effortlessly into its windswept surroundings. The panoramic views more than make up for the property's bland, Scottish theme-park décor, and both service and amenities bristle with good ol' American efficiency.

Restaurants range from the Mediterranean-style Esperante, all Tuscan terracotta and olive-green tones, to the Squire, named after legendary US golfer Gene Sarazen, one of only four players to have won all four majors and renowned for his gentlemanly demeanour. And from the glass-roofed, fountain-featuring Atrium, to the cosy Kittocks Den (Scottish for "a flighty lady" and titled after the forested ravine that runs through the estate and is home to its herd of deer).

There is also a Clubhouse, which does hearty home cooking for hungry golfers (try the Pitenweem haddock in beer batter), straddling the Devlin (after Australian Bruce) and the Torrance (Scottish Ryder Cup captain Sam) courses. Spa, pool and gym, well - this is offshire USA, after all.

Rates from: 🐚🐚🐚🐚
Star rating: ★★★★★
Overall rating: 🐾🐾🐾🐾

Ambience :	8.67	Cleanliness:	8.75
Value:	7.92	Facilities:	8.86
Staff:	8.42	Restaurants:	8.58
Location:	8.92	Families:	8.75

Old Course Hotel, Golf Resort & Spa

St Andrews, Kingdom of Fife, KY16 9SP, Scotland
T: +44 1334 474 371 **F:** +44 1334 477 668
www.HotelClub.com

To stay here if you don't like golf is a bit like dining in a private box at Wembley if you don't like football. St Andrews is the game's Mecca, boasting literally dozens of courses, and the Old Course is where it all began - about 600 years ago. But first, its time to dispel a few myths.

The hotel has no connection with the Old Course, except a wonderful view over its celebrated Road Hole. Being a guest will give you no playing privileges - you'll have to take your chances in the daily lottery like everyone else (and although it's a public course, you'll have to produce your handicap certificate to be allowed on it).

Second, the hotel - once owned by British Transport - is not especially old, and its stylistic influences are more Japanese than Scottish, though it is now owned by the Kohler group.

Having said all that, it's still an excellent hostelry, with 144 comfortably furnished rooms and suites, recently refurbished at a cost of £5 million. The Road Hole Grill is one of the best restaurants in a town not lacking in eateries, while Sands offers a more casual dining experience, and there's pub grub in The Jigger Inn. A Bar & Grill - Duke's - adjoins the property's own private golf course of that name.

The new Kohler Waters Spa is world-class. But still the biggest attraction for aficionados is to be able to sit on their own private balcony and watch the golfers traipse across what is probably the most photographed tiny bridge in the world, over the Swilken Burn.

Rates from: 🛏🛏🛏🛏🛏
Star rating: ★★★★★
Overall rating: 🎭🎭🎭🎭 ½

Ambience :	9.05	Cleanliness:	9.57
Value:	8.33	Facilities:	9.24
Staff:	9.25	Restaurants:	9.15
Location:	9.38	Families:	8.57

Wales

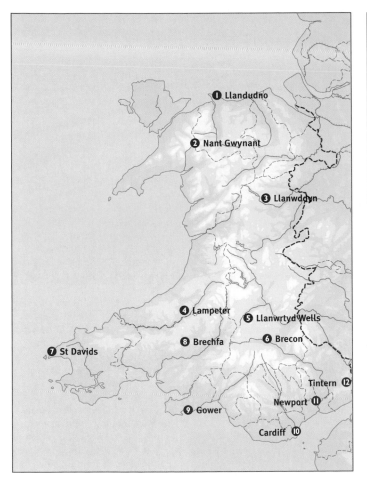

To the possible relief of a fair proportion of readers, Eco Retreats - a very rustic conglomeration of teepees and yurts near Machynlleth - does not appear in this guide. But it does presage the revolution that is currently overtaking Welsh accommodation, and by the same token, the changes that are taking place in the world's largest principality.

For a more familiar (and very much five-star) sort of overnight stay, look no further than the St David's Hotel & Spa in Cardiff, the *sine qua non* of urban regeneration; or indeed the rather more economical Big Sleep, which lies a short way off and is probably one of the wittiest ways so far devised to cope with a 1960s former office block. Outside Wales' primary city, country house estates and their ilk encourage visitors to soak up this country's many pleasures, best described as

bucolic with an utterly capital B.

Brought under English dominion in the 15th century, and not without a struggle, Wales maintains a sturdy independence to this day, no matter how a certain Charles Windsor might be dubbed. Public notices displayed in Welsh as well as English are not simply cosmetic, as the local language is in healthy day-to-day use. The National Eisteddfod is an annual celebration of culture that has no equal in any of the other parts of the United Kingdom, while the National Assembly (established in 1998 to oversee local government issues, and centred around the magnificent Senedd debating chamber designed by Lord Richard Rogers) is no mere talking shop.

Most of the country's three million residents live in the main cities by the coast, leaving the mountainous interior relatively wild. The border with England roughly follows Offa's Dyke (an 8th-century earthwork rampart thrown up by the King of Mercia) and incredibly runs straight through the Lion pub in the village of Llanymynech. Three National

Parks - Snowdonia, the Brecon Beacons, and the Pembrokeshire Coast - attract loads of outdoors types year round.

Softies and gricers can take the easy way to the top of Mount Snowdon (1,085 metres, and more usually referred to nowadays as Yr Wyddfa) aboard the mountain

railway, which was built in 1896, as solid a tribute to Victorian engineering as might be imagined. Indeed, the 19th century saw Wales become increasingly industrialised, exporting vast quantities of coal and steel although these have recently been overtaken by the service sector.

Tourism now forms a substantial part of the Welsh economy, and the country's best-known sons and daughters attract a stream of heritage trailers. Richard Burton is the obvious thespian, with Christian "Batman" Bale following close behind. Tom Jones and Dame Shirley Bassey head the list of well-known crooners (take in a Sunday chapel service if you are in any doubt about Wales's continuing musical abilities). Tommy Cooper, Dawn French, Terry "Python" Jones and Max Boyce sharpened their early comic wits here. Of course, this is the spiritual home of rugby, witness legends such as Gareth Edwards and JPR Williams. And for the record, TE Lawrence ("of Arabia") was born in Tremadog in 1888, followed by design guru Laura Ashley (Merthyr Tydfil, 1925).

One of Wales many claims to fame is its numerous castles, with Caernarfon heading the list,

reportedly modelled on Constantinople and whose 18-year construction ended in 1301. The area is actually the heartland of Welsh nationalism, though less fervently so than in 1969 when an attempt was made to blow up the train carrying the aforementioned C. Windsor to his investiture as Prince of Wales.

A more recent construction than Caernarfon Castle, though just as quintessentially Welsh, is the Rhondda Heritage Park. Based around the former Lewis Merthyr Colliery, it's a poignant reminder of the days when miners were among the country's principle breadwinners, and a proud and cleverly designed showcase for a major part of Wales' heritage.

Equally fascinating is Hay-on-Wye (YGelli), the second-hand book capital of Britain, just inside the border and the site of a well-regarded literature festival that attracts top authors every summer.

As in other parts of Britain, gloriously sunny days in Wales can turn into unglorious wet ones faster than it takes to say "blizzard", though in fairness it should be noted that Welsh beaches are highly popular in summer. Needless to say, there's plenty of entertainment indoors, and the words "croeso i Gymru" - welcome to Wales - are uttered heartily and genuinely whatever the weather, and especially in Llanfairpwllgwyngyllgogerychwyrn drobwllllantysiliogogogoch, which is still the most cunning tourist come-on as well as the longest domain name in the world.

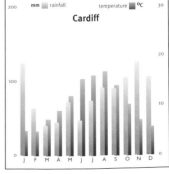

WALES' BEST HOTELS

Ty Mawr Country Hotel

Brechfa, Carmarthenshire, SA32 7RA, Wales
T: +44 1267 202 332
www.HotelClub.com

Ty Mawr means "big house". But it's all relative. By the standards of the tiny village in which it is located Ty Mawr is a substantial building. As hotels go, it's as intimate as it gets, with just five bedrooms. What it lacks in size it makes up for in character. A former farmhouse dating from the 15th century, Ty Mawr is filled with those textbook period features that provide the perfect canvas for rustic interior design. Thick stone walls, low ceilings, log fires, old beams, cosy nooks and crannies... Ty Mawr has got the lot.

You won't sacrifice anything in the way of comfort, for this gleaming ex-farmhouse has been sympathetically remodelled. The well-equipped cottagey-style bedrooms have antique pine furnishings and bathrooms come with Italian tiled floors and Victorian-style claw-foot baths.

Food and drink play their part in Ty Mawr's popularity. There's an emphasis on local organic ingredients in the restaurant, while the old bakery next door has been converted into the Flock Inn, a microbrewery producing five varieties of beer (aficionados of real ale might want to take Ty Mawr's residential brewing course),

Ty Mawr's other trump card is its location. Brechfa is an utterly tranquil spot, fringed by forest and set beside the Cothi, a hugely popular fishing river. Yet for all its peace and quiet it's not remote. The bustling market town of Carmarthen is just 15 minutes' drive away, and across the hill there's the National Botanic Garden of Wales, which is more than worth the trip.

Rates from: 🛏🛏
Star rating: ★ ★ ★
Overall rating: **Editors' Pick**

Ambience :	n/a	Cleanliness:	n/a
Value:	n/a	Facilities:	n/a
Staff:	n/a	Restaurants:	n/a
Location:	n/a	Families:	n/a

Llangoed Hall Hotel

Llyswen, Brecon, Powys, Mid Wales, LD3 0YP, Wales
T: +44 1874 754 525 **F:** +44 1874 754 545
www.HotelClub.com

Well-known names and Llangoed seem to go together. When the Hay Literary Festival ("The Woodstock of the mind", according to Bill Clinton) is held each year at the nearby "town of books", all the international celebrities stay here. The iconoclastic architect Sir Clough Williams-Ellis redesigned the house, which dates from the Middle Ages, in 1919. And in 1990 it opened as a hotel after being acquired by Sir Bernard Ashley, husband of the late Laura Ashley.

Llangoed Hall lives up to its pedigree. It's a true country house, as opposed to those less exalted country house hotels that crop up just about everywhere. Discretion and quiet professionalism set the tone. There's no reception desk, for example, though you will be greeted warmly and courteously. Llangoed prefers to think of its clients as house guests. And it's fair to say that all the accoutrements necessary for a weekend at a grand country house are readily to hand: the drawing room scattered with the day's newspapers and warmed by a massive fireplace; the drinks cabinet and attentive butler; the panelled library and billiard room, to which gentlemen (and even ladies) can retire; the fresh flowers and antiques; the carved timber staircase leading to a long upstairs gallery. And everywhere, paintings from Sir Bernard's personal art collection.

As you'd expect, none of the 23 bedrooms is the same. They have all been individually - and richly - decorated with fabrics from Elanbach, Sir Bernard's textile design and printing company based in the grounds, which extend to the banks of the River Wye.

Rates from: 💰💰💰💰
Star rating: ★★★★★
Overall rating: 🐾🐾🐾🐾

Ambience :	10.0	Cleanliness:	9.67
Value:	8.50	Facilities:	7.33
Staff:	9.67	Restaurants:	9.17
Location:	9.50	Families:	6.40

The Big Sleep Hotel Cardiff

Bute Terrace, Cardiff, CF10 2FE, Wales
T: +44 2920 636 363 **F:** +44 2920 636 364
www.HotelClub.com/hotels/The_Big_Sleep_Hotel_Cardiff

The Bogart and Bacall of British hotels, Cosmo Fry and Lulu Anderson (an entrepreneur and former fashion journalist) brought a welcome scattering of zest to the industry when they opened The Big Sleep in a refurbished 1960s office block just before the turn of the Millennium. Refreshingly unburdened by any preconceptions, other than to provide somewhere stylish to stay at affordable prices, they've done rather well. BS (unfortunate abbreviation) might not appeal to more traditional tastes, but its Ikea-like functionality and lack of frills certainly provide an experience that's different. Of the 81 rooms here, there's a choice of Budget for penny-pinchers, or Family for ankle-biters, while top of the range - Penthouse - is still shy of 100 quid. Quite the best aspect of the accommodation is the enormous windows, granting views over the city and a feeling of freedom even when the weather is at its most Welsh. Breakfast is Continental (commendable coffee, croissants, cereal) and may be packed as a takeaway, the bar facilities are fairly slim, but at least there are modem ports, 14-channel TVs and a kettle in the rooms. Fry and Anderson (who count actor John Malkovich as a partner) certainly didn't ignore the age-old dictum for hotel success ("location, location, location") and the staff seem to be inspired by their surrounds and the owners' vision. In short, this is a cheap, chic, kip, and a welcome counterpoint to GB's steeply priced accommodation tally. A second Big Sleep is performing similarly well in Cheltenham, a town generally regarded as Middle England's solar plexus. Watch out, Hilton.

Rates from: 🛏
Star rating: ★★
Overall rating: 🛏🛏🛏🛏

Ambience :	7.80	Cleanliness:	8.70
Value:	8.70	Facilities:	7.08
Staff:	8.40	Restaurants:	3.00
Location:	9.00	Families:	5.50

Churchills Hotel

Cardiff Road, Llandaff, CF5 2AD, Wales
T: +44 2920 400300 **F:** +44 2920 568 347
www.HotelClub.com/hotels/Churchills_Hotel_Cardiff

At first glance it looks just like any other town-house style hotel but Churchills prides itself on showing guests some of the friendly hospitality the Welsh are known for - through the little touches. Take for example the homey looking duvet and patchwork cushions in any one of the 22 bedrooms, or better yet, any of the 13 suites contained in mews-cottages; or the specials chalked on the small blackboard in the lounge bar. The Llandaff suite offers conference facilities for up to 110 delegates while more intimate meetings can be arranged in the Cathedral Suite which can host up to 15 people. And with a host of nearby attractions such as Castell Coch, Dyffryn Gardens and Bute Park, guests may find themselves saying *cymraeg* (hello) again before long, instead of simply *hwyl fawr* (goodbye) for good.

Rates from: 🌑🌑
Star rating: ★★★
Overall rating: 🌙🌙🌙🌙

Ambience :	8.00	Cleanliness:	9.00
Value:	9.00	Facilities:	8.88
Staff:	10.0	Restaurants:	9.00
Location:	8.00	Families:	9.00

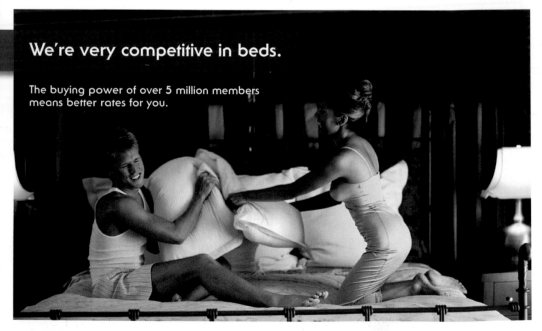

Hilton Cardiff

Kingsway, Cardiff, CF10 3HH, Wales
T: +44 2920 646 300 **F:** +44 2920 646 333
www.HotelClub.com/hotels/Hilton_Hotel_Cardiff

In a city where rugby is the lingua franca the Hilton stands out like a good fly-half, with plenty of style and flair and not a hint of cauliflower ear. The hotel opened in 1999 in a converted office building and remains the city centre's only five-star, and with the Millennium Stadium (the cauldron of Welsh rugby) just around the corner, it has become the hotel of choice for visiting teams - although this may be more to do with the generous buffet breakfasts than the proximity of the pitch.

The 197 rooms range from PlayStation-equipped Hilton Rooms to spacious Junior Suites, all with beds and bathrooms generous enough to accommodate even the largest prop forward; the most popular rooms also boast superb panoramic views over Cardiff Castle (although the best views are from the Executive Lounge on the seventh floor).

As well as the castle and the Millennium Stadium, the hotel is within a short stroll of the National Museum, the greenery of Bute Park and Queen Street - the city's main shopping strip. The Hilton's location proves to be a match winner in the evening too, as the surrounding bars and restaurants on Greyfriar Road provide plenty of choice for cocktail sippers and tapas grazers.

Within the hotel, the bright and airy Razzi Restaurant also offers an excellent contemporary Welsh menu to scrum down on, with the adjoining Razzi Piano Bar adding a true touch of class. The whole package is neatly rounded off with a cool gym and a very welcome heated, 20-metre pool.

Rates from: 🛏🛏🛏
Star rating: ★ ★ ★ ★ ★
Overall rating: 🌀🌀🌀🌀

Ambience :	9.04	Cleanliness:	9.46
Value:	7.82	Facilities:	8.65
Staff:	8.56	Restaurants:	8.88
Location:	9.36	Families:	8.00

Jolyon's Boutique Hotel

5 Bute Crescent, Cardiff, CF10 5AN, Wales
T: +44 2920 488 775 **F:** +44 2920 488 775
www.HotelClub.com/hotels/Jolyons_Boutique_Hotel

means cosy, cuddle and cupboard under the stairs), serves up a hearty Welsh breakfast in the morning using locally sourced, organic food.

In the evening diners can enjoy modern Welsh cuisine, or share a platter of local cheeses, before sinking into large leather sofas and sinking a few glasses of wine. Jolyon Joseph, the owner, can often be found serving behind the bar and will happily provide recommendations on hotspots for evening entertainment, and with over a dozen bars and restaurants in the neighbouring Mermaid Quay, there's plenty of choice.

Cardiff's foremost boutique hotel is a perfect fit for the city. Like the Welsh capital, Jolyon's is cosy, compact and instantly likeable. Six individually designed rooms are crammed into this Grade II listed Georgian townhouse, and each has its own merits. Several rooms look across to the Wales Millennium Centre (home of Welsh National Opera), some are filled with grand four-poster beds, others feature beautiful slate floor bathrooms with

Philippe Starck loos. Head to the top floor and the room spills out onto a rooftop terrace - an ideal spot to watch the sun set over Cardiff Bay. Lavish and colourful furniture from across the globe seems to have been stuffed into every nook and cranny, but there's no forgetting that this hotel has its heart in Wales. The small cellar bar, aptly named Cwtch (pronounced "cutch" and one of those handy Welsh portmanteau words that

Rates from: 🐾🐾
Star rating: n/a
Overall rating: 🐾🐾🐾🐾

Ambience :	9.00	Cleanliness:	9.00
Value:	9.00	Facilities:	7.25
Staff:	8.50	Restaurants:	7.50
Location:	9.00	Families:	9.00

The St David's Hotel & Spa

Havannah Street, Cardiff, CF10 5SD, Wales
T: +44 2920 454 045 **F:** +44 2920 313 075
www.HotelClub.com/hotels/The_St_Davids_Hotel_Spa_Cardiff

The flagship of Cardiff's hotel fleet was designed to mimic the prow of a cruise liner slicing through the waters of Cardiff Bay, its distinctive rooftop sail matching the sweep of the waves, and since opening in 1999 it has left all other Welsh hotels floundering in its wake. The Rocco Forte venture (now owned by Principal Hotels) was ahead of its time when it first opened its doors; the glitz and glamour of Wales' first five-star out of place in the less than ship-shape Tiger Bay, but the red carpet events, champagne cocktails and the chiselled looks of the grand, seven-storey atrium gave a much needed jumpstart to the city, which has now grown into an A-list short break destination.

Rooms here range from the Classic King, with marble bathrooms and generous proportions, up to Deluxe Master Suites (the preferred living quarters of visiting celebrities) on the upper three floors - and thanks to the hotel's angular profile all 132 rooms boast private, sea-view balconies, with vistas stretching far across the Bristol Channel on clear days. Bay views, and a healthy dose of sea air, are also plentiful from the outdoor terrace of the Tides Grill, where in the summer months al fresco diners can enjoy an à la carte menu of fresh seafood or modern twists on classic Welsh dishes - all beautifully presented (even the potato chips are neatly stacked). The adjoining Tides Bar offers an opportunity to splurge out and uncork a bottle of Krug Grand Cuvée, or indeed sample the entire range (Tides is the only Krug champagne bar in Wales), and the expert mixologists will prepare an

armada of signature cocktails, on the rocks or otherwise, with masterful skill. Further dining options and several champagne, cocktail and dim sum bars can be found five minutes' walk away at Mermaid Quay, and after indulging in the city's nightlife, the following morning can be spent detoxing below decks in the St David's marine spa.

Oohs and aahs of relaxation bubble from salt-water spa pools, underwater jet beds and the hydrotherapy corridor; a crew of specialists armed with an array of hot stones, mud masks and algae wraps maintain the pampering, and perhaps catering to Cardiff's legions of visiting football and rugby stars, the spa has also created a menu of massages and facials just for men.

Between treatments freshly massaged bodies can stay poolside and call upon the services of the spa butler for refreshments, or head to the Waves buffet restaurant, where a dress code of spa robe and slippers applies and light lunches are served on a sun drenched outdoor terrace.

Naturally, prices here are a touch higher than most other hotels in Cardiff, but its package of prime location, top-notch service and luxury facilities keeps it leagues ahead of the competition, and as patron saint of Cardiff's tourism industry, the St David's is a shining example for the city to follow. As the locals would say: "Bendigedig". Which means to say - quite outstanding.

Rates from: 🐧🐧🐧🐧
Star rating: ★ ★ ★ ★ ★
Overall rating: 🐧🐧🐧🐧 ½

Ambience :	9.00	Cleanliness:	9.53
Value:	8.26	Facilities:	9.31
Staff:	9.35	Restaurants:	9.06
Location:	9.05	Families:	8.19

Fairyhill

Reynoldston, Gower, Swansea, SA3 1BS, Wales
T: +44 1792 390 139 **F:** +44 1792 391 358
www.HotelClub.com

Boutique hotels are all the rage nowadays. It could be argued that Fairyhill was one of this new breed long before the term was coined. With just eight bedrooms, and the accent firmly on good living with a contemporary twist, Fairyhill has been a consistent player in Wales' top accommodation for many years.

The well-proportioned 18th-century house is surrounded by ten hectares of grounds consisting of lawns, mature woodland, a trout stream and beautiful lake (there's even a croquet lawn). So it's a genuine country retreat. But within, Fairyhill is far removed from the stuffy, faux gentility of many country house hotels. It's laid back and casual, but impeccably run with an easy but highly professional touch - it's the kind of place with the kind of ambience that appeals to today's tastes.

And talking about tastes, Fairyhill's other big plus-point is its food. The restaurant's reputation has spread far and wide. Non-residents are happy to make the longish trip from other parts of South Wales just to eat here, choosing from inventive menus that make the most of local ingredients like Gower seafood and Welsh Black beef. Fairyhill was ahead of the game in this respect, too, championing locally sourced food long before it became the culinary fashion. Foodies also appreciate the outstanding wine cellar.

The bedrooms are plush, exceedingly comfortable and individually designed. It's an idyllic hotel in an idyllic location, on the Gower Peninsula - Britain's first Area of Outstanding Beauty - close to spectacular beaches and headlands.

Rates from: 🪙🪙🪙
Star rating: ★ ★ ★ ★ ★
Overall rating: 🎗🎗🎗🎗 ½

Ambience :	10.0	Cleanliness:	10.0
Value:	8.00	Facilities:	7.00
Staff:	10.0	Restaurants:	9.50
Location:	9.00	Families:	10.0

Falcondale Mansion Hotel

Falcondale Drive, Lampeter, SA48 7RX, Wales
T: +44 1570 422 910 **F:** +44 1570 422 559
www.HotelClub.com

Although located on the outskirts of the busy little country and university town of Lampeter, Falcondale Mansion has an air of splendid isolation. Set within six hectares of secluded countryside overlooking a mix of ornamental woodland, lawns and gardens, the hotel is approached by a long drive. But it's no cold or distant grey-stoned country pile. The mansion was built in the mid-19th century in an exuberant Italianate style, a design accentuated by a striking, white-painted façade.

The Italianate influence has rubbed off within. The Falcondale is a surprisingly light and airy house, with lots of windows - and a large conservatory - that make the most of its south-facing aspect. And there's also genuine warmth in the way you are looked after by the Falcondale's friendly staff (or is this better described as a warm-hearted Welsh welcome?). Whatever its source, it sets the tone for a hotel with the full complement of country comforts but without any attendant pomposity or pretension.

Relaxed informality is also the keynote at the hotel's restaurant and separate brasserie. Both serve excellent food that relies heavily on home-made and locally sourced ingredients.

The 20 bedrooms are individually designed with rich colour schemes and furnishings in keeping with the house's character. Most also benefit from wonderful views across the grounds and exquisite gardens (come in May or June and you'll be rewarded with spectacular displays of rhododendrons and azaleas). At any time of the year you may spot the red kite, a rare bird of prey, wheeling in the skies.

Rates from: 💰💰💰
Star rating: ★★★
Overall rating: 💗💗💗💗

Ambience :	10.0	Cleanliness:	9.00
Value:	6.00	Facilities:	8.86
Staff:	9.00	Restaurants:	9.00
Location:	9.00	Families:	8.86

Bodysgallen Hall & Spa

Llandudno, North Wales LL30 1RS, Wales
T: +44 1492 584 466 **F:** +44 1492 582 519
www.HotelClub.com

Bodysgallen is one of those historic hotels that pioneered fine country house living. Still very much at the top of its game, Bodysgallen is rightly regarded as one of the best hotels in Wales. The formula is simple - restoring an historically and architecturally significant property (a 17th-century house set in 80 hectares of grounds just inland from the Victorian seaside resort of Llandudno) to provide the ultimate in luxury and hospitality.

Sensibly, they have steered well clear of the minimalist, über-cool design ethos. It just wouldn't work here. The rooms are rich and warm, with all the classic, traditional features: lots of oak wood panelling, stone mullioned windows, ornate fireplaces, four-poster beds, patterned fabrics, and an abundance of antiques, fine pictures and fresh flowers. The theme continues out of doors in Bodysgallen's magnificent garden, with its terraced lawns, walled rose garden, and - the horticultural highlight - a rare 17th-century knot garden of box hedges filled with sweet-scented herbs.

The service is discreet, the atmosphere restful. Guests at this 33-room hotel have the choice of staying in the main building or in cottage suites within the grounds. Some so-called spa hotels make do with modest facilities. Not so in Bodysgallen's case. Its large spa and leisure complex includes the full complement of treatment, sauna, steam and fitness rooms plus a generously sized 15-metre swimming pool. The hotel is noted for its fine dining. Unsurprisingly, it comes highly recommended for those two British staples - Sunday lunch and afternoon tea.

Rates from: 🪙🪙🪙
Star rating: ★★★★
Overall rating: 🦢🦢🦢🦢🦢

Ambience :	9.25	Cleanliness:	10.0
Value:	8.75	Facilities:	10.0
Staff:	7.75	Restaurants:	9.75
Location:	9.50	Families:	9.39

Lake Hotel Vyrnwy

Llanwddyn, Powys, SY10 0LY, Wales
T: +44 1691 870 692 **F:** +44 1691 870 259
www.HotelClub.com

There's no argument about this hotel's primary feature. Just look out of the window. Lake Vyrnwy has a world-class view.

The hotel sits on a wooded hillside overlooking the waters of its eponymous lake, encircled by thick forests that rise into wild Welsh mountains. The sense of theatre is enhanced by a spiky, Gothic water tower - a cross between fairytale and Frankenstein - that pokes out of the lake's inky black waters.

Guests sit and stare for hours at this vista. And they do so in some considerable comfort, for the hotel has other special qualities that set it apart from the usual country house experience. For a start, there's the building itself. It's something of a misfit, looking more like a baronial Scottish shooting lodge than Welsh hotel. Inside, the look continues - wood panelling, subdued lighting, comfy, weathered leather chairs and sofas, log fires, a plush drawing room complete with grand piano,

and a liberal scattering of hunting, shooting and fishing memorabilia. This is all entirely in keeping, for Lake Vyrnwy is Wales's premiere country sports hotel, taking full advantage of the fact that it's part of a 9,700-hectare estate.

But you don't have to be a hunting enthusiast to enjoy Lake Vyrnwy. There's birdwatching and walking too, and within doors a brand-new spa with tropical and mist showers and all kinds of exotic treatments. The hotel's 52 rooms, many with lake views, come with all contemporary comforts but are decorated in classic rather than chic style - entirely in keeping with the hotel's dignified character.

Rates from: 💰💰💰
Star rating: ★★★
Overall rating: 📷📷📷📷 ½

Ambience :	8.75	Cleanliness:	9.50
Value:	8.75	Facilities:	8.67
Staff:	9.50	Restaurants:	9.25
Location:	9.75	Families:	9.50

Carlton Riverside

Irfon Crescent, Llanwrtyd Wells, Powys, Wales LD5 4ST, Wales
T: +44 1591 610 248
www.HotelClub.com

The Carlton Riverside is a "restaurant with rooms". It makes no pretence at offering anything other than comfortable, convenient accommodation. Why the reticence? Let's put it down to old-fashioned Welsh honesty. Bluff and nonsense is for those who live across the border. It helps that the restaurant has one of the best reputations in the country and helped spark an epicurean sea change in Wales.

It's a reputation that would be the envy of many a celebrity chef owned eatery somewhere far more cosmopolitan, but the Carlton is located in Britain's smallest town, Llanwrtyd Wells, a blissfully tranquil place that straddles the River Irfon and nestles in the shadow of the Cambrian Mountains. It's on the side of the Irfon that the Carlton sits, though in November 2006 it moved 300 yards along the riverbank. The relocation did nothing to diminish the quality of the cuisine, or alter the standards of the five guestrooms. They are still comfortable but unfussy. Not all of them have views to die for and none are likely to inspire a photo shoot for *Country Life*, but owners Alan and Mary Ann Gilchrist will not pull the wool over your eyes - they are far too busy arranging your meals. While Mary Ann attends to the locally sourced produce in the kitchen, Alan presides over the front of house.

And once you're sated on their sumptuous fare you can retire safe in the knowledge that the same care will be lavished upon you come breakfast time.

Rates from: 🦢🦢
Star rating: ★★★★
Overall rating: 🦢🦢🦢🦢

Ambience :	7.00	Cleanliness:	7.00
Value:	8.00	Facilities:	7.86
Staff:	10.0	Restaurants:	10.0
Location:	8.00	Families:	7.86

The Celtic Manor Resort Hotel

Coldra Woods, The Usk Valley, Newport, South Wales, NP18 1HQ, Wales
T: +44 1633 413 000 **F:** +44 1633 412 910
www.HotelClub.com/hotels/Celtic_Manor_Resort

So what exactly is Celtic Manor? The answer lies in the "resort" appellation. It's marketed as a complete destination rather than mere hotel, and for once the salespeople haven't gone over the top. Everything about Celtic Manor is larger than life. Drive along the M4 motorway into Wales and there it stands, filling the skyline like some medieval castle. The statistics are impressive too. There are two hotels, over 400 rooms, three championship golf courses, a world-class golf academy, two health clubs, two spas, four restaurants, a children's entertainment centre and cavernous, state-of-the-art convention and conference centre, all set within a sprawling 570 hectares of hillside.

All of this has cost a great deal of money. It may even have dented the wallet of its owner, the fabulously wealthy Welsh telecoms entrepreneur and golfing enthusiast Sir Terry Matthews. But this hotel is no rich man's plaything. It is sleekly and professionally run, humming along like a Rolls-Royce. And unlike many large, bland corporate hotels, it retains its own personality and identity.

The cathedral-like atrium - one of its most architecturally successful features - is a huge space guarded by carved wooden dragons symbolising Wales and decorated with wall hangings depicting Welsh scenes. It's the central feature of the 330-

bedroomed modern resort hotel. For something a little more traditional there's a 70-roomed 19th-century manor house next door.

Whatever you choose, you'll see lots of golfers. Celtic Manor effortlessly matches most of Scotland's famous golfing hotels - and in 2010 it is due to host the Ryder Cup, the world's most prestigious golfing tournament.

Rates from: 💰💰💰💰
Star rating: ★ ★ ★ ★ ★
Overall rating: 👍👍👍👍

Ambience :	8.81	Cleanliness:	9.19
Value:	7.97	Facilities:	9.30
Staff:	8.81	Restaurants:	8.88
Location:	8.25	Families:	8.21

Pen-y-Gwryd Hotel

Nant Gwynant, Gwynedd, LL55 4NT, Wales
T: +44 1286 870 211
www.HotelClub.com

No TV or telephone, no locks on the doors, no credit-card payment accepted, few ensuite bathrooms, an unheated "natural pool" and set mealtimes ... who on earth would want to stay here? Thousands of climbers and hikers and fans of old-fashioned, down-to-earth hospitality, that's who. For this place is a classic.

The original 1810 farmhouse in the heart of Snowdonia went through a lot of ups and downs until Chris Briggs bought it in 1947 and set about turning it into a mountaineers' Mecca. (George Mallory had stayed there as early as 1924 and Sir Edmund Hillary used it as a "base camp" prior to his pioneering conquest of Everest in 1953 - as the many souvenirs around the walls attest.)

Breakfast and dinner are announced by a gong - at 9am and 7.30pm sharp - and they're both worth being on time for: porridge and kippers, Welsh black beef or lamb chops, with plenty of home-made "puds". There is a wood-panelled, slate-floored residents' lounge and a large games room. And a sauna in the garden.

Rooms are simply furnished, with toilets and bathrooms mostly in the corridors outside, though one has a four-poster bed and all are equipped with fluffy towels and heaps of blankets. Service is cheerful and efficient, albeit with a touch of eccentricity: amble into the dining room in a baseball cap or bare feet, or start drinking water straight from the bottle, and you're liable to get a lecture. And quite right too, Pen-y-Gwryd's legion of loyal patrons would maintain.

Rates from: 💰💰
Star rating: n/a
Overall rating: 🏩🏩🏩🏩 ½

Ambience :	10.0	Cleanliness:	8.00
Value:	9.00	Facilities:	10.0
Staff:	9.00	Restaurants:	8.00
Location:	10.0	Families:	10.00

TYF Eco Hotel

Caerfai Road, St Davids, Pembrokeshire, SA62 6QS, Wales
T: +44 1437 721 678 **F:** +44 1437 721 838
www.HotelClub.com

Without wishing to be ageist about it, this place is probably better suited to those who put an adrenalin rush before creature comforts.

If you dig surfing, wind-surfing, kayaking or what the TYF people term "coasteering", the Eco Hotel - just 10 minutes from one of the best beaches (in terms of water quality) in the UK, in the heart of the dramatic Pembrokeshire Coast National Park - you couldn't pick a better crash-pad.

A 200-year-old converted windmill is at the centre of this 12-roomed property - you can climb the spiral staircase to where the sails used to be for a magnificent view of the peninsula - and there is self-catering accommodation in a stone cottage next door.

And it comes with squeaky-clean "green" credentials: wind-up solar radios and "Indigo" lanterns in the rooms and a commitment to fair trading and offsetting carbon-dioxide emissions. Turn up to stay without a car and you'll be treated to a drink on the house.

It is also the first certified organic hotel in Wales. All food served in the restaurant, which is open to non-residents, has been organically grown, with stacks of veggie choices and even organic wine and cider.

There is activity equipment for hire and you can sign up for various skills courses. The owners, who also run a management consultancy, specialise in team-building. But what does TYF stand for? Target Your Future? Tell Your Friends? The Yately Forums? The Theophilus Youth Fellowship? None of the above, apparently. How about T'rrific Young Fun?

Rates from: 🐚🐚
Star rating: n/a
Overall rating: **Editors' Pick**

Ambience :	n/a	Cleanliness:	n/a
Value:	n/a	Facilities:	n/a
Staff:	n/a	Restaurants:	n/a
Location:	n/a	Families:	n/a

Parva Farmhouse Hotel & Restaurant

Tintern, Nr. Chepstow, Monmouthshire, NP16 6SQ, Wales
T: +44 1291 689 411 **F:** +44 1291 689 941
www.HotelClub.com

This 17th-century building on the banks of the River Wye, just a short way from Tintern Abbey, is what country hotels used to be all about. Cramped and quaint but bursting with character. With only eight rooms (one with a four-poster bed), it's almost a B&B - except that they all have TV and radio alarms, hairdryers and tea- and coffee-making facilities, Wi-Fi Internet access and room service.

Doors are closed with a latch, ceilings are slopey, the bathrooms are miniscule (but with excellent showers) and there are old-fashioned sheets and blankets on the beds. Dogs are welcome in a couple of the rooms, but no children under 12.

Food at this family-run establishment is gloriously home-made (they even offer a local wine) and served in the intimate Inglenook Restaurant, which boasts a four-metre beamed fireplace. The comfortable lounge - wood-burning stone fireplace adorned with horse brasses, thick stone walls, leather armchairs and sofas on a flowered carpet, and a selection of magazines (no TV says the hotel, proudly) - has an "honesty" bar. And there is a "suntrap" garden with views over the Wye Valley.

Why would you be there in the first place? The area has literally hundreds of picturesque walks, some organised by the local Forestry Commission, there are six golf courses within a 25-kilometre radius, riding stables nearby and fishing on the doorstep (pheasant shooting can be arranged). Chepstow racecourse is just down the road, as is the Royal Forest of Dean with its Roman iron mines. And Tintern Abbey. Reason enough?

Rates from: 💰💰
Star rating: ★★
Overall rating: 🏠🏠🏠🏠

Ambience :	9.00	Cleanliness:	9.00
Value:	10.0	Facilities:	10.0
Staff:	7.00	Restaurants:	9.00
Location:	9.00	Families:	8.88

We're very competitive in beds.

The buying power of over 5 million members
means better rates for you.

Membership is free.
The rewards are unlimited.
Use Member Dollars 365 days a year.

Hotel ratings index

Facilities

Facilities	Restaurants	Families	🏉	🍸	📈	🌐	♿	🌷	1	✚	🐼	📖	🎵	⬛	🛏	✖	🤿	🏠	🚣	🎾	🏃	P	📶
9.88	9.98	9.41		•				•						•	•					•		•	•
8.06	10.00	9.67	•	•				•					•	•	•	•				•	•	•	•
8.33	9.27	7.67	•	•			•		•				•	•	•	•							•
n/a	n/a	n/a	•	•	•			•			•			•	•	•				•		•	•
7.24	9.25	7.71						•	•			•		•	•	•				•		•	
4.00	9.00	6.33		•				•						•								•	
9.08	9.64	8.40	•	•			•	•	•	•		•		•	•	•	•	•		•		•	•
n/a	n/a	n/a		•	•									•	•	•						•	•
8.80	9.13	8.33		•			•	•		•		•		•	•	•	•	•		•		•	•
8.62	9.46	7.60		•				•		•		•		•	•	•		•	•			•	
6.40	9.21	8.40	•	•				•		•		•		•	•	•			•	•	•		•
8.21	8.64	8.00	•	•	•		•	•		•		•		•	•	•					•	•	•
8.11	8.29	7.36	•	•	•			•		•		•		•	•	•					•	•	•
8.81	8.14	7.90	•	•				•		•		•		•	•	•							•
7.87	9.08	7.11	•	•				•		•		•		•	•	•							•
8.89	8.67	8.40	•	•	•			•		•		•		•	•	•		•					•
8.04	8.67	7.58		•	•			•		•		•		•	•	•							•
9.07	9.25	8.50		•	•			•		•		•		•	•	•							•
8.29	7.73	8.07		•	•			•	•		•			•		•		•		•	•	•	•
9.20	9.25	8.70		•				•	•		•			•	•	•		•	•				•
8.63	9.22	7.86		•				•	•		•			•	•			•					•
8.34	8.71	8.18		•	•			•			•			•	•	•		•			•	•	•
8.52	8.79	8.70	•	•	•			•		•	•	•	•	•	•	•		•					•
n/a	n/a	n/a						•															•
8.82	9.23	7.91	•	•	•			•			•			•	•	•	•	•					•
7.35	9.45	6.89		•							•			•	•						•	•	•
7.92	8.81	7.60		•				•	•		•			•	•	•	•	•		•	•	•	•
6.83	8.50	6.50		•				•	•					•	•	•							
4.25	6.67	6.67	•					•						•	•	•						•	•

Hotel ratings index

		PAGE	★	☞	Ambience	Value	Staff	Location	Cleanliness
							Ratings		
Grove	Chandler's Cross	39	5	4	8.82	6.82	8.41	8.18	9.41
Grosvenor	Chester	40	5	4.5	9.19	8.15	9.08	9.54	9.38
Crabwall Manor	Chester	41	4	4	8.85	8.08	9.33	8.77	9.54
De Vere Carden Park	Chester	42	4	4.5	8.92	8.92	9.35	8.54	9.63
Highbullen	Chittlehamholt	42	4	n/a	n/a	n/a	n/a	n/a	n/a
Coombe Abbey	Coventry	43	4	4	9.73	8.40	9.13	9.20	9.67
Crewe Hall	Crewe	43	4	4	9.25	8.25	9.00	8.63	9.38
Lumley Castle	Durham	44	4	4	9.63	8.56	9.44	9.06	9.50
Grand	Eastbourne	45	5	4	9.10	7.95	8.90	9.20	9.35
Acorn	Evershot	46	4	n/a	n/a	n/a	n/a	n/a	n/a
Babington House	Frome	47	n/a	4	9.00	7.75	8.25	9.25	9.25
Balmoral	Harrogate	48	3	n/a	n/a	n/a	n/a	n/a	n/a
De Vere Slaley Hall	Hexham	49	4	4	8.68	8.14	8.68	8.55	9.32
Four Seasons	Hook	50	5	1	8.83	7.83	8.33	9.17	8.83
Hell Bay	Isles of Scilly	51	3	5	10.00	9.00	9.00	10.00	10.00
42 The Calls	Leeds	52	n/a	4	9.25	8.00	8.81	9.50	9.31
De Vere Oulton Hall	Leeds	53	5	4	9.25	8.46	8.96	8.50	9.25
Hilton	Leeds	54	4	4	8.33	8.33	8.90	8.57	9.38
Marriott	Leeds	55	4	4	8.77	8.64	8.91	9.41	9.45
Malmaison	Leeds	55	4	4	8.86	8.43	9.07	9.07	9.50
Park Plaza	Leeds	56	4	4	8.71	8.53	8.31	9.18	9.29
Quebecs	Leeds	57	5	4	9.10	7.90	8.50	8.60	9.30
Queens	Leeds	59	4	4	8.83	8.61	8.94	9.72	9.11
Britannia Adelphi	Liverpool	60	3	4	8.35	7.35	7.85	9.45	7.85
Crowne Plaza	Liverpool	61	4	4	9.00	7.71	8.62	9.07	9.79
Marriott	Liverpool	62	4	4	8.77	8.73	8.91	9.32	9.45
Radisson SAS	Liverpool	62	4	4.5	9.15	8.65	9.20	8.80	9.55
Andaz	London	63	5	4	9.16	7.68	9.11	8.84	9.16
Ascott Mayfair	London	64	5	4	9.14	7.71	8.79	9.36	9.21
Bonnington	London	65	4	4	8.00	7.82	7.25	8.83	8.67

Facilities

Facilities	Restaurants	Families																					
8.99	8.59	7.55	●	●	●		●	●	●	●	●	●		●	●	●	●	●	●	●		●	●
8.88	9.38	8.50	●	●			●			●		●		●	●	●						●	
9.19	8.85	8.78		●	●		●	●		●				●	●	●	●		●		●	●	●
9.11	9.17	8.67	●	●	●		●	●	●	●		●		●	●	●	●		●	●	●	●	●
n/a	n/a	n/a		●	●		●	●	●	●				●	●	●	●	●	●		●	●	●
7.44	9.00	7.33	●	●	●		●	●				●		●	●	●	●		●		●	●	●
8.90	9.13	9.00	●	●			●	●		●		●		●	●	●	●	●	●		●	●	●
7.44	9.13	8.08		●			●	●	●	●		●		●	●	●						●	●
8.07	9.15	8.54	●	●	●		●	●		●	●	●		●	●	●	●		●		●	●	●
n/a	n/a	n/a		●				●		●				●		●	●	●		●		●	
8.83	9.00	8.00	●				●	●		●	●			●	●	●	●	●	●		●		●
n/a	n/a	n/a		●				●						●	●							●	●
8.90	8.45	8.93	●	●	●		●	●	●	●		●		●	●	●	●		●		●	●	●
7.40	8.33	7.75	●	●	●		●	●		●	●	●		●	●	●	●	●	●		●	●	●
9.57	9.00	9.57	●	●	●		●	●	●	●		●		●	●	●	●		●		●	●	●
6.45	8.60	6.88		●			●					●		●	●	●						●	●
9.00	9.21	7.27	●	●	●		●	●	●	●		●		●	●	●	●				●	●	●
8.47	8.90	8.76		●	●		●			●		●		●	●	●	●				●	●	●
8.35	8.68	8.00		●	●		●			●		●		●	●	●	●				●	●	●
8.85	8.79	7.33	●	●			●			●		●		●	●	●					●		●
7.69	8.86	6.88		●	●		●			●		●		●	●	●							
7.17	8.00	7.50		●			●							●	●						●	●	
8.13	8.65	9.00	●	●	●		●	●						●	●	●					●	●	●
8.25	8.44	8.21		●				●		●		●	●	●	●	●		●			●	●	●
8.96	8.77	8.88		●	●		●			●		●		●	●	●		●	●		●	●	●
9.03	8.82	8.62		●	●		●			●		●		●	●	●		●			●	●	●
9.28	8.94	7.89		●	●		●			●		●		●	●	●	●	●			●	●	●
8.23	8.81	7.82		●	●		●			●		●		●	●	●							●
7.94	8.85	7.78		●	●		●			●		●		●	●	●	●						●
7.17	8.06	6.86		●	●			●						●	●	●							●

Hotel ratings index

		PAGE	★	☞	Ambience	Value	Staff	Location	Cleanliness
					Ratings				
Brown's	London	65	5	4	9.43	8.07	9.08	9.86	9.43
Cavendish	London	66	4	4	8.93	8.57	9.14	9.64	9.08
City Inn Westminster	London	67	4	4	8.63	8.31	8.97	8.78	9.38
Claridge's	London	68	5	4.5	9.65	7.76	9.36	9.53	9.67
Connaught	London	70	5	4	8.75	8.25	9.00	9.00	9.56
Copthorne Tara	London	71	4	4	7.85	8.05	7.90	8.74	8.65
Covent Garden	London	72	5	4	9.21	8.36	9.21	9.71	9.86
Crowne Plaza	London	73	4	4	9.07	8.71	9.36	9.36	9.50
Cumberland	London	73	4	4	8.52	8.12	8.48	9.31	8.65
Dorchester	London	74	5	4	8.96	7.49	8.83	9.41	9.22
Grosvenor House	London	76	5	4	9.13	8.03	9.00	9.53	9.53
Hempel	London	76	5	4	9.40	7.80	8.60	8.53	9.47
Hilton Hyde Park	London	77	4	4	8.44	7.88	8.38	8.63	8.88
Hilton Kensington	London	77	4	4	7.50	7.86	8.23	8.71	8.43
Hilton Metropole	London	78	4	4	8.31	7.91	8.33	8.94	8.97
Hotel Russell	London	79	4	4	8.30	7.52	8.37	8.74	8.93
Hoxton	London	79	4	4	8.83	9.08	8.71	7.79	9.33
Hyde Park Towers	London	80	3	4	8.45	8.20	8.70	9.05	8.55
InterContinental Park Lane	London	81	5	4	8.41	6.90	8.31	8.86	8.72
Jurys	London	83	4	4	8.65	7.82	8.35	9.24	9.24
Landmark	London	84	5	4	9.39	8.00	8.93	8.90	9.45
Lanesborough	London	85	5	4	9.20	7.80	9.27	9.40	9.40
Langham	London	86	5	4	8.89	8.19	9.26	9.41	9.44
Le Méridien Piccadilly	London	87	5	4	8.54	7.27	8.24	9.48	8.65
London Bridge	London	88	4	4	8.91	8.32	8.87	8.93	9.27
London Hilton on Park Lane	London	89	5	4	8.43	7.32	8.41	9.36	9.14
Marriott	London	89	5	4	8.89	7.89	8.58	9.30	9.33
Malmaison	London	90	n/a	4	8.78	7.50	8.94	8.72	9.50
Mandarin Oriental	London	91	5	4.5	9.40	7.87	9.37	9.53	9.70
Metropolitan	London	92	5	4.5	9.55	7.30	9.10	9.00	9.73
Milestone	London	92	5	4.5	9.27	8.50	9.36	9.27	9.67

Facilities

Facilities	Restaurants	Families	🍴	🍸	🖼	🌐	♿	🌷	1	✚	🧸	🎿	🎵	☕	🍽	✂	🏊	🏠	⛵	⚽	🏃	P	📶
8.35	9.00	9.17	•	•	•		•			•			•		•	•	•	•			•	•	•
8.36	8.55	8.00		•	•		•						•		•	•	•					•	•
8.21	8.41	7.92	•	•	•		•			•			•		•	•	•				•	•	•
8.76	9.63	8.53	•	•	•		•			•			•		•	•	•						•
7.33	9.07	6.88	•	•	•		•			•	•		•		•	•	•		•	•			•
7.64	8.22	7.88	•	•	•		•			•			•		•	•	•				•	•	•
8.41	8.83	8.13		•			•			•			•		•	•	•						•
8.37	8.85	8.38	•	•	•		•	•		•			•		•	•	•	•				•	•
8.19	8.57	7.61	•	•	•		•			•			•		•	•	•			•		•	•
8.57	9.00	7.86	•	•			•			•			•		•	•	•					•	•
8.50	8.93	8.65		•	•		•			•			•		•	•	•						•
7.59	8.92	6.88	•	•	•		•	•		•			•		•	•	•					•	•
8.01	8.50	7.69	•	•	•		•						•		•	•	•					•	•
8.00	8.25	8.14	•	•	•		•			•			•		•	•	•	•				•	•
8.56	8.69	8.53	•	•	•		•			•			•		•	•	•		•			•	•
7.02	7.86	7.00	•	•	•		•						•		•	•						•	•
7.22	7.76	6.87		•	•		•						•		•	•							•
8.12	8.12	8.07		•				•					•		•	•						•	•
8.34	8.32	8.00	•	•	•		•			•			•		•	•	•	•				•	•
7.54	7.81	8.33		•	•		•			•			•		•	•	•				•		
8.69	9.17	8.03	•	•	•		•			•			•		•	•	•	•				•	•
8.32	9.00	7.75	•	•	•		•			•			•		•	•	•					•	•
8.73	8.88	8.21	•	•	•		•			•			•		•	•	•	•			•	•	•
8.28	8.48	7.90	•	•	•		•			•			•		•	•	•						•
8.48	8.56	9.04	•	•	•		•			•			•		•	•	•				•		•
7.96	8.67	7.63		•	•		•			•		•	•		•	•	•	•					•
8.65	8.88	8.33		•	•		•			•			•		•	•	•	•				•	•
7.91	8.19	6.73		•	•		•			•			•		•								•
8.92	9.00	8.25	•	•	•		•			•			•		•	•	•						
9.09	9.71	8.60	•	•	•		•			•			•		•	•	•					•	•
8.61	9.00	8.60	•	•	•		•			•			•		•	•	•	•	•			•	•

Hotel ratings index

		PAGE	★	👆	Ambience	Value	Staff	Location	Cleanliness
Millennium	London	93	4	4	8.53	8.33	8.71	9.60	9.07
Park Lane	London	94	5	4	8.86	8.00	8.57	9.07	8.71
Park Plaza Victoria	London	95	4	4	8.29	8.12	8.88	8.88	8.94
Radisson Edwardian	London	95	5	4	9.00	7.76	8.71	8.41	8.76
Renaissance Chancery Court	London	96	5	4	9.50	8.19	9.25	9.06	9.31
Ritz	London	97	5	4	9.50	7.64	9.22	9.42	9.76
Royal Garden	London	98	5	4	8.67	8.04	8.54	9.54	9.17
Royal Horseguards	London	98	4	4	8.96	8.38	9.26	9.58	9.29
Rubens at the Palace	London	100	4	4	9.24	8.65	9.18	9.71	9.59
Sanderson	London	100	n/a	4	9.43	7.30	8.72	9.20	9.48
Selfridge	London	101	4	4	8.38	7.90	7.95	9.67	9.05
Sheraton Park Tower	London	102	5	4	8.20	7.87	8.53	8.87	9.07
Sheraton Skyline	London	103	4	4	8.48	7.62	8.52	8.67	8.76
Sofitel	London	104	5	4	9.06	8.06	9.35	9.39	9.50
Soho	London	105	5	4	9.31	7.56	8.21	9.44	9.38
St George's	London	106	3	4	8.43	8.43	8.36	7.75	9.23
St Martins Lane	London	106	5	4	8.94	7.06	8.51	9.40	9.57
St Giles	London	107	3	4	8.03	8.72	8.26	9.53	8.19
Strand Palace	London	108	3	4	7.88	8.26	8.31	9.33	8.58
Swissôtel The Howard	London	108	5	4	8.36	8.04	8.32	9.28	9.44
Tower	London	109	5	4	8.50	7.80	8.60	9.38	8.88
Waldorf Hilton	London	109	5	4	9.00	8.04	8.98	9.50	9.41
Westbury	London	111	5	4	9.00	8.41	9.00	9.12	9.24
Britannia	Manchester	112	3	4	8.60	8.85	8.45	9.00	8.70
Hilton	Manchester	113	4	4	8.40	7.60	8.67	8.50	8.60
Lowry	Manchester	114	5	4	8.95	7.84	9.06	8.54	9.65
Malmaison	Manchester	115	n/a	4	9.07	8.29	8.96	9.46	9.43
Midland	Manchester	115	4	4	9.11	8.26	9.22	9.38	9.43
Palace	Manchester	116	4	4	9.14	8.81	9.24	9.43	9.05
Radisson Edwardian	Manchester	116	5	4	8.82	8.18	9.03	9.30	9.30
Best Western Three Swans	Market Harborough	117	3	4	9.00	7.50	8.50	7.50	9.50

Facilities

Facilities	Restaurants	Families	F1	F2	F3	F4	F5	F6	1	F8	F9	F10	F11	F12	F13	F14	F15	F16	F17	F18	F19	P	📶
7.65	8.64	7.64	•	•	•		•			•			•		•	•	•					•	•
8.04	9.00	7.89	•		•		•			•			•		•	•	•					•	•
8.41	7.64	8.50	•	•	•		•			•			•		•	•	•					•	•
7.79	8.75	8.15	•	•	•					•			•		•	•	•					•	•
8.84	9.07	8.33	•	•	•		•			•		•	•		•	•	•		•			•	•
8.58	9.31	8.52	•	•	•		•		•	•			•		•	•	•		•			•	•
8.28	8.82	7.87	•	•	•		•			•			•		•	•	•		•			•	•
8.26	8.68	8.67		•	•		•			•			•		•	•	•					•	•
8.28	9.27	8.36	•	•			•						•		•	•	•						•
8.67	9.03	6.38	•	•	•		•	•		•			•		•	•	•		•			•	•
7.90	8.35	8.46	•	•	•		•			•			•		•	•	•					•	•
8.33	8.64	8.00		•	•	•	•						•		•	•	•					•	•
8.15	8.30	8.31		•	•		•	•		•	•		•		•	•	•		•			•	•
8.39	8.43	7.89	•	•	•		•			•			•		•	•	•						•
8.60	9.00	6.33		•			•						•		•	•	•						•
7.27	8.29	7.46															•						•
8.14	8.69	5.89	•	•	•		•			•			•		•	•	•					•	•
8.30	7.61	8.00		•			•								•								•
7.55	8.27	7.95		•	•		•						•		•	•	•				•		•
7.97	8.06	7.50	•	•	•		•	•		•	•		•		•	•	•					•	•
8.27	8.88	7.78		•	•		•			•			•		•	•	•					•	•
8.97	9.05	8.43		•	•		•			•			•		•	•	•			•			•
7.49	9.00	8.10	•	•	•		•			•			•		•	•	•					•	•
7.73	8.32	8.33		•										•	•	•	•					•	•
6.81	7.80	8.00		•	•		•			•			•		•	•	•		•	•			•
8.56	9.03	8.38	•	•	•		•			•			•		•	•	•		•			•	•
8.86	8.88	7.82		•			•			•			•		•	•	•						•
8.55	8.81	8.74		•			•			•			•		•	•	•		•	•	•		•
7.94	9.53	8.00		•	•		•						•		•	•	•						•
8.72	8.52	8.13		•	•		•			•			•		•	•	•		•	•		•	•
7.50	9.00	7.50		•									•		•	•	•					•	•

Hotel ratings index

		PAGE	★	👆	Ambience	Value	Staff	Location	Cleanliness
					Ratings				
Rookery Hall	Nantwich	118	4	5	9.50	9.00	10.00	10.00	9.50
Chewton Glen	New Milton	119	5	4	9.30	7.41	9.31	9.22	9.56
Malmaison	Newcastle	120	n/a	4	8.97	7.85	8.88	9.29	9.26
Headland	Newquay	121	4	4	9.25	8.63	9.31	9.69	9.06
Lace Market	Nottingham	122	4	4	8.67	7.33	7.67	9.00	9.00
Whipper-In	Oakham	123	3	4	9.00	8.00	10.00	9.00	9.00
Le Manoir aux Quat' Saisons	Oxford	124	5	4	9.50	7.38	8.69	8.56	9.81
Macdonald Randolph	Oxford	125	5	4	9.32	8.42	9.42	9.68	9.47
Malmaison	Oxford	126	3	4	9.54	8.42	9.21	9.08	9.83
Royal Oak	Sevenoaks	127	3	4	10.00	9.00	10.00	10.00	10.00
Hotel Du Vin & Bistro	Tunbridge Wells	128	4	4	8.79	8.15	8.57	8.50	9.36
Miller's at Glencot House	Wells	128	3	n/a	n/a	n/a	n/a	n/a	n/a
Estbek	Whitby	129	4	n/a	n/a	n/a	n/a	n/a	n/a
Hilton	York	130	4	4	8.64	8.60	8.80	9.47	9.29
IRELAND	**Area**								
Adare Manor	Adare	135	5	4	9.31	8.38	8.83	8.62	9.00
Dunraven Arms	Adare	136	4	4	9.19	8.62	9.00	8.90	9.62
Hodson Bay	Athlone	137	4	4	9.13	8.42	9.03	8.82	9.29
Radisson SAS	Athlone	138	4	4	8.20	8.07	8.31	9.47	9.20
Shamrock Lodge	Athlone	139	4	4	8.75	9.75	9.75	9.75	10.00
Slieve Russell	Ballyconnell	140	4	4	8.86	8.27	8.83	7.64	9.33
Great Northern	Bundoran	142	4	4	8.93	8.36	9.21	9.29	9.21
Glenlo Abbey	Bushypark	142	5	4.5	9.46	8.08	9.54	9.62	9.69
Breaffy House	Castlebar	143	3	4	8.71	9.14	8.62	8.67	9.10
Cavan Crystal	Cavan	144	4	4.5	9.36	8.79	9.36	7.64	9.93
Radisson SAS Farnham Estate	Cavan	145	4	4.5	9.33	9.20	9.47	8.27	9.80
Abbeyglen Castle	Clifden	146	4	4.5	9.67	9.50	9.70	9.46	9.54
Inchydoney Island	Clonakitty	147	4	4.5	9.42	7.92	9.17	9.75	9.42
Ashford Castle	Cong	148	5	4	9.49	8.13	9.10	9.24	9.49
Ballynahinch Castle	Connemara	150	4	4	9.74	7.89	9.24	9.48	9.44
Ambassador Best Western	Cork	151	4	4.5	9.20	9.33	9.57	9.07	9.73

Facilities

Facilities	Restaurants	Families
9.00	10.00	9.50
8.93	9.56	7.69
8.02	8.60	8.00
8.13	9.06	9.00
7.50	9.00	8.35
9.00	9.00	9.00
6.84	9.44	7.50
8.53	9.37	8.25
8.29	9.05	7.36
7.07	9.00	7.56
7.87	9.08	7.11
n/a	n/a	n/a
n/a	n/a	n/a
8.60	9.07	9.00
8.42	9.03	7.76
7.63	8.95	8.75
8.80	9.03	8.84
8.88	8.50	7.90
5.75	7.67	10.00
9.00	9.06	8.91
8.35	8.85	9.45
8.76	9.25	9.00
8.90	8.40	8.82
8.84	9.21	9.50
9.47	8.79	8.43
7.51	9.58	9.31
9.13	9.33	8.88
8.30	9.28	8.33
6.90	9.15	8.13
8.03	9.29	9.17

Hotel ratings index		PAGE	★	☞	Ambience	Value	Staff	Location	Cleanliness
				Ratings					
Hayfield Manor	Cork	152	5	4.5	9.52	8.11	8.57	8.97	9.55
Jurys Inn	Cork	153	3	4	8.43	8.71	8.37	8.93	9.14
Maryborough	Cork	154	4	4	8.00	8.00	9.00	8.00	9.00
Rochestown Park	Cork	155	4	4	8.73	8.54	8.56	8.42	9.15
Dingle Skellig	Dingle	156	4	4	8.86	8.54	8.81	9.46	9.14
Harvey's Point	Donegal	158	4	5	9.57	8.79	9.38	9.64	9.77
Arlington	Dublin	159	3	4	8.47	8.43	8.63	9.57	8.53
Beacon	Dublin	160	4	4	8.67	7.83	8.83	7.33	9.50
Bewleys Ballsbridge	Dublin	161	3	4	8.23	8.80	8.58	8.16	9.00
Brooks	Dublin	163	4	4.5	9.06	8.47	9.56	9.29	9.35
Cassidys	Dublin	164	3	4	8.24	8.71	9.13	9.06	9.12
Citywest	Dublin	165	4	4	8.73	9.23	9.10	8.27	9.30
Clarence	Dublin	165	5	4	9.18	8.02	9.25	9.60	9.47
Clontarf Castle	Dublin	166	4	4	9.00	8.48	9.14	8.52	9.52
Conrad	Dublin	167	5	4	9.27	8.05	9.18	9.27	9.73
Fitzpatrick Castle	Dublin	168	4	4	9.21	8.43	9.08	9.07	9.36
Fitzwilliam	Dublin	169	5	4	8.90	8.00	9.10	9.50	9.50
Four Seasons	Dublin	170	5	4	9.23	7.50	9.08	8.70	9.60
Gresham	Dublin	172	4	4	8.88	8.41	8.94	9.63	9.24
Merrion	Dublin	174	5	4	9.26	8.19	9.26	9.60	9.53
Morgan	Dublin	174	4	4	9.00	7.29	8.50	9.36	9.29
Morrison	Dublin	175	4	4	8.54	7.86	8.41	9.40	9.23
Royal Marine	Dublin	176	4	5	10.00	10.00	10.00	8.00	10.00
Radisson SAS St Helen's	Dublin	177	5	4	9.03	8.24	9.06	8.73	9.49
Shelbourne	Dublin	177	5	4	9.21	8.12	8.93	9.76	9.45
Temple Bar	Dublin	178	3	4	8.00	7.73	8.07	9.47	8.13
Trinity Capital	Dublin	179	3	4	8.87	8.60	9.13	9.40	9.27
Westbury	Dublin	180	5	4	9.26	7.80	9.17	9.82	9.45
Westin	Dublin	181	5	4	9.00	8.26	9.00	9.64	9.45
Castle Durrow	Durrow	182	4	4.5	9.54	8.77	9.69	8.92	9.31
Marriott Johnstown	Enfield	183	4	4	8.79	8.64	9.21	8.07	9.21

Facilities

Facilities	Restaurants	Families	🍼	🍸	🖼	🌐	♿	🌷	1	✚	🧸	📖	🎵	🍽	🛏	🎿	🏊	🏠	🎾	🕐	ⓘ	P	📶
8.88	9.32	9.00	•	•	•		•	•		•				•	•	•	•	•				•	•
8.25	8.60	8.62		•	•		•			•				•								•	•
8.50	10.00	9.00	•	•	•		•	•		•		•		•	•	•	•				•	•	•
9.13	8.88	8.56	•	•			•	•		•		•		•							•		
8.38	8.96	9.04	•	•			•	•		•	•	•		•	•	•	•	•			•	•	•
8.43	9.79	9.58		•			•	•					•	•	•	•	•						
6.85	8.40	8.47		•			•					•	•	•	•								•
7.83	7.67	5.50	•	•	•		•			•				•	•	•					•	•	•
7.38	8.51	8.59	•	•	•		•	•		•				•		•					•	•	•
9.28	9.00	9.00	•	•	•		•			•		•		•	•	•					•	•	•
7.29	8.35	9.13	•	•			•			•		•		•		•					•	•	•
8.84	8.87	8.50	•	•	•		•	•	•	•		•		•	•	•	•				•	•	•
7.83	8.88	7.70	•	•			•			•	•	•		•		•					•	•	•
8.25	9.09	9.13	•	•	•		•	•		•		•		•		•					•	•	•
8.70	8.95	8.41	•	•	•		•			•		•		•		•					•	•	•
8.73	9.36	9.00	•	•	•		•	•		•		•		•	•	•	•				•	•	•
7.87	8.71	8.60	•	•	•		•			•		•		•	•	•					•	•	•
8.91	9.21	8.39	•	•	•		•	•		•		•		•	•	•	•				•	•	•
8.09	8.72	8.62	•	•	•		•			•		•		•	•	•					•	•	•
8.67	9.18	8.23	•	•	•		•	•		•	•	•		•	•	•	•				•	•	•
6.85	7.92	6.17		•	•		•							•	•	•							•
7.31	8.48	6.00	•	•			•					•	•	•	•						•	•	•
10.00	10.00	10.00	•	•	•		•					•		•	•	•					•	•	•
8.58	9.03	8.62	•	•	•		•	•		•		•		•	•	•					•	•	•
7.83	9.03	8.31	•	•	•		•					•		•									•
7.12	7.67	8.00		•			•						•	•	•								
7.90	8.50	9.56	•	•			•			•		•		•								•	•
8.29	8.96	8.41	•	•	•		•			•		•		•							•	•	•
8.28	8.78	8.25		•	•		•			•		•		•									•
8.35	9.08	9.33	•	•				•			•		•	•	•			•		•		•	•
8.60	8.50	8.27	•	•	•		•	•		•		•		•	•	•	•	•				•	•

Hotel ratings index

Facilities

Hotel ratings index

		PAGE	★	☞	Ambience	Value	Staff	Location	Cleanliness
Dromoland Castle	Newmarket-on-Fergus	209	5	4	9.58	8.00	9.31	8.92	9.52
Marriott Druids Glen	Newtownmountkennedy	211	5	4	9.06	8.55	9.20	8.74	9.48
Heritage	Portlaoise	212	4	4	8.43	7.69	8.62	8.86	9.50
Kelly's	Rosslare	213	4	4.5	9.27	8.79	9.32	9.27	9.42
Galway Bay	Salthill	215	4	4	8.95	8.50	8.98	9.52	9.40
Clarion	Sligo	216	4	4	8.87	8.70	8.97	8.59	9.40
Radisson SAS	Sligo	217	4	4	8.78	8.52	8.60	8.52	9.33
Parknasilla	Sneem	218	4	4.5	9.57	8.50	9.41	9.86	9.32
Tullamore Court	Tullamore	218	4	4	8.00	8.20	8.25	8.60	9.40
Mount Wolseley	Tullow	219	4	4	9.10	8.57	9.00	8.10	9.10
Faithlegg	Waterford	220	4	4	8.76	8.29	9.00	8.90	9.38
Tower	Waterford	220	3	4	8.56	8.67	8.89	9.67	9.22
Waterford Castle	Waterford	221	5	4.5	9.62	9.00	9.54	9.77	9.62
Carlton Atlantic Coast	Westport	222	4	4	8.95	8.85	9.06	9.10	9.30
Castlecourt	Westport	222	3	4	8.93	8.79	9.32	9.28	9.48
Hotel Westport	Westport	223	4	4.5	8.80	9.20	9.25	9.50	9.47
Knockranny	Westport	223	4	4.5	9.33	8.73	9.54	9.10	9.57
Ferrycarrig	Wexford	224	n/a	4	7.00	9.00	9.00	10.00	9.00
Talbot	Wexford	225	4	4.5	9.10	9.25	9.35	9.55	9.45
Whites of Wexford	Wexford	226	4	4.5	9.10	9.15	9.60	9.45	9.35
ISLE OF MAN	**Area**								
Sefton	Douglas	227	4	4	9.17	8.00	9.40	9.50	9.50
NORTHERN ISLAND	**Area**								
Hastings Culloden Estate	Belfast	230	5	4.5	9.39	8.45	9.19	9.15	9.64
Hastings Europa	Belfast	232	4	4	8.63	8.31	9.00	9.63	9.06
Hilton	Belfast	233	n/a	4	8.40	7.96	8.58	9.00	9.12
Jurys Inn	Belfast	234	3	4	8.24	7.94	8.82	9.35	8.94
Malmaison	Belfast	234	4	4	9.00	7.79	8.93	9.00	9.50
Merchant	Belfast	235	5	4	9.40	7.47	9.13	9.53	9.53
Stormont	Belfast	236	4	4	8.78	8.72	8.89	8.83	8.94
Radisson SAS Roe Park	Limavady	237	4	4	8.95	8.33	9.00	8.48	9.05

Facilities

Facilities	Restaurants	Families	Facilities (icons)
8.68	9.31	8.66	• • • • • • • • • • • • • • • • •
8.98	8.90	8.55	• • • • • • • • • • • • • • •
8.65	8.08	7.89	• • • • • • • • • • • • • •
8.40	9.61	9.75	• • • • • • • • • • • • • •
8.58	8.80	9.20	• • • • • • • • • • • • • • •
8.86	9.04	9.12	• • • • • • • • • • • •
9.00	8.46	8.83	• • • • • • • • • • • • •
8.39	8.78	9.39	• • • • • • • • • • • • •
8.02	8.60	8.93	• • • • • • • • • • • •
8.80	8.90	9.21	• • • • • • • • • • • • •
8.72	8.86	8.13	• • • • • • • • • • • • • • •
7.90	8.67	8.85	• • • • • • • • • • • •
8.11	9.15	9.50	• • • • • • • • • • • • •
7.86	9.60	8.60	• • • • • • • • • • • • •
8.52	8.48	9.46	• • • • • • • • • • • • • •
8.64	9.11	9.40	• • • • • • • • • • • • •
8.73	9.52	9.05	• • • • • • • • • • • •
9.00	9.00	10.00	• • • • • • • • • • • •
9.24	9.60	9.64	• • • • • • • • • • • • •
9.26	9.42	8.89	• • • • • • • • • • • • • • •
9.60	9.20	9.50	• • • • • • • • • • •
9.42	9.30	8.59	• • • • • • • • • • • • •
7.91	8.63	8.38	• • • • • • •
8.43	8.91	8.63	• • • • • • • • • •
7.82	8.60	8.71	• • • • • • • •
7.05	9.00	8.00	• • • • • •
7.64	9.08	7.83	• • • • • • • • • •
8.91	8.73	8.17	• • • • • • • • • • • •
8.77	8.95	9.06	• • • • • • • • • • • • • •

Hotel ratings index

Hotel	Area	PAGE	★	☞	Ambience	Value	Staff	Location	Cleanliness
Hastings Slieve Dornard	Newcastle	238	4	4	8.85	8.04	8.63	9.59	9.23
SCOTLAND	**Area**								
Gleneagles	Auchterarder	244	5	4.5	9.54	7.97	9.36	9.21	9.48
Hilton Coylumbridge	Aviemore	246	4	4	8.93	8.60	9.15	9.27	9.00
Crieff Hydro	Crieff	247	4	4	8.00	7.50	7.50	7.50	8.00
Apex City Quay	Dundee	248	4	4	8.25	8.81	8.50	8.56	9.38
Hilton	Dunkeld	249	4	4	8.76	8.35	8.76	9.12	8.88
Balmoral	Edinburgh	250	5	4	9.02	7.69	8.74	9.70	9.42
Bonham	Edinburgh	252	4	4	8.94	8.88	8.56	9.38	9.50
Caledonian Hilton	Edinburgh	253	5	4	9.00	8.03	8.92	9.36	9.28
Dalhousie Castle	Edinburgh	253	4	4.5	9.77	8.92	9.46	9.31	9.85
George	Edinburgh	254	4	4	8.75	8.15	8.89	9.75	9.20
Glasshouse	Edinburgh	255	5	4	8.88	8.00	9.04	9.04	9.54
Macdonald Roxburghe	Edinburgh	256	4	4	8.65	8.18	8.88	9.41	9.00
Malmaison	Edinburgh	257	n/a	4	9.07	8.41	9.12	8.26	9.41
Marriott Dalmahoy	Edinburgh	258	4	4	9.06	8.53	8.94	8.29	9.24
Paramount Carlton	Edinburgh	258	4	4	8.50	7.50	9.50	9.50	9.00
Point	Edinburgh	259	3	4	9.21	8.38	8.71	9.14	9.00
Prestonfield	Edinburgh	260	5	4	10.00	7.50	9.63	8.63	9.88
Scotsman	Edinburgh	260	5	4	9.31	8.06	8.78	9.66	9.38
Sheraton Grand	Edinburgh	261	5	4	8.63	8.29	8.90	8.95	9.34
Thistle	Edinburgh	262	4	4	8.19	7.88	8.60	9.06	8.81
Tigerlily	Edinburgh	262	4	4.5	10.00	8.50	9.25	9.50	9.75
Witchery by the Castle	Edinburgh	263	5	4	9.94	8.24	9.41	9.82	9.59
City Inn	Glasgow	263	4	4	8.67	8.80	9.20	8.60	9.64
Marriott	Glasgow	264	4	4	8.61	8.52	9.00	8.57	9.59
Hilton	Glasgow	265	5	4	8.40	8.15	8.81	8.30	9.10
Du Vin	Glasgow	266	5	5	10.00	9.33	9.33	10.00	10.00
Jurys Inn	Glasgow	268	3	4	7.69	8.14	8.14	8.86	9.14
Malmaison	Glasgow	269	n/a	4	8.40	7.87	8.60	8.33	8.80
Marks	Glasgow	270	4	n/a	n/a	n/a	n/a	n/a	n/a

Facilities

Facilities	Restaurants	Families	1	2	3	4	5	6	7	8	9	10	11	12	13	14	15	16	17	18	19	20	21	22
9.20	8.73	8.38		•	•		•	•		•						•	•	•	•	•				•	•
9.29	9.51	8.69	•	•	•		•	•	•	•	•	•				•	•	•	•	•		•	•	•	•
7.47	8.20	9.33	•	•			•	•			•					•	•		•					•	•
8.50	9.00	7.50	•	•	•		•	•	•	•	•	•				•	•	•	•	•		•	•	•	•
8.55	8.13	7.70		•			•			•		•				•	•	•	•	•				•	•
8.55	8.88	8.75	•	•			•	•		•		•				•	•	•	•	•		•		•	•
8.54	8.86	8.36	•	•	•		•			•		•				•	•	•	•	•				•	•
6.96	9.07	7.44	•	•						•		•				•	•	•	•					•	•
8.11	8.76	8.12		•	•		•			•		•				•	•	•	•	•				•	•
8.42	9.38	9.30	•	•			•	•			•	•				•	•	•	•	•			•	•	•
8.15	8.80	8.50		•	•		•				•	•				•	•	•	•					•	•
7.67	7.77	7.67	•	•	•		•	•			•	•				•	•		•				•	•	•
8.64	8.60	8.45	•	•	•		•			•		•				•	•	•	•	•			•	•	•
7.81	8.92	7.50		•			•	•		•	•	•				•	•	•	•					•	•
8.90	9.06	9.17		•	•		•	•	•	•		•				•	•	•	•	•		•	•	•	•
7.00	8.00	7.00	•	•	•		•			•		•				•	•	•	•	•				•	•
8.06	9.00	8.43		•			•				•	•				•	•	•	•						•
8.02	9.75	7.00		•	•		•	•	•	•		•				•	•	•					•	•	•
8.71	8.55	7.11	•	•			•			•		•				•	•	•	•	•			•	•	•
8.88	8.81	8.52	•	•	•		•			•		•				•	•	•	•	•	•			•	•
6.60	8.13	8.36		•	•		•				•					•	•	•					•	•	•
7.75	9.67	9.10	•	•	•		•							•		•	•	•							•
4.30	9.29	6.50														•		•							
7.61	8.93	9.00		•	•		•			•						•	•	•					•	•	•
8.98	8.77	8.92		•	•		•			•						•	•	•		•				•	•
8.91	8.89	8.57		•	•		•			•						•	•	•	•	•				•	•
9.00	9.00	9.48	•	•	•		•	•		•		•				•	•	•	•			•	•	•	•
7.56	7.62	8.11		•	•		•				•	•				•	•	•						•	•
7.99	8.00	7.00		•			•			•		•	•			•	•	•							•
n/a	n/a	n/a		•			•				•	•				•	•	•						•	•

Hotel ratings index

Facilities

Facilities	Restaurants	Families																					
8.76	8.35	7.75	•	•	•		•							•	•	•					•	•	
n/a	n/a	n/a						•						•	•						•	•
n/a	n/a	n/a		•				•	•					•		•			•			•
n/a	n/a	n/a		•				•						•							•	
10.00	7.00	7.00	•	•				•						•	•					•	•	
n/a	n/a	n/a						•						•								
n/a	n/a	n/a		•										•						•	•	•
9.08	9.26	9.12	•	•	•		•	•	•	•	•	•		•	•	•	•	•			•	•
n/a	n/a	n/a					•	•		•				•		•	•	•		•	•	
5.25	10.00	10.00		•				•					•	•	•						•	•
8.86	8.58	8.75	•	•	•		•	•	•	•		•		•	•	•	•	•		•	•	•
9.24	9.15	8.57		•	•		•	•	•	•		•		•	•		•	•			•	•
n/a	n/a	n/a		•				•						•							•	
7.33	9.17	6.40	•	•	•			•						•	•	•				•	•	•
7.08	3.00	5.50		•			•					•		•		•				•	•	•
8.88	9.00	9.00		•			•	•						•	•					•	•	•
8.65	8.88	8.00		•	•		•			•		•		•	•	•	•	•			•	•
7.25	7.50	9.00		•				•						•							•	•
9.31	9.06	8.19		•	•					•		•		•	•	•	•	•			•	•
7.00	9.50	10.00		•				•				•		•							•	•
8.86	9.00	8.86		•				•				•		•	•						•	•
10.00	9.75	9.39		•	•		•	•		•		•		•	•	•	•	•			•	•
8.67	9.25	9.50	•	•	•		•	•		•		•		•	•	•	•	•	•		•	•
7.86	10.00	7.86		•										•								
9.30	8.88	8.21	•	•	•		•	•	•	•	•	•		•	•	•	•	•	•		•	•
10.00	8.00	10.00		•			•	•						•	•			•			•	
n/a	n/a	n/a		•	•			•						•		•				•	•	•
10.00	9.00	8.88		•				•			•			•							•	

Index